VIKINGS
ON A PRAIRIE OCEAN

VIKINGS

ON A PRAIRIE OCEAN

The Saga of a Lake, a People, a Family, and a Man

GLENN SIGURDSON

GREAT PLAINS
PUBLICATIONS

Great Plains Publications
233 Garfield Street South
Winnipeg, MB R3G 2M1
www.greatplains.mb.ca

Great Plains Publications gratefully acknowledges the financial support provided for its publishing program by the Government of Canada through the Canada Book Fund; the Canada Council for the Arts; the Province of Manitoba through the Book Publishing Tax Credit and the Book Publisher Marketing Assistance Program; and the Manitoba Arts Council.

Design & Typography by Relish New Brand Experience
Printed in Canada by Friesens
Cover painting by Robert Pollack

LIBRARY AND ARCHIVES CANADA CATALOGUING IN PUBLICATION

Sigurdson, Glenn, 1947- author
     Vikings on a prairie ocean : the saga of a lake, a people, a family and a man / Glenn Sigurdson.

Includes bibliographical references and index.
ISBN 978-1-926531-93-9 (pbk.)

     1. Sigurdson, Glenn, 1947-. 2. Sigurdson family. 3. Fishers--Manitoba--Winnipeg, Lake, Region--Biography. 4. Icelanders--Manitoba--Winnipeg, Lake, Region--Biography. 5. Icelandic Canadians--Manitoba--Winnipeg, Lake, Region--Biography. 6. Folklore--Iceland. 7. Winnipeg, Lake, Region (Man.)--History. 8. Winnipeg, Lake, Region (Man.)--Biography. I. Title.

FC3395.W5S53 2014   971.27'2   C2013-908749-4

ENVIRONMENTAL BENEFITS STATEMENT

Great Plains Publications saved the following resources by printing the pages of this book on chlorine free paper made with 100% post-consumer waste.

TREES	WATER	ENERGY	SOLID WASTE	GREENHOUSE GASES
27	12,441	12	833	2,294
FULLY GROWN	GALLONS	MILLION BTUs	POUNDS	POUNDS

Environmental impact estimates were made using the Environmental Paper Network Paper Calculator32. For more information visit www.papercalculator.org.

FSC
www.fsc.org

MIXTE
Papier issu
de sources
responsables

FSC® C016245

This book is dedicated to my mother and father,
Sylvia and Stefan Sigurdson.

"takk fyrir ferðina" Thanks for the journey

PREFACE

Stefan Sigurdson was a special man with a quiet way. He was born into an Icelandic-Canadian fishing family in Hnausa, Manitoba on the shores of Lake Winnipeg on November 21, 1921. He spent the first 70 years of his life in the village of Riverton, the family home and headquarters of Sigurdson Fisheries Ltd., with its own legacy of more than a century on Lake Winnipeg. Dad was known as a statesman within the Lake Winnipeg fishery. His gentle wisdom and charisma were felt in the communities around the lake, in Winnipeg doing business, or selling fish into the markets of Chicago. He formed deep relationships with the indigenous people, always mindful that they had lived around the lake and off the lake—and the mighty rivers that enter and leave it—long before the arrival of any Icelanders. Dad gave strong leadership by giving strength to others without ego, and always with respect.

When he returned from three years of duty on a Royal Canadian Navy corvette in the North Atlantic during the Second World War, he saw a beautiful young woman walking down the street in Riverton. He soon identified her as Sylvia Brynjolfson, whose family had recently relocated to Riverton from nearby Hecla Island. His strategy was simple. Talking fish with her father "Malli," one of the iconic Lake Winnipeg fishermen, was sure to be the best way into her heart and then her life. They married in 1946 and in each of the 66 years that followed they were a powerful team. Together they built a life, brought up three children, and worked in the business, the church and the community as dedicated citizens and untiring contributors. In their retirement years they moved to Whiterock where they became active members of the Icelandic Canadian community in Vancouver.

No two people better epitomize life on Lake Winnipeg, the vast prairie ocean, than my mother and father, Sylvia and Stefan. The lake defines them; it is inside them. That wisdom has also shaped my life. Dad worked with me over several years as I gave birth to this labour of love, and he shares its authorship. Before he died in 2012, he knew that this book would one day be completed.

LAKE WINNIPEG SURROUNDING AREA

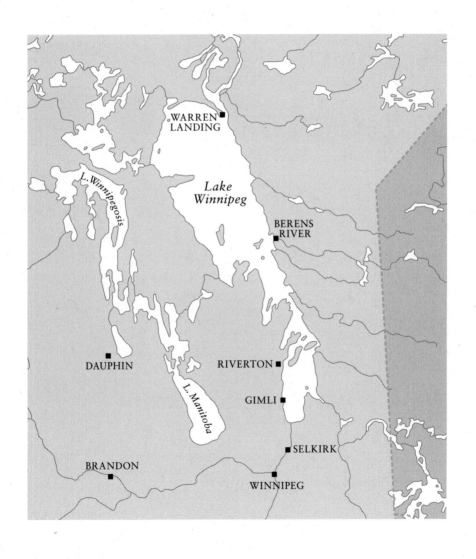

FOREWORD

In 1961, Glenn Sigurdson was a student of mine at the Riverton Collegiate. Since then he has gone on a great journey, beginning in a small Manitoba town and growing up in an Icelandic Canadian fishing family on Lake Winnipeg, becoming a prominent lawyer, and then transitioning into an internationally recognized mediator. He credits those early beginnings with much of the success. I agree and I expect you will as well, for he reveals in these pages how the lessons learned in his community, his family, and the people of the lake, have been put to work in resolving seemingly intractable disputes, across Canada and beyond.

With *Vikings on a Prairie Ocean*, Glenn has woven together anecdotes, events and facts into a narrative that has brought back to life the personalities from an earlier era of the life on the lake. Glenn offers new and important insights into the early Icelandic immigration to Canada, and the central role that fish and fishing played in that experience.

Outside of the Icelandic Canadian community, the story of Icelandic immigration to Canada is not well known. Iceland, on the far side of Greenland, only has a population of about 300,000. During the late 1800s the population was much smaller and the island was only visited now and again by adventurers or by commercial traders. Subsistence farming and fishing provided just enough food and trade goods in good years for the people to survive. Even in good years, there were not enough frost free nights for grain to grow and ripen. That meant that hay was the staple crop. Dairy cattle, sheep, and horses were bred, the first for the many products that could be made from their milk, the second, for meat and wool, and the third, for transportation as there were no roads, no wheeled vehicles, but only trails from one isolated farm to another.

In the 1870s volcanic eruptions destroyed precious grazing land, the weather turned cold so that there was a shortage of fodder for animals and in some places the sea froze so that fishing was difficult if not impossible. Marginal land was no longer productive. Although there was a welfare system of sorts with the indigent sent to farms in the district in which they were born, the burden of supporting more and more people became great. Finally, some Icelanders decided to emigrate. Some went to Brazil, some to the United States but a large number came to Canada. The majority of those who came were desperately poor. Many of them had been labourers on isolated farms. Their worldly goods often were not much more than a quilt, a spoon and a wooden bowl from which they ate all their meals. The decision to leave was heart wrenching both for those who were going and those staying.

They came to Canada ill prepared in every conceivable way. Ocean nets and techniques did not catch fish. The lake froze over in winter. There were no big game animals in Iceland so Icelanders had no hunting skills. Few trees grow in Iceland so there they built with turf and stone. In Canada they faced impenetrable forest. Brutal cold and hip-deep snow brought near starvation, and then smallpox struck. The cost in lives was high. They found themselves trapped in a situation even more desperate than the one they had left. That they persevered through those early years is a miracle.

Glenn draws on the diary of his great-great-grandfather, Sigurdur Erlendson, to tell this story with both its heartbreak, and hope. It would be the fish of the lake that would be the salvation of the early settlers enabling them first to feed themselves, and in the following generations to build an economy around fishing. Sigurdur's sons would in the Icelandic tradition become Sigurdson, and they would plant the family's roots in the business of fishing for many generations to follow. Within the first few years, the colony had been reduced to a few hundred souls. Many of the first settlers had left for other parts of North America because of the difficulty of providing for themselves. It was news of the emerging prospects in the fishery that would bring new settlers to Canada. Among these new arrivals were his mother's family who would also soon join the ranks of what would become the Icelandic fishing families of Lake Winnipeg.

Fishing on Lake Winnipeg was difficult and often dangerous. Remote fishing camps, bad weather, difficult living conditions, negotiating fish prices, buying supplies, planning ahead for the next season, working with groups of people from many different ethnic backgrounds, all provided lessons that would be valuable in Glenn's later career. But the heart of the fishery was its people who took risks, endured hardship and had the vision to create an industry that has continued to the present day. An important dimension of this story is the strong connections that developed between the Icelanders and the indigenous people of the Lake through fishing. It is the people of the Lake, the families and communities and their relationships that Glenn brings to life for the reader, and it is their stories which would shape his life and his work.

Icelanders and Icelandic Canadians are writers. They frequently write autobiographies. Each one adds to the story of the Icelandic immigration and its aftermath. However, *Vikings on a Prairie Ocean* goes beyond being an autobiography, although Glenn is the narrator and also a character in the book, his experience with fishing has allowed him to fill the book with information that will be of value for readers and researchers in the years to come. His description of the trip north with his mother, siblings and dog brings the journey to life, shares it with the reader, and makes it more than a statistic.

His facts about the fishing itself provides information about the details of the fishing life that only could be provided by someone who had intimate knowledge of the industry. While this book will be a valuable source of information on the fish and the people of Lake Winnipeg in an earlier era, it does so within a much wider historical context with many surprising facts and important insights. Icelanders had all lived on isolated farms. There was little communication between various parts of the country. Now, people from all parts of Iceland found themselves living in the same small communities. New Iceland would be created from a mix of classes and regions of their homeland, bound together through a common struggle.

Lake Winnipeg is the centre of this story because its waters and the lands along its shores gave these immigrants a distinct sense of place which moulded and formed the families and the community. The relationship to Lake Winnipeg became part of how people defined themselves. The lake took labour and lives. It gave back a living. It helped make people independent but it also made necessary a highly interdependent network within and beyond the community for fish cannot move themselves from Lake Winnipeg to distant markets. It made the community stretch beyond their ethnicity to do business with people of all races and creeds.

The hardship faced by the community forced it not only to form a work ethic that often pushed people to their limits but also forced them to reach for new solutions to new problems. Those characteristics lie behind the many members of this small ethnic community to succeed at the national and international level. Glenn chose law, then mediation. These areas may seem solely Canadian but in Iceland, from the very first days of its settlement, law and mediation were critical parts of society. Glenn's choices have been firmly rooted in Iceland's history and applied in Canadian society.

— W. D VALGARDSON

Glenn and his partner, Major

INTRODUCTION

This book was born out of nostalgia. I became enamored with capturing the incredible places and characters I knew growing up in a fishing family on Lake Winnipeg. The first Icelanders arrived on Lake Winnipeg in 1875. My ancestors came one year later. Our history on the lake began that year, with a few fish pulled through a hole in the ice, a bounty that pushed back starvation during the family's first winter, spent in a shack on Hecla Island. By 1882, the fledgling steps of fishing as a business had begun off the island's shores. What became a family legacy of more than a century began with my great-grandfather and his brother who emerged as leaders in the blossoming industry and the development of the Icelandic community in Canada. People build their lives on foundations laid from the beginning. For me, it was more than that, for it was on the lake where I learned the essential "tools of my trade," a trade still in search of a name.

I work within and among diverse organizations—companies, communities, groups and governments—in the public and private sectors, building partnerships and resolving seemingly intractable disputes, often in the vortex where the economy, the environment, and society meet. My role is to deliver a special kind of leadership as the "man in the middle" between big problems and big groups and organizations.

My work has taken me throughout Canada and to many other parts of the world. Navigating the divide between fighting and talking is a tricky journey. The longer people have been in the fight the more it defines who they are, and the more difficult it is to detach them from it. But I also know that the longer they talk the more likely they will stay talking. And as the investment in talking grows the potential to deal with differences takes root in the form of actions enabling individuals and organizations to better live and work together.

I have put these tools to use among many people and in many places, but Lake Winnipeg and its people have stayed alive in my mind, just around the corner every day. How could it be otherwise, with my mind fertilized so richly by remarkable places and captivating characters? Thank God for those experiences, for these memories provided me with countless movies of the mind that continue to move me in new ways. These memories often elicited spontaneous tears or laughter in me, sure signs that they were coming from a deep emotional place. I have drawn strength from them and have shared the stories with many others. They have become my calling card. I am known by them.

This book started on an airplane. I found myself breathing life back into the people and times of the Lake Winnipeg I had known, translating the memories dancing inside my brain onto the digital screen of my Blackberry. At some point, these efforts became a duty, for there are few still around who knew that world well enough to bring it to life, to tell the stories of those who once fished the lake and made this history what it was.

I often think of myself as having been born in a time warp, for my entry into the life of Lake Winnipeg was not much different than my Dad's had been as a boy, nor my grandfather's, nor his father before him. Icelanders could drink in the beer parlors, but not the Indians with whom they worked and lived on the boats and in fish camps. Men were still out of touch for months in remote winter fishing camps, and women and kids stayed home. Dog teams no longer pulled fishermen out to their nets when I was a boy, but the last of the teams was still alive. Men still chiseled holes through five feet of lake ice with a steel bar. Ice augers were several years away. Fish receipts were tabulated with the same ancient adding machine that the first settlers used, pulling the handle hundreds of times a day. There were no transistor radios, and the phone lines out in the country weren't private, but were "party lines." At least adding machines and typewriters had been invented by 1972 when I started practising law. Xerox machines were still to come, so you made your copies on the typewriter with carbon paper. Telegrams were the only alternative to the letter and the phone.

My quest to transfer my memories onto paper evolved over time. I needed to explain the "life and times" so these places and people would be brought to life as real human beings, not caricatures. Using my own family as a story spine was a convenient way to do so. What began taking shape moved beyond a "Lake Winnipeg sketchbook" to something more like "the life and times of a Lake Winnipeg family." That's when I got Dad involved, about eight years ago. My sense of duty deepened. By the time my dad, Stefan, was eight, he knew he would spend his life on Lake Winnipeg. That was 1930. In 1955, when I was eight, I was far from knowing how I wanted to spend my life. Nevertheless, Dad and I both started our work lives nailing together wooden boxes for packing and shipping fish. Dad's boyhood wage was five cents a box. Mine was the same. The partners of Sigurdson Fisheries Ltd., or "Sig Fish" which is how everybody referred to the company, were obviously not big on cost-of-living increases.

My contribution to Lake Winnipeg's history focuses on the Icelanders whose fate became tied to this remarkable body of water. And yet, I am ever mindful that the Icelanders represent but one slice of the lake's history. No people have so long been entwined with the fortunes and misfortunes of Lake Winnipeg and her mighty rivers as the indigenous people. I've spent much of my career working with Canadian indigenous communities, continuing connections to the Cree and Ojibway (known as the Saulteaux in the West) developed from my earliest remembrances. "First Nations" is the common term today for Canada's indigenous people, but I respectfully use the term "Indian" to discuss a period in which they were known, and knew themselves, by that term, for it would be artificial to do otherwise.

The reach of the story kept expanding. It was impossible to tell the story of the Icelanders on Lake Winnipeg, and the role of fish and fishermen, without setting it on the wider stage of the Icelandic settlement in Canada, and the creation of the "Republic of New Iceland." In 1875 when within weeks of their arrival on the shores of Lake Winnipeg, treaties with the Indians were being concluded at the North End of the lake, and Louis Riel had only been banished months before from the Red River Colony in the vicinity of the convergence of the Red and Assiniboine Rivers for his leadership of the insurrection of his Métis countrymen. My enterprise was beginning to take the form of "a prairie ocean saga."

Lake Winnipeg has been at the heart of the continent's history from time immemorial. Indigenous peoples have occupied the surrounding territories for millennia. In colonial times it was the strategic centre where great English and French mercantile empires—the Hudson's Bay Company and the North West Company—and their Indian Nations allies collided and eventually converged. The Norway House Cree and Métis were the great York boatmen of the "Company of Adventurers" trading into Hudson Bay, moving supplies 1,000 miles south down the Nelson River and Lake Winnipeg to the trading post at Lower Fort Garry, then carrying furs back to ships awaiting in Churchill Bay. Meanwhile, from east to west, the cargo ship of the fur trade was the canoe as the master canoeists, the "courier de bois," moved across thousands of miles on the mighty river systems from the east to the west.

The Icelanders became neighbours with the First Peoples of these lands, alongside the existing settlers and those from many places who followed. Writing the Canadian story had just begun, and this group from an island in the middle of the North Atlantic was there helping to write it, adding their own story, and adding another chapter to the history of the Vikings. Their saga was unlike that of many immigrants who came after to find their way by fitting into a new land. The Icelanders arrived with a vision of building a New Iceland within "the Icelandic Reserve" set aside for them and began the arduous task of creating a society with its own institutions and identity.

The final iteration of my project followed a couple of years later. Those to whom I had looked for advice set before me a further challenge: "Write yourself into this." I never intended this book to be about me, but my advisors persisted. "Who you are and what you do are so vitally intertwined that you are in a unique position to have each inform the other. So do it." Their guidance was well founded.

I have written thousands of pages over a long career. But writing this book was the hardest assignment I have ever tackled, by far. The material in these pages is factual, not the artful combination of truth and fiction my Viking forbears blended into their "sagas." But I hope it is not too bold to honour that history by describing what follows in these pages as a saga.

The more I wrote, the more I came to realize that this saga was a journey of self-exploration about how the lake, its Icelandic and First Nations fishermen, and the communities and people around it, had shaped and inspired me. But as I wrote myself into the book it became much more. My career would take me to the lands of the Cree and Ojibway living alongside the multitude of rivers that flow into Lake Winnipeg, and the sole river, the mighty Nelson that takes all this water north to Hudson Bay. These rivers and people would also come to deeply inform and shape my work and my life in the memoir that follows.

History is much more than facts, dates and events, kings and heroes. History is to a people what memory is to a person, a story that defines them and unites them. The story lives inside them. It is their identity, orientating the way they see and understand the world. I have come to understand that writing this story was deepening and sharpening my understanding of who I am, what I do, and why.

I have been blessed with relentless curiosity and a rambunctious spirit. I have always resisted being "caged in" by conventional wisdom. Those attributes have served me well, shaping many insights that are cornerstones in my life and work. Complex problems populate the landscape in which I work. I have come to understand that the ostensible problem is not the real problem. The challenge is not mines, or fish, gas wells, or dams; the problem is the organizational cultures and structures around them. The problem grows larger and more interconnected when we pull back the curtains to reveal organizations sliced into silos and knowledge diced up into disciplines. Inside communities and non-governmental organizations (NGOs), the complexity is different but no less, for here we find factions, families, coalitions. And government? Far too small a word for too big a thing that walks and talks like a cumbersome giant, thinks in terms of policies and programs, but is ill-equipped to solve problems and develop enduring relationships. Often when I work in teaching settings, especially with professionals whose training has imprinted the ways they think, interact and work, I describe the challenges we collectively confront as trying to "put Humpty Dumpty together again."

Connecting the dots between the present and the past to understand the story of one's life is deeply human. Examining history enables you to see the future more clearly. I think of this in other ways in terms of my work. The jurist Oliver Wendell Holmes had a powerful message: "I give not a fig for someone who sees simplicity before understanding complexity, but I would give my life for someone who sees simplicity beyond complexity."

At this point in life, I am searching for the simplicity of which Holmes speaks, and am increasingly persuaded that the key to unlocking it is to search into the human condition and affairs in the past that were shaped in more basic times. It means understanding that what you think you have told people and what they hear may be two very different things. Simplicity emerges with the ways and the words to cross that divide. Like the Huldufolk, the little people who have tickled the Icelanders' imagination for centuries, simplicity is an elusive trickster hiding behind rocks and in crevices, in forests and beside rivers, and popping up when least expected, and only fleetingly. As I wrote this book it became clear that I needed to focus my search on what was already inside me, a gift from the lake, its rivers and its people.

I developed from my earliest years an awareness and acceptance of people and an understanding of the similarities and differences in their worldviews. Icelanders, indigenous peoples, Ukrainians, and many other immigrant groups melded together as Canadians before my eyes. For the people indigenous to this land, this was home, the only place attached to their identity. For the rest of us the "old country," however distant, was kept alive as a big or small particle in our identity. This nurtured an orientation inside me that is fundamental to how I think and act.

I start with the presumption that we are all the same. We have hopes and fears, most profoundly with respect to the security and happiness of our children. I am comfortable with differences—different people, different languages and different situations driving different ways of looking at the world and acting within it. Differences provide the potential to deliver strength, not weakness, to provide opportunities, not erect barriers. Since boyhood I have come to realise that I was living within this dialectic, and it was shaping me.

And there was yet another discovery. As I struggled to fuse my life and career together, I was coming to understand that this act of writing and remembering enabled me to capture my mysterious and elusive calling in new words and new ways, explaining what I do in what I hope will be a compelling way.

Many Icelanders journeyed from their island home expecting a new life beside a prairie ocean. They understood that independence and interdependence were intrinsically interconnected. They understood that creating an economy as a basis for self-sufficiency was the foundation of independence. Mostly sheep farmers, they came to find land, but confronted with heavily forested terrain and long, snowy winters, the futility of farming soon became apparent. Within a few years the farmers became fishermen, and began building "New Iceland" inside a country itself engaged in the business of nation building.

This prairie ocean became home for many, but many also left. Wherever they are today, part of their history and identity is lodged in and around Lake Winnipeg. I hope in some small way they will see in my story a part of their story. I have taken the heart and wisdom of the people of the lake with me on many journeys since my boyhood. I hope this book will contribute to giving their personal and collective stories an enduring voice.

— STEFAN GLENN SIGURDSON, QC
   APRIL, 2014

PART ONE

KIDS AND DOGS WERE FREE

CHAPTER ONE

Goldeye

"So, what do you do?"

Not in the mood for chitchat, at least not until a glass of wine and dinner, I gave a terse but true answer: "I'm a recovered lawyer."

He looked at me quizzically. He seemed pleasant enough. I didn't want to be rude, nor encouraging, so I simply added: "I help people have difficult conversations." And with a smile, I told him, "I'm a bit preoccupied now getting something finished."

I put on my headphones and turned to the airplane window. I was back in my own world, on my inner journey with the people and places of Lake Winnipeg.

My memory always seems energized at 35,000 feet, where I've spent more of my life than I could have ever imagined as a boy. Not surprisingly, my mind often wanders back to my first airplane ride, which I remember like yesterday, perhaps because my memory was so well fertilized that day! Now I fly for work; then I was going for fish.

That great adventure starts with the goldeye, the famed fish of Lake Winnipeg. In 1906, the greatest of the cathedral-like railway hotels of the time, the Canadian Pacific Railway's Royal Alexandra, opened its doors to the city, and Winnipeg opened up to the world. "Chicago North," as Winnipeggers were wont to think of their city, was still reaching its stride. The Royal Alex, as the *Winnipeg Tribune* proclaimed, was a "guarantee in brick and stone that the future growth of Winnipeg is assured."

The grand hotel was noted for its elegance, its service and its cuisine. It was a Royal Alex chef who debuted goldeye as a "local delicacy," and launched its fame.[1] It soon appeared on gourmet tables across North America—from elegant meals in the dining cars of the passenger trains to the stately hotels of Chicago and New York. In 1919, goldeye was served to President Woodrow Wilson and King George VI as they dined together in the luxurious Grand Café.

By the 1950s, goldeye were all but fished-out on Lake Winnipeg. It was rumours of a small interior lake packed with goldeye that prompted the establishment of a fishing outpost on a lake 30 minutes east from Berens River, a First Nations community 250 miles north of Winnipeg on the eastern shore of Lake Winnipeg. The Sigurdsons first began operating in Berens River in 1895. They had known the Boulanger family for many decades. Old Tom Boulanger first brought the goldeye news to Dad, for this was the area where he and his sons had their trap lines, and it was his family that would set up the fishing operation there. The allure soon proved to be an illusion. The "goldeyes" were actually mooneyes. They looked alike, but that's where the similarity ended, for they lacked the Midas name, the taste, the texture and the price. Like gold turning into fool's gold, the prospect of a fishing bonanza quickly dimmed, but the pickerel (walleye) fishing was reasonable, so the operation continued for a few years. Transport of the fish by air was the only option.

That takes me to Jack Clarkson, a former Mountie turned pilot. His exploits were already becoming the stuff of legend around the lake when I was a boy. Jack had many lives—nine is probably far too small a number. He had a way of staying alive in the air and on the ground no matter what misfortunes befell him. A couple of years before, he had made an emergency river landing that ripped both wings off the airplane. Nothing deterred Jack. He took on a new mission for Sigurdson Fisheries enthusiastically. He began flying the 30-minute trips in his tiny two-seat Cessna 180, taking supplies and equipment in one direction, and fish on the return. Every day the sight of Jack landing in front of the station pulled me more deeply into his orbit. I pleaded incessantly with Mom and Dad to let me go on a trip. They finally relented.

It wasn't a great day for my first flight with Jack. A stiff breeze made for a bouncy take-off, the pontoons bumping along the wave tops as we struggled to achieve lift. Then we were up, and away to the east. Our little craft couldn't ascend beyond the turbulence in minutes like the big jetliners. We had to fly through it.

My eyes were riveted to the ground, my stomach alive with a mix of exhilaration and terror. I knew the propeller was pulling us through the air, but I marvelled at how it had become invisible. My anxiety rose with each twist and bump, and it slowly dawned on me that the feeling had left my legs. I looked down to make sure they were still attached. I explained this fearful development to Jack through the headset. "Don't worry about it," was all he had to offer. I flew on legless, frozen with fright, obsessed with getting solid ground beneath my feet, should they happen to reappear.

Jack pointed to a small lake ahead as we began to descend into the heavier turbulence again. The lake was alive with whitecaps. Jack circled and then moved down into the landing approach. The strong wind made it difficult for him to position the aircraft. About to touch down, Jack suddenly pulled sky-ward again, uneasy about the prospect of a safe landing. Again we circled, ap-proached, and pulled up at the last minute. Jack was not prone to giving up. He'd flown there with supplies for the men and knew they had fish waiting to be taken away. They counted on him, and nothing would stop him from complet-ing his mission. In a carnival of bounces and splashes we finally made it down.

My fears during our struggle to land gave way to a greater terror as I con-templated a future without legs. How could I have been so stupid as to insist on taking this trip? What was wrong with my boat at Berens River? Was my whole life about to change? It's comical now in a Stuart McLean Vinyl Cafe-gone-bad sort of way, but it was anything but amusing at the time. My fear-fuelled imagination was making plans for the legless years ahead. Finally, the door of the plane was thrown open and someone yanked me out. To my enor-mous relief, I was standing upright on the shore. I walked about to celebrate, but I had a strange, disconnected feeling running through my limbs.

Jack wasn't about to waste time on the ground. The second the last box of supplies was offloaded, the first fish box was being pushed inside. He collapsed my seat to make room for as many boxes as possible in the cramped, cone-like compartment. Frightened that he was going to leave me there, I blurted, "Jack, where is my seat?"

Jack scooped me up, plunked me on top of a fish box, and strapped me down with one seamless motion. Weather was closing in fast, and Jack had no time for talk. He jumped across the pontoons and bolted into the pilot's seat. He fired up the engine and we taxied out onto the lake. Into the wind at full throttle, we bounced for a few moments, and then wind grabbed beneath the wings. We were in the air, but just barely, and the shoreline was approaching fast. Bug-eyed, I watched the scene unfold as we struggled up over the trees at the last second.

My legs were already detached. At least I knew now that they would be-come part of me again when we were back on the ground. Not something I wanted to pursue with Jack, I let it be, assuming it was just one of the things one has to deal with when flying. Anyway, the overwhelming smell of fish around me was much more distracting than my leg problems.

I was used to the smell of fish; standing at the gutting table as the fishermen dressed their catch was part of my daily routine. The fish slime from the sheds was a magnet for perch. I pulled the hearts from the pickerel heads, the tight red particles of muscle, to bait my hook shaped from a safety pin. I spent hours every day plucking perch from their frenzied swim below the dock. Often Dad sent me down with orders to have the fishermen push the guts over to me, and

I would pull out the livers for Dollie to cook for supper. But I had never been in such close quarters with this much fish. The air in the cabin was becoming hotter, the engines were roaring, and the stink was becoming unbearable. Jack could see my distress, or see that I was turning white, and he reached over and opened a vent. Fresh air streamed onto my face and I gobbled it up.

I could see the shoreline of Lake Winnipeg ahead. My focus shifted to making it to land in one piece so I could relate the triumph of my trip to everyone who would listen. Any vomiting would destroy my triumphal ending—I needed to avoid that at all costs. It was blowing much harder than when we left, and there were big waves just out from the station. It didn't deter Jack. He literally dropped us into the trough between two waves, the wing tips dipping into the crests. We wobbled to the dock.

I jumped out the instant the door was pulled open, anxious to bypass Dad and Mom, who were almost surely on their way to greet me. I knew if I saw them I could never hold back my tears. But with the fishermen I could boast! I ran to the gutting shed to brag of my adventures. I didn't share my secret oath to never set foot on a plane again. That would have been an oath broken, for I could never have anticipated how much of my life would be spent in airplanes travelling to communities large and small, across Canada from Haida Gwaii to Cornerbrook, and around the world from London to Papua New Guinea.

Reliving those stories of the lake, its history and its people was like comfort food at the end of a long day. Often the memories would make me laugh or cry inwardly. One day I found my thumbs sprang into action on my Blackberry to capture some scene or moment from the past. And then I did another, and another. Soon my chronicling grew into an obsession. Whether travelling on business or for pleasure I was glued to that "damn Crackberry," as my wife Maureen fondly described my Blackberry when she was with me, usually adding, "You're an addict," just to make sure I got the point.

Usually by the time dinner arrived and a glass of wine was served, I would be more conducive to conversation with airplane seatmates I had ignored as I drifted into memories. When there was an opportunity to restart the conversation, I brought us back around to "what we did" and supplied a less obtuse, if simplified and insufficient response: "I work in the middle of complicated problems around resources, land and the environment."

"That sounds interesting. What kinds of things do you work on, exactly?"

It was easy to respond in broad terms, but I was cautious about getting into too much detail. Beneath the apparent "problems" over fish or water, forests or mines, are real people, with real hopes and fears. If I'm going to be helpful, I must earn their trust so they can confide in me, without worry that I will share their confidences with others. That's the foundation that enables me to have quiet conversations with them. It empowers me to raise tough questions about where their interests truly lie.

I have come to understand that there are no "little things," for what is little to some is big to others. I often say of the work I do that, "if you want to work on the big stuff sweat the small stuff, not the other way around." So I must always consider carefully what I say and do in my work and how I respond to the stranger or write for others to respect the privacy and sensitivity of what is told to me.

Maybe the best way to begin understanding how I've spent my career, the countless difficult conversations I've been part of, is to join me for one. It's the spring of 1994, 7:00 a.m., in the restaurant of the Crest Hotel on the harbour in Prince Rupert, BC. I'm there to deal with a major conflict that has arisen between the Department of Fisheries and Oceans and the different communities of interest around Prince Rupert.

"Paul? Glenn Sigurdson. Good to meet you."

With a name like Paul Paulson, and being a top fisherman, I had figured Paul must be an Icelander, and almost certainly from Manitoba. A call to my mother Sylvia the night before had confirmed my instincts. Before I meet someone for the first time I like to have some sense of who they are. I am in the people business. This time, I had struck gold. Paul was from Hecla Island, where my mother grew up, and where Dad's family settled when they first arrived in Canada in 1876.

"I have a bone to pick with you, Paul," I said as I slid into my chair across the table. "Your father used to bully my mother at school. He pulled her ponytail and was always poking and pinching her from behind when the teacher was not looking. But Mom tells me she remembers you as a nice young man, and sends her regards as she lost touch after your family moved to the Coast."

Paul's eyes were trying wildly to place me for a moment, and then: "Who in the hell are you?"

He sat across from me, fit and taut, as you would expect of a man who spent nine months a year far out at sea in a small boat in some of the roughest waters in the world. Paul was a genuine "Heclinger," that was for sure. I liked him immediately. Icelanders always liked a bit of frisky conversation and Paul was no exception. I finally told him who I was, and we moved quickly from the playful to the immediate.

"I'm here to see if I can help sort out the fishing wars up here," I told him.

"How in the hell are you going to do that?"

"Well, I don't know, yet. That's why I'm talking to you. As the head of the Pacific Gillnetters Association I was told you were a guy I had to talk to. So here I am talking to you. What do you think it will take to cool things down and change direction here? Or maybe you guys just like fighting."

"Goddamn DFO is shutting us down over some bullshit about steelhead. There's more of those damn fish than there has ever been. Some of the boys were so pissed off with Al Lill's announcement that he was going to cut steelhead interception by 50 percent that they wrapped the DFO building in gill nets. One of my buddies got a little too excited and jumped in the offices through some damn barred window…now he's in shit. There's nothing to sort out."

I listened to Paul. I do a lot of listening in my business. He had many opinions about who was to blame, who the troublemakers were, what issues were at hand. As my partner Jerry Cormick says, "People save the best for last, after most people have quit listening to get ready to do their own talking. That is the most important time to listen." I could sense Paul's deep frustration and despair. His way of life was under threat. His own son had to leave the fishing business to become a tradesman so he could comfortably support his family. Paul, along with all the gillnetters, was feeling pain.

Paul asked me what I did. I explained that I worked "in the middle of other people's wars," between companies, governments, associations, communities, First Nations, environmental groups and others, to bring them into a space where they can explore the prospect of talking on the same playing field, leaving the fight outside in the parking lot for the time being.

"So, Paul, what do you want?"

"Tell DFO to back off. That would be a good first step."

"Well, you and I both know that's not likely to happen. These constraints are coming to try to boost the steelhead returns. There is a lot of concern about those stocks, particularly within the province. What do you think is the likelihood they are going to back off?"

He knew the answer. I ask a lot of questions like that, where people already know the answer. They don't need me to tell them, and then argue with me about what I said.

"Ok, Paul, so let's just work with the reality for a moment. What might you be able to do in your operations to keep fishing and reduce steelhead interceptions?"

"What is being talked about is 'weed lines,' to drop the nets six feet or so and avoid the steelhead, which swim closer to the surface than salmon. But that will never work."

I let that hang out there. I didn't know whether it would work or not, and I didn't need to know, at least at this point.

"What about run timing? Are the steelhead coming in at certain times more than others?"

"That's usually the pattern. What the hell are you writing on that damn paper?"

"What you want. What you are worried about."

"On the place mat. Doesn't a hotshot like you have paper?"

"I probably have some, but right now I prefer this. What else?"

Paul continued describing his worries about friends and their families, guys fearful about paying their mortgages and kids' music lessons, and the First Nations guys from upriver who fish in the estuary of the river on the coast each year. It was the smallest guys that were facing the biggest impact.

Eventually, we travelled back to Lake Winnipeg together. He wanted to know more about my connection with the lake, which I could see was still deep inside his heart. We spoke of Hecla Island and Riverton. It came out that I was indeed from the Sigurdson family of Sigurdson Fisheries, and that my mother's father was Malli Brynjolfson, an iconic fisherman from Hecla, whom Paul remembered. I also told him that Mom had written a book, *Thora's Island Home*, for young adults. It was about a young girl growing up on Hecla Island in the 1930s, and Mom was now working on a sequel. We reminisced about some of the old characters on the island, and I told him of other Icelanders who had moved west, as he seemed keen to hear.

I asked Paul whether he had taken a look at the computer model Greg Taylor, the Ocean Fish Manager, had on his desk. It had been developed by DFO and the province, and could be used to demonstrate how changing fishing locations and timing could affect interception rates on steelhead. Paul allowed that he had seen it.

"Paul, everybody has choices ... to fight, sue in the courts, go to the media, cause trouble, or talk. I am in the talking business now, but for twenty years I was a lawyer in Winnipeg until I headed west in 1989. I've done lots of heavy fighting in my career."

"Ok, so what do you want from me?"

"If there is interest from all sectors would you be prepared to come to an initial meeting to talk about this?" I asked.

"The sporties will never come. As soon as they have a rod in their hands, they think they own the river."

"Paul, I know they will come. I spent two days with them in Terrace. John Brockley, the chair of that caucus, seems like a very solid guy. He told me to get up here to talk to you guys as he and his group are prepared to sit down and see whether there is a better way of going forward."

"Well, I guess there's no harm in talking, but I don't think we'll get anywhere."

"Paul, let me get back to you. I have to go over to meet with Bob Hill, the head of the Tsimshian Tribal Association."

"Bob's a good guy to talk too. He knows the industry. Is he prepared to come to this deal?"

"I'm going to find out. I will call you later."

"Good to meet you, Bob. I just came from meeting with Paul Paulson. Earlier I met with Joy Thorkelson at the Union. I understand you're a guy I should be talking to."

"The First Nations have been fishing these waters long before there were any white guys around here. Your job, as I recall from our phone call, is to get a bunch of unreasonable people into a room, and play peacemaker. That's going to be one hell of an assignment. Who are you working for? DFO?"

"Nobody yet, but if I do go to work, I either work for everyone or no one. I only work in the middle. If this goes forward, DFO has told me they will pay for my services, but it will be on that basis. I have a small contract now to pay for my expenses and some time to explore possible interest in moving discussions forward involving all the sectors, including the government sectors, all at one table. That is the basis on which I am here. To have some exploratory discussions, and if they do go forward, I will want to get paid but do not care who pays me. Anyone will be able to fire me."

"Who else have you talked to?"

"One of the first contacts I made was with Don Ryan, given his role with the Skeena Fish Commission, which as I understand includes all the First Nations along the Skeena, including the Tsimshian."

"That's right. Don's a key guy to talk too. What did he say?"

"Actually, his first words were, 'We need one place on the Skeena to talk about issues like this. We have too many different processes and places to be already, so if we can create one place to do business, I'm in.' He said he would send Mark Duiven, who works with him, to an information session I ran in Terrace just after Christmas. Mark is the deputy commissioner of the Skeena Fish Commission. He said they were interested in seeing whether something could get going here with all the players. They told me you were someone I should talk to you when I got to Rupert."

The next thing Bob asked was as direct as it gets: "What do you know about fish? Or working with First Nations?" That was exactly the question he should ask. People with whom I work have a right to know me and what I am all about.

There are many truths. Only if those with whom I work are comfortable that I understand and feel their particular truth will they have the confidence in me that's so critical to working with them effectively. I need to get to know them. Being able to draw upon a broad base of experience has been a critical asset enabling me to find points of connection with the diverse range of people I encounter in so many different places. So too is a proven track record. So Bob and I chatted for some time, comparing notes.

I answered straightforwardly, in the same manner in which Bob asked. "I know quite a bit about fish. I grew up in a fishing family on Lake Winnipeg. Icelanders and Indians had worked and fished together there for over a hundred years," I explained. "I was a lawyer in Winnipeg until 1989, when I moved out here. From 1973, I was the lawyer for 12,000 Cree people in the six communities affected by the massive hydro developments on the Nelson River in northern Manitoba. Later in the '80s, I was the lawyer for the Ojibway people of Whitedog affected by the mercury from the Dryden pulp mill."

I told Bob my years as a lawyer had caused me to conclude that negotiations were the only way difficult problems could be solved. The tools the courts had at their disposal were insufficient to shape proper remedies. So I had become the "man in the middle," advocating for the process and a solution, not for any party. I told him about the case I had just completed on Haida Gwaii involving the construction of a marina. I also mentioned my friendship over the years with several prominent people he would know, like National Chief Phil Fontaine, a long-time friend. Just like I make a few calls to get the lay of the land as a first step in difficult conversations, I know that folks check me out, as they should. Word travels quickly within the First Nations world. Giving people a point of contact is important.

I gave Bob a booklet I had been involved in developing: *Building Consensus for a Sustainable Future: Guiding Principles*. I explained that it was a set of ten principles describing key points that anyone attempting to build a process for a problem like this might want to consider. It was negotiated over two years among the multi-stakeholder Round Tables of Canada and all the provincial and territorial Round Tables signed on by them. I thought Bob might find it interesting.

The next morning at 8:30, the phone rang and it was Bob on the other end. He was pleased with the little orange booklet and wanted to meet.

He got to the point as soon as I arrived. "These are good principles. Consensus. That's what First Nations understand because that's how we work. Nobody being forced into doing something; we have to reach an agreement amongst everyone. Good information that is clear and understandable. A level playing field with everyone having a voice. This is the kind of thing I took from this book. Is that right?"

"That's the gist of it, Bob. If you want to get to the end, then people have to be part of the solution from the beginning. There is no way that either the DFO or the Fisheries is going to be able to pay for a fish cop on every boat much less find enough people qualified to do that. You have to create an environment where people understand it is *their problem*—they own it—and they are responsible and accountable for resolving it, and the future of the fish."

"Well, if this is what you are trying to do, then we can work with you."

Within a few weeks, all the players had agreed to come to an initial exploratory meeting. The quickest way to have a meeting go sideways is for some of the parties to be caught by surprise.

John Brockley, the head of the Sport Fishing Coalition in the Skeena, a forester by occupation, arrived late in the evening after a six-hour drive as I was wandering about the front entrance after a walk. He called me over. I hauled myself into the giant floor-stick four-wheel-drive and he said:

"Glenn, if these government people want the rest of us to work together, they better get their own act straightened out. I want you to tell that to Chris Dragseth from DFO and Art Tautz from the province."

"I will connect with them first thing in the morning. I might wake them up if I call so late."

"No, I want you to call now. Tell them they better meet first thing in the morning and get their act together or this will go nowhere."

I made the calls. There was a breakfast meeting next morning. Chris and Art assured me that they had already started working together. I called John.

We went "off script" within moments. As we went around the circle in opening introductions someone used the word conservation; a firestorm erupted. A commercial guy boomed out "Conservation for you is allocation as far as we are concerned." We had only climbed on the boat, and we are already sinking. The word war got more heated. John just listened. Suddenly, he interjected: "Can't we just agree that we are trying to get more fish up the river, and down?" Everybody took the hook, ever so deftly delivered. A university course in a few moments. Beginning is always the toughest. "Them's fighting words" is still real; it's the shootouts at the O.K. Corral that are gone.... Kind of gone. In my work these kind of natural leaders emerge with their unique brand of magic.

It was two months of hard slogging, but a comprehensive agreement was struck involving all the players on the Skeena, and for the next three years every fishery opening was by consensus. Within a few weeks an unprecedented joint memorandum was signed between DFO and the province agreeing to collaborate on fisheries management. I became the chair of the ongoing process.

I have lived much of my professional life in the space where big problems meet big organizations. Here, interests, values and power collide around difficult decisions and complicated disputes. Communities, companies, departments and ministries, civil society groups, First Nations, local governments. Unlikely as it can seem, these groups are all interconnected in one way or another, to certain problems, and because of the problems, connected to each other. What I've learned through hard experience is that the real problem is not usually the ostensible problem. The implications and uncertainties around fish, mines or gas fields are challenging in and of themselves. However, the far greater challenge is the inability of organizations to resolve problems when the solution requires engaging with other parties who see the world differently. These challenges are deep-seated. To be sure, many challenges are "cross-cultural," to use a popular term, but challenges are far more pervasive than the term implies, reaching deep inside organizational and professional cultures and the values, behaviors and competencies that come with them.

I often say I work in the spaces between A, B, C, D and E. In the courses I teach, I sometimes draw a few circles in a cluster and ask folks what they see. Not surprisingly, they say a bunch of circles. Then I draw a circle around the circles and ask what they see. Most say a bunch of circles inside a circle. The more creative types occasionally suggest pepperoni pizza, or maybe an Easter basket. Only one person, a First Nations guy, has ever said "the space between." Eventually, I shade in the areas between the circles. And that, I tell them, is my workstation. My job is to understand the big and little things that happen inside that space. Sometimes I use a picture of the intricate little gears inside a Swiss watch working to keep time with precision, the failure of any one of which will grind the mechanism to a halt.

Next, I ask the students to name each circle after an organization. Their imaginations now energised, the possibilities start to flow. If it's a business class, they may suggest a bunch of companies, maybe a supply chain. Soon the list widens out to include external players with which businesses must interact to be successful: corporations, government agencies and departments, indigenous communities or unions, for example. Inside each organization lives a spectrum of interests and a cascade of decision makers. Inevitably, there are tensions and frictions up and down and across the organization. Finance and legal, engineering and human resources, all have their own turf, their own ways of doing things, and their own vice presidents. It's the same in government agencies and ministries, and NGOs too have divisions between their wonks and their warriors.

I explain to the classes that the alphabet surrounding me is almost always made up of groups of some kind, large and small. My real-life circles are multiple parties with diverse views of the world and their places within it. It is a world where people worry about themselves, but also speak for others. More often than not, the complex collage of interests I encounter are nested in resource, environmental or land use issues, often with First Nations interests at stake. I have worked most everywhere in Canada—every province and territory, every major city, and small settlements across the country. My assignments have spanned a diversity of sectors and situations: energy to water, rendering plants to nuclear waste, municipal conflicts to treaty negotiations, hydro utilities to mining projects, sky trains to pipelines, and the list goes on.

I have worked with complex organizations from companies to governments to achieve greater alignment and integration across internal divides, and as far afield as Papua New Guinea, Lima, Berlin, and London. Sometimes I operate with organizations like school boards, wine festivals, and many different kinds of non-governmental organizations. Sometime it is with global companies; other times they are as small as a community fish plant. In each, power and authority meet fear and hopes. Each player sees the world through different lenses, and the world sees them—the attributes and beliefs that define them—as it will.

The relationships of which I speak are between and among groups and organizations. Interpersonal chemistry between individuals is helpful, but not sufficient. To be durable and resilient, relationships must withstand the constant migration of people in and out of organizations. Relationships require structure. They must be flexible and adaptive. And they are based on the capacity to deal with the inevitable differences that arise as problems, people and context evolve over time. It is differences in perspectives, talents, resources, histories and beliefs that give any society energy. The challenge is not the fact of the difference, it is how to deal with our differences. "Differences are OK." Respecting that diversity is key to managing together how we can live with it, making our differences work for us, not against us. Diverging perspectives are opportunities to deepen and strengthen relationships as parties build abilities to deal with difference.

I work in busy places, but my space is lonely. Usually I work alone, or with one or two colleagues. Working in the middle of other people's "wars" is not easy. The work has been pioneering. To be sure, there have been intermediaries throughout history. That role is as old as civilization, but it has been implicit and pragmatic, and not the subject of study and research. Only in the last forty years has there been increasing focus on research and practices associated with the resolution of complex, multi-party situations, often with a public dimension, through negotiation-based strategies. A distinct body of practice and knowledge, and a small but very experienced professional community has developed. I am privileged to have been part of building that community.

When all the fancy covers are pulled back, organizations are just a bunch of people, and wars are a bunch of people fighting. The people business is tricky business. Logic takes a back seat, as hard as some would like to fight that reality. When it comes to people, if you want to work on the big stuff, sweat the small stuff. What is small to some is big to others. People's hearts measure the small stuff—the gentle kindnesses, the marks of trust. The participants in a complicated tangle involving a marina on Haida Gwaii years ago gave me a plaque that sits above my desk. It is a quotation from the Chinese philosopher Lao Tzu, written in the sixth century BC:

> Go to the people. Learn from them. Live with them. Start with what they know. Build with what they have. Work with the people, love the people and when the work is done they will say that they have done it themselves.

I have come to understand that the wellspring of this ancient wisdom is respecting people's "right to be" who they are, and that means that before agreeing or disagreeing with what they say or do I must first hear them to understand them. I gave a talk some years ago to the American Fisheries Society. I called it "Fish and People: Who is Eating Who?" Fish have been central to my life from the beginning, and professionally I have been in the middle of a lot of "fish wars," but that has been only one component of a very diverse body of work. You can learn a lot from fish, and from the people whose lives and lifestyles revolve around them. I have taken that experience and wisdom and applied it in many different contexts. There are no more complex problems than those of a fishing identity and culture. They embrace the past and the future, mystery and uncertainty, traditional knowledge and scientific reasoning, knowns and unknowns, lives and livelihoods. If you can work on fish problems, you can work on anything. My place in the world is grounded in people and fish, and that in the deepest sense of the word, is "home."

CHAPTER TWO
Going North

The scene was the same every year. Mom hauled the trunk out of its nook in the basement, wiped off the dust and spider webs, and the two of us lugged it up the stairs and into the bedroom. Nothing started my young heart racing like seeing that battered grey wooden trunk on the move once more.

Every year at the end of May, Dad left before the rest of us for the North End of Lake Winnipeg. As soon as school was finished for the summer, we'd be on our way to join him. We'd be going north. There was something very grown up about the way that expression sounded. For a young boy, "going north" meant the promise of adventure and excitement. The expectation of the trip had been no different for my dad, his dad, or his dad before him.

Our village, Riverton, was 80 miles north of Winnipeg, alongside Lake Winnipeg. There were adventures to be had in Riverton, for sure, but not enough to keep those of us lucky enough to have dads involved in fishing from dreaming about summer life in the fish stations. We made sure everyone in town knew where we were going. Anticipating the voyage made it easier to bear down and study for exams. Soon I'd be free from the cramped little desk where Mom insisted I sit to do my homework. Learning, at least the kind done with books, would be behind me for two endless-seeming months. Doing well in the first two terms meant the possibility of being exempted from June finals, and that translated into finishing school earlier. In the early years, my sister and brother weren't in school yet, so the burden was on me; the sooner I was out, the sooner we got going.

Mom's packing started weeks before school ended. Our home was a little bungalow, and my younger brother Eric and I shared a small bedroom, so our sister Elaine inherited the trunk as her roommate while we prepared for the trip. The trunk became logistics central. It filled a little more every day as Mom layered in the clothes and supplies we'd need up at the station.

The long-awaited departure began when a blue, five-ton Chevy truck, driven by a couple of Dad's men, came to pick up the trunk—along with a creaky spring frame and bulky mattress—and haul them six miles to the dock at Hnausa for loading onto our fish freighter, the *JR Spear*. A couple of hours later, a car picked us up for the drive to the boat. We bumped down the narrow gravel road along the lake, and then, twisting around the potholes, turned toward the harbour and the lonely, windswept shoreline.

This was no small dock. It was majestic enough to serve as one side of a man-made harbour along a straight shoreline. The enormous dock seemed perfectly natural to me back then, but it really was an anomaly. It was constructed through the initiative of my father's grandfather in 1896. Ten years later, the "Big House" was built on the shoreline facing the dock. This grand home, once presiding palatially, had long since burnt to the ground. Initially built with wood, the dock was now an imposing solid concrete structure, stretching out some 600 feet with a half-cocked elbow mid-way. A straight wooden breakwater reached out from the shore 300 feet to the south, angling toward the dock to create an almost-enclosed harbour. Vessels entered through the gap at the front where the distance between the dock and the breakwater narrowed to about 75 feet.

The open expanse of Lake Winnipeg lay in every direction. This was the domain of the *JR Spear*, at dock now, and many other freighters like her. They plied these waters, hauling men, equipment and supplies north to the fish stations and then returning south to Selkirk or Winnipeg, their holds full of 100-pound wooden boxes—two feet long, 16 inches wide and 12 inches deep—of ice and fish. From there the boxes were loaded onto rail cars destined for the great markets in Chicago and New York.

As we drove onto the dock, our most enthusiastic greeter was Major, my Scotch collie, my inseparable buddy, who had been tossed onto the back of the truck with the trunk and mattress. The crew had him tied to the stem at the front of the *Spear*. He could hear us on the dock before we were in sight, and his barking reached a frenzied crescendo as we drew closer.

The *JR Spear* was an ocean liner as far as I was concerned. It was 84 feet long and carried a crew of eight or nine, including a captain, mate, two engineers, two wheelsmen, a cook, and often one or two deckhands. It had an upper deck, where the wheelhouse was located along with four cabins where the crew bunked. The kitchen was on the lower deck.

Captain Clifford Stevens, the fourth generation of his family to captain the tugs of Lake Winnipeg, was quick to welcome us aboard in his quiet way, but Major's barking overwhelmed any reasonable communication. Beside the captain was Gestur Bouchie, a young guy from Berens River who greeted us with a smile and a joke. He was as talkative as the captain was quiet. Before the final pieces of luggage were carried aboard, I had already darted across the wooden gangway between the dock and the main deck.

Men's backs were spared the burden of carrying boxes of fish and supplies on and off the boat by a set of rollers, a temporary track with rugged iron rails held together by a corduroy of smooth steel rollers riding on a cushion of ball bearings. The 10-foot-long track lay flat, a little more than knee high, stretching from the dock to the center of the deck. Its sections were locked together in a chain, supported at the join by two empty wooden fish boxes. As soon as the loading was completed, the rollers would be piled onto the main deck with the boxes, waiting for action at the next port of call.

Mom passed Elaine (six) and Eric (three) into the hands of the ever-watchful crew, and then the captain steadied her as she stepped down from the dock onto the deck. The last supplies had arrived from Winnipeg and been loaded, and the other passengers were aboard. We usually pulled out around eight at night. Twelve hours later we'd be in Berens River.

With departure imminent, the elevator platform was secured at the bottom of the hold and a heavy wooden cover positioned over the opening. The men pulled the gangway onto the boat and mounted back into position the waist-high wooden gate that covered the lower half of the main hatch. The upper part of the hatches would only be covered when heavy seas or cold warranted.

The bed was already set up on the *Spear's* main deck, four fish boxes supporting each corner. As the tug moved out through the gap of the harbour, Mom was making up the bed with sheets and a warm comforter, readying it for the four of us to tumble into with the growing darkness. It was an unlikely scene, this beautiful young woman with her three youngsters, all moving with familiarity and ease over the rough-hewn timbers of the open deck.

The sun would soon drop below the horizon, and on clear nights, away from the lights of town, the stars seemed so close. The Northern Lights sometimes danced across the sky, shimmering up and down, disappearing for a moment and then pulsing back.

Peering out from under the covers, I could see the cables in the metal framework of the elevator. Just beyond that was a small gas engine, with metal levers and pedals the engineer used to send the little elevator platform up and down with piles of fish boxes. The ceiling above me was two-by-fours painted white, topped by the planking of the deck above, with a couple of bulbs providing a feeble light. I could almost touch the ceiling on tiptoes. Anyone over six feet (like the captain) had to bend their head sideways as they walked the deck.

My mind was still abuzz with the recent action. This little area on the main deck, now our bedroom, had been alive with the smell of the engine at work, and the grinding of cables and grunting of the elevator as it jerked along its route. After they took 1,000 boxes of fish off the boat—100 pounds each, 60 pounds of fish and the rest ice—the supplies had to be loaded. At least two men worked the hold, two more at the top of the elevator, moving boxes on and off the rollers onto the platform, and men pushing boxes on and off the rollers, and on and off trucks. And finally the 45-gallon barrels of fuel were rolled down the gangway and positioned on the decks.

Out on the lake, the clean, fresh air washed away the smells of the tug, but when it was windy and dark and the hatches were down, the smell of fish and diesel commingled. Through the doorway of the kitchen wafted the smell of coffee, and at daybreak, the unmistakeable scent of frying bacon.

The first milestone we passed on the way north was the lighthouse at Gull Harbour, on the north end of Hecla Island, the largest island on the lake at 20 miles long and six miles wide. At the south end is a vast marsh, home to legions of ducks and geese. The marshland gives way to low-lying plains, heavily blanketed with birch and poplar, and populated by moose and deer. When I was a kid, a small car ferry traversed the mile-wide channel separating the island from the mainland. Today, travellers cross over on a causeway in a couple of minutes.

Hecla Island rises gradually over 20 miles to imposing limestone cliffs at the north end. The first sign of houses is near the middle of the island, where the tree cover starts giving way to open spaces and fields. The roadway arches to the east and the scene soon bursts onto the open expanse of the lake ahead, and from there you travel north along the shoreline. The community is spread across the shoreline, with narrow lots reaching back into meadows, houses placed neatly along the gravel road that winds its way across the island. On the tip of the point that defines Gull Harbour stood the iconic lighthouse, elegantly crowned with its beacon of light that reached across the covers of our makeshift bed.

On a clear night, as we passed by the centre of the island, Mom often pointed to the church tower to remind us she grew up in the house next to the church. She explained how by the young age of 19, our Afi (grandfather in Icelandic) had saved enough money to buy a prime piece of land. Afi's mother and he lived in a small shanty there until he married, and it was in that shanty that my mother and my aunt Solveig began their lives. Mom explained how Afi in 1927 had bought fir lumber from a big hardware store, Brown and Rutherford, in Winnipeg, to build the new house on this choice property. This home has operated for many years as the only guesthouse on the island, Solmundson Gesta Hus. Whenever we were on Hecla as kids, and we drove by the house, Mom pointed up to the second floor window on the right, just above the balcony, to show us where her bedroom had been. I was all ears to hear anything about Mom's childhood and my Afi (grandfather). He was deep in my heart from the day he started pretending he was a bear, grunting and growling around on all fours with a blanket pulled over him, chasing me across the living room floor after a big Christmas dinner.

Afi was the quintessential Lake Winnipeg fisherman, our "old man and the sea." He started fishing in his 13th year and didn't stop for 62 more. With his pipe chugging Old Chum tobacco, and a cup of coffee in his hand, he plied his way across the shallow and treacherous waters of Lake Winnipeg every summer and fall and traversed the even more dangerous ice that covered the lake for six months in winter. Mom used to say that the lines of his face told the story of his life. Perhaps five-foot-eight, he was trim and and wiry. He was a good-looking man, with a warm face, despite having no teeth. When this first hit me and I blurted out "Afi, you have no teeth!" he promptly responded that he most surely did. "They are in the drawer. I only use them 'for best.'" It was the unhappy legacy of thousands of cups of coffee he drank before he was forty, sucking each sip through a sugar cube—"Moli Kaffi" as it was known amongst the Icelanders. Afi had false teeth made when his originals fell victim to the dentist's pliers, but he never had the patience to get used to them. Remarkably, unless you knew already, you never noticed that he had no teeth. Even more remarkably, his biggest challenge as a result was not eating a steak, but chewing hamburger. I suppose it must have been because eating a soft hamburger was like chewing sand.

The Lake Winnipeg shoreline dips and swings, especially along its western side, creating a series of bays, some that swoop deep into the landscape others little more than a gouge. As you move north from Hecla Island, one of the largest indentations on the west shore is Washow Bay, which morphs northeastward into an expanse of often-fearsome water known as Humbug Bay. Twenty miles farther north this "sea within a sea" starts narrowing into "the Channel," winnowing down to a narrow opening between the two points known as the Dog Heads.

The lake is at its narrowest there, two-and-a-half miles across. As if by a knife, the geology of Canada is split, granite to the east and limestone to the west. Small granite islands and inlets reach out from a jagged shoreline to form the eastern point, East Dog Head. Beyond, the granite vastness of the Precambrian Shield extends its rugged arms across Ontario and Quebec to the Labrador Coast on the North Atlantic. On the west, a short shale bar of flat, white, rounded rocks beckons like a crooked finger from a long, sweeping bay. This is West Dog Head. Behind it are flatlands and swamps that become the Prairies, and then the long push to the Rocky Mountains.

If you could reach down to the mud below Lake Winnipeg, 60 feet in some places, more than 80 in others, you would be touching the bottom of the mightiest lake the world has ever known, with fifteen times the volume of Lake Superior and so vast that it once spread over the entire centre of the continent. When the glacial ice dam that formed the shores of Lake Agassiz broke up and disintegrated 8,500 years ago, it released a monumental torrent of fresh water into Hudson Bay, lifting global sea levels by as much as three meters. Some have linked this momentous event to the great flood in the time of Noah. Today, the legacy of a glacial past is a massive patchwork of lakes and rivers, now the catch basin of an expanse stretching across the interior of North America from the Rockies to the Canadian Shield, from the cornfields of the Midwest to the tundra of the North. The centre of this inland empire of water and land, Lake Agassiz's greatest legacy, is Lake Winnipeg.

The South Basin reaches down roughly 100 miles from the Narrows, spreading out to an average width of about 20 miles. The North End is 60 miles wide by 200 miles long. The Narrows are the bottleneck the water must squeeze through from one basin to the other. Each change in wind direction brings dramatic and often sudden changes in the water level at either end, as the water rushes to and fro as in a tipped hourglass.

The curious name Dog Heads may make one ponder, but still ahead to the north are Black Bear Island, Lynx Harbour, Rabbit Point, Catfish Creek and Poplar Reefs. The names are echoes of a far older story reaching deeply into the history of this place and its Aboriginal inhabitants since time imme-morial. Names like Matheson Island, Cox's Light, Berens River, Humbug Bay, Hecla, Gimli and Selkirk are signposts of the arrival of European colonisers and settlers.

I always claimed the outside edge of the bed, so I could slip away unde-tected. My bedmates were long asleep, and at last my excitement eased enough that I felt I could join them. Once I let go and relaxed, the *Spear's* enormous old Fairbanks Morse two-stroke engine and its thump-thump, thump-thump put me to sleep almost instantly. Thankfully, the noise also drowned out con-versation or footsteps from the wheelhouse directly above.

It seemed that no sooner had I shut my eyes than they were popping open again as dawn crept onto the distant shoreline. I slipped from under the covers and padded my way to the wheelhouse for a visit with the captain and wheels-man. This meant climbing the steep steps alongside where Major was lodged in the few square feet between the elevator and the bow. He was only a few strides away from the bed, but it might have been a mile as far as he was con-cerned. I have little doubt that Major brought genuinely mixed emotions to this voyage. I knew him well enough to interpret his yips and moans and gauge the meaning of the position of his tail or the way he held his head. Even in the dark he must have sensed we were close. But on nights when the full fury of a storm was upon us, as he pitched and tossed, determined to maintain his hold with the deck rising and falling relentlessly, Major would let out long, eerie groans peppered with bursts of frantic barks. On the same nights Major let loose those mournful complaints, my own nighttime activities were severely limited, not just because Mom refused to let me wander around on a pitching boat, but because I shared the internal agony Major must have been feeling. Having the lake in my blood didn't make me immune to queasiness, or worse!

Lake Winnipeg's mood swings are those of a temperamental, but alluring, goddess. At peace, the lake glistens under the intense Manitoba sun, never more restfully than at daybreak after a calm night. You know by dusk whether it will be a restful night. And on those mornings, as the sun appears, the lake is eerily still, as if in a deep, impenetrable sleep. The winds come gradually back to life with a gentle and steady rhythm, and by mid-morning the sun transforms what had been a shimmering glow into a vibrant glittering.

Then there are the times the wind rises as night comes. It's then that fishermen and freighters await the lake's fury. Lake Winnipeg's storms come quickly. Five minutes can transform quiet calm into a raging swell. The lake is shallow, probably an average depth of 20 to 25 feet in the South End and 60 to 70 in the North End. The waves break hard, with glistening white crests, a mountain range with churning snowcaps on every peak. Her storms are often punctuated by the rolling rumble of thunder, and jagged snakes of lightning darting through the blackened sky. Fog is rare, but as winter approaches, and during the spring thaw, there is a risk of snow. In July and August some years, galloping forest fires spread thick smoke across the lake.

As long as we weren't too close to our destination, where the voyage could be treacherous, I was sometimes allowed to steer the tug. Gestur Bouchie, the mate, let me sit in front of him on the stool and "take control" of the huge wooden steering wheel. It was taller than I was, and more likely to take control of me, but Gestur's hand was never too far off. As I steered, I imagined myself standing like I'd seen Dad and my afis do so many times, craning their necks out toward the water, faces drawn in concentration.

Full with the pride of having been in charge, I'd next make the first of my nighttime visits to the kitchen, always the cosiest and warmest place aboard. Even the captain was subservient to the commands of the cook. "Mamma" Sinclair from Fisher River spent years in the small space in front of that gas stove, looking after her boys. Her high-pitched voice and constant giggle were always a little out of synch with this large-framed, robust woman. The ambience in the kitchen was decidedly less cozy when old Herb Baldwinson was

behind the stove. Tall, lean and irascible, I always entered Herb's domain tim-
idly, pulling the door open slowly and poking my head inside. I would slide
carefully onto the bench, squeezed between the wall and the oilcloth-covered
table. But soon that old master pie-maker had milk and raisin pie in front of
me, and all was right in my world.

There was never a shortage of food or talk between those kitchen walls.
The crew drifted in and out for coffee, and appeared for a meal every six hours
with the changing of the watch. I often found Mundi Tomasson, the engineer,
sitting there. Mundi had tended the engines for many seasons. Up the painted
red ladder he would climb after his regular check of the engines, and then he'd
step across the latticed steel platform through which he could see the engine
below, and over to the small back hatch where he'd lean for hours gazing out
to the open water.

I often sauntered up to Mundi as he stood watch. I stood there quietly beside this bulky man, with a perpetually worried but gentle look on his broad
face, transfixed on the water sweeping by, whether calm or rough. Words came
sparsely for Mundi, and whatever he said sounded most serious. "Bad weather's coming," he might murmur. Or, if it looked like we'd be getting in late to
Berens River, meaning he'd be on watch till midnight, then unloading most of
the night before another watch at six, he might say, "Not much sleep. Why in
the hell did they pull out of Hnausa so damn late?" Then silence. And a moment later, "The engine's been acting funny," and he was gone.

When he wasn't in the engine room or at the hatch, Mundi was manning
the controls of the elevator on the main deck just behind the stem of the boat.
He commanded the operation, watchful as the deckhands in the front hold below loaded boxes and drums onto the elevator platform. When everything was
ready, he engaged the clutch and the load groaned its way up to the main deck.
It went from there onto rollers and down onto the dock. One of the thoughts
that kept Mundi preoccupied as he peered out the open hatch was whether
he'd be able to get the motor for the elevator started. He'd ponder and I'd
watch him ponder, and then he'd turn and go without a word, back down the
ladder into the engine room to check his gauges once again. I would wander
off, back to the wheelhouse or up to the galley, and Mundi would soon be in
for yet another coffee.

Sometimes when Mundi clambered down to the engine, I followed and
peered through the iron grid as he stepped down the steel ladder. The engine
room was Mundi's home for nearly five months every year. The Fairbanks Morse
engine was scary big, as big as a Volkswagen Beetle. Its monstrous iron flywheel
was taller than me until I was at least eight. It was brand new in 1934 when

it was first lowered into the hold, one of the first, if not the first, diesel marine engines on the lake. Although now near antiquity, it still got the job done, and the steady, distinctive thump of its pistons showed no signs of fatigue.

A shiny steel walkway ran around the entire motor. Mundi had made that tour thousands of times, alert to any sign or sound of trouble, examining every moving piece that enabled the old beast to maintain its relentless rhythm. Contrary to expectation, the engine room was brightly lit, more so than any other place on the boat, and almost hospital clean. You knew you were entering a special place the moment your hands slid over the smooth, bright red metallic paint on the railings alongside the ladder. Keeping that engine running was not just a matter of business efficiency; it was the frontline of defence in averting tragedy in a Lake Winnipeg gale. A cord stretched down from the wheelhouse to the engine room, and the captain or mate pulled it to ring a bell to alert the man at the controls in the engine room. The old Fairbanks switched instantly from forward to reverse—one bell ahead, two reverse—which was especially critical for manoeuvring into harbour and to the dock.

Having finally completed my tour, I crawled stealthily back into bed. Lying on the deck, my mother, brother and sister breathing softly beside me, I dreamed up elaborate tales to help the time pass until I saw Dad. As we lay bundled together on the bed, I stared at the stars beyond the open hatches. No street lights dimmed or obscured them here.

Mom had told me about the great sagas of the Vikings. In fact, Mom told me a lot of mysterious things about our family. We were Icelandic, she said. And the Icelanders came from the Vikings. At school we had a picture of some Vikings; they had long wooden boats and hats with horns and fur. It was fertile terrain for my young mind, free of cares and full of the spirit of travel and adventure. I learned later that the Vikings had indeed founded Iceland.

The *Spear* changed course sharply from north to east at Cox's Light and proceeded into the mouth of Berens River, on course for the navigational ranges that would lead us to our destination. The sun was still rising, but the sky was flooded with first light as we slid past tiny granite islands. Millions of seagulls nested there. They clustered on every island and rock outcropping, filling land and sky. Soon, the eggs covering the rocks would be alive with fuzzy grey chicks that would track morsels from the gut boats as soon as they were strong enough to fly. For now, the watchful parents kept guard with an almost unimaginable cacophony of squawking.

Daybreak came around four, and the profile of the islands was at its clearest. I imagined my dad walking to the side of the island and listening for the boat right about then. He said that when the breeze was soft and low, he could hear the thumping of the engine when we were still four hours away. Sometime between six and seven in the morning the two-way radio would crackle to life, and we'd hear Dad's voice loud and clear (although what we knew as clear on a two-way would have been inaudible to most).

"Berens River to the *JR Spear*. Do you read me?" Even through the static, I always knew it was him.

"Roger, roger."

"How are things this morning, Captain? Over."

"Things are good, Stefan. We had a good run last night. It looked like the weather might be turning when we left Hnausa but it stayed steady all night. Over."

"Have you got my gang aboard? Over."

"Roger, roger."

"I see you on the ranges now. We'll see you in a few minutes. Over."

Technology like the two-way radio was beginning to make life easier, if not a little noisier. The two-way we know now is not as it was then. Without the privacy of varying channels, your business, others' business, the fish business, was everybody's business. The growing number of companies on the lake was not only intensifying the competition for and pressure on the fish resource, but also on air time.

Starting in 1947, conversations about everything from business to chitchat went on every hour, on the hour, from seven to seven each day. The new radios were an outgrowth from the war, where advances in shortwave radio had become part of modern warfare. With the purchase by Sigurdson Fisheries of shortwave radio surplus from a dealer in Winnipeg, they soon became an intrinsic part of life on the lake. Sig Fish was one of the first to introduce the technology, but others soon followed. Prior to that the only communications on the lake were CBC radio messages broadcast daily at noon. They were terse at best: "Harry Goosehead. Your wife just had a baby. Get home. Halldór Einarson. Your dad is failing. Come home." That was it, but it served well for some time.

Often in those years the conversation amongst the Sigurdsons shifted into Icelandic, particularly when fishing was heavy, in an attempt to limit the knowledge listeners could glean. When the possibility of establishing private channels arose, the Sigurdsons were the first to insert their own crystal into each of the sets to assure greater privacy.

Shortwave had a dramatic impact on almost every aspect of the Lake Winnipeg operations, especially safety and logistics, both in terms of ordering supplies and planning for the transportation of the fish south. And that's not to mention the perk of being able to call home and receive news from home, a welcome complement to the regular flow of letters that went back and forth with each trip.

Shortwave also changed the ambience in the old offices and stores. (The station manager and the tugs were "on sched" every hour mom explained how.) Sometimes it was for a moment or two of what was essentially gossip (although the men might not have admitted it), and other times they were dealing with a crisis. They were noisy square boxes those first radios. Signals were often out, or weak, and it would be barely possible to hear through a wall of static, if anything made it through at all. Particularly if the tugs weren't reaching each other, there was always concern about why. Usually it was just a matter of the signals or a wheelsman tired of listening to all the squawking on an otherwise peaceful trip up the lake.

The two-ways were embedded in our lives by the time my mom, brother, sister and I were heading north. It was all I could do to contain myself when that big box boomed the one voice I was dying to hear: my dad's.

I knew we were almost there when I woke up on deck. We were approaching Berens River, passing along the string of granite pearls stretching out six miles from the river mouth. We would soon be at the "ranges," the navigational markers that helped vessels traverse the tricky channel into the station. For some distance we could see the white, wooden structures reaching above the horizon, like skeletons of lighthouses, with triangular pieces of plywood mounted to their frames. The captain would take out his binoculars and search the mainland until he spotted a similar triangular marker.

At the buoy at Barrel Rock, I'd charge up to the wheelhouse to watch Gestur Bouchie, the mate, turn the big wheel hard right to take us due east, charting a course along the line between the two points defined by the ranges. When I arrived at the wheelhouse, after promising Major I'd stop on the way back down, Gestur and his younger brother Charlie, his wheelsman, always had on big grins as I burst through the open doors. Their younger brother Peter and I had become friends hammering millions of nails into the porch in front of our small camp when we were three. We didn't stop until it was solid steel. Gestur and Charlie liked to joke with me: "Your netchimoose [sweetheart] will be on the dock waiting for you, Glenn. She's been sitting there waiting for you since you left. We told her to go home, but she wouldn't leave."

Gestur needed to keep a close eye for buoys as we made our way through the treacherous waters to the Berens River fish station, on a small granite island about a mile out from where Berens River empties into Lake Winnipeg. As we turned on the last range in the direction of the station, the full view of the river mouth about a mile across the bay came into view. On the right, we could now see the largest and most inland island, and soon the red buildings of the fish station. To the left (the east), in a gentle bay north of the entrance to the river, were the pearly white buildings of the Catholic mission and hospital bathed in the morning sun.

One or two times a week I would head over there on the gut boat with a gang from the station. This was the domain of Brother Cartier's movie nights. As squat as he was short, he had a full, round face that welcomed you before he said a word. Brother Cartier had been around the mission a lot longer than I had been alive, and the movies were his gift to the community. He took admission, set up the benches, sold the drinks and the chocolate bars, managed the exuberance of the kids, and ran the big old projector in the centre of the hall. No cushy seats here, just benches with no backs, 15 rows deep and 15 feet across. The adults stood around the hall talking and laughing, the kids chasing each other around, until Brother Cartier sat on the chair beside the table where the projector was perched, pulled the film off one spool and threaded it through to the spool on the screen side and flicked the switch.

The movies were almost inevitably Westerns. None of us dwelled much on how it was Indians those cowboys were shooting, and vice versa. I didn't look any more like a cowboy than my Indian friends looked like the Indians on the screen. I had no six guns and they had no war paint!

Whether it was Roy Rogers and Dale Evans, or Tonto and the Lone Ranger, as long as I had an Oh Henry! in one hand and a Coke in the other, all was right in my world. That is, at least, until the panic of the inevitable moment the film broke as it clacked its way through the projector, and the screen went black. Brother Cartier would scurry to turn on a feeble light, and with a determined grimace set about piecing the film together and rethreading it. He often lost a good chunk in the gears, but the show went on. It could be hard to hear the movie with all the Coke bottles tipping onto the concrete floor and clunking to the front as one kid after another gave them a push under the benches, the bottles' bulged middles gracing them with a wobble all their own. It wasn't a luxury theater, but we didn't expect one, either.

When we passed the final island, we took dead aim at the last of the ranges, a big white beacon on a small rock outcropping. We were almost there. The tug began to arc back to the south, and as it swung about the front of the station came into full view, one long contiguous structure, every building barn red. To the far left was the small, cozy camp that would be home for the summer. Our lodging was perhaps twenty feet by ten. Mom and Dad's spring mattress would be carried over, and two double-decker metal bunk beds were waiting, one for Eric and me (me on top) and one for Elaine (on the bottom). From my bunk I could reach the top of the two-by-four along the unfinished wall, where I hid my secret treasures, like the pocket knife I'd tote every day on the island, just like all the other fishermen.

The Berens River settlement was just upriver, where it widened into a bay before making its long reach over the Canadian Shield toward the Ontario border. The river and the community were named after Joseph Berens, governor of the Hudson's Bay Company when the first trading post was built in 1814. The Hudson's Bay Store, with the RCMP detachment as its neighbour, sat on the height of land on the inside of the bay.

On September 20, 1875, the lieutenant governor of Manitoba, Alexander Morris, came to the community on the MS *Colville*—commissioned into service that year by the Hudson's Bay Company—the first steamboat to sail Lake Winnipeg. Morris came to make treaty with the Ojibway people on the east shore and the Cree people at the North End of Lake Winnipeg. The hereditary chief, Nah-wee-kee-si-quah-yash, signed the treaty that day on behalf of his community. He took the name Jacob Berens at that time, and Berens soon became the name of one of the most prominent families on Lake Winnipeg.[2] His home was on the height of land with a commanding presence over the bay and the river. My great-grandfather Stefan Sigurdson first arrived in Berens River ten years later, and ten years after that, in 1895, established the base for his fishing operations on a small island in the bay a long stone's throw from Chief Berens' home.

Contrary to Gestur and Charlie's teasing, there was no sweet little netchi-moose (that's how the name sounded to me, but I have little doubt that I've completely distorted this term of endearment) waiting at the station dock to warm my young heart. But there were usually a few kids hanging around, amongst them a few girls at least as shy as me, avoiding eye contact if I ever glanced in their direction.

Often, several Indian families from the settlement had pole tents set up on the island. That way their summer homes were much closer to the fishing grounds. Gestur and Charlie's mom and dad had a three-poled tent set up next door to us. I thought I could make out Alice Swain rubbing clothes on the washboard. She and her husband Henry had built a little hut just beyond our camp. It was their summer home, with a fire going most of the time out front. Her long, thick braid of hair and immaculate red and yellow apron were hard to miss.

The cookhouse was next to our camp. It was like a community hall. Up to 50 men squeezed onto benches along the long table for breakfast at four and supper at six. Across the back of the cookhouse, facing me as I looked at the dock looming ever closer, was a wall of huge windows opening out onto the river mouth. Many cooks and their assistants, "the cookies," presided over this domain through the years, but none as long as Alice Berens, known always as Dollie, whose lineage traced directly back to Chief Jacob Berens. The number of men living at the station dwindled over the years as the centre of the white-fishing operations moved northward. That made it possible to convert some of the dining area into a bedroom, and for several months each year Dollie and her husband Jacob Gibeault made their life together there, he as a fisherman, she as the reigning queen of the island.

The focus of my attention was a bulky copper propeller on a rope hanging from a nail in the eave at the front of the cookhouse. Along the edges of its four chubby blades were the bites and bruises from rocks struck in bygone days. These wounds ended its days on the lake, but it found a new life as the kitchen bell. My job was to strike it with an iron rod every day at 9:30 for coffee, 12 for dinner, three for coffee, six for supper, and nine for coffee again. (Someone else would attend to the four a.m. breakfast bell. That was our one concession to life on the island; we had our breakfast at eight.) The propeller twisted around furiously with each hit, clanging out its message of invitation. I'd whack it again and again, aiming to strike each of its fins before I was finished, if I could keep track of which was which in the excitement of the moment. A sense of power surged through me as I bashed at the prop and started the sudden rush of men out of every nook and cranny of the island, up from the boats tied along the docks, and out from the shanty-roofed bunkhouses.

Directly in front of the boat now were the three peaks of the giant icehouse. It stored over 800 tons of ice cut from the lake in the winter and pulled block by block from the lake up a slide that looked like a section of an old roller coaster. The chunks were dropped down from the top of the icehouse and positioned into a giant iceberg held in place by two-foot-thick walls filled with sawdust. On top of the iceberg, a thick layer of hay had been woven to further protect the ice from the summer heat. The shore hands would climb up each day and with big picks chunk out ice pieces into the crusher below, which was driven by old two-cycle engines. Soon I'd be scrambling up there with them, smelling the sweet scent of hay.

Beside the icehouses was the dressing shed, covered with its shanty roof. The fishermen unloaded their catch on the small dock in front and pushed it in boxes over steel rollers into the shed. There, they dressed the fish at makeshift tables—plywood painted white, a diamond-shaped hole cut in the middle, positioned on top of a 45-gallon drum with its top cut off. The fishermen beheaded each fish, cut open the belly, pulled the guts out, scraped, and then swished the offal down the opening to the drum below. Beside the dressing shed was the packing shed, another shanty-roofed structure, where the fish was sorted and weighed. They packed 60 pounds of fish into a box and then filled each one with ice up to 100 pounds.

With the blood of the Icelandic fishermen in my veins, I took to anything related to fish and water. As I sat patiently, waiting for the next nibble on my line, there were invariably two or three seagulls perched on the pilings at the end of the dock. When I became conscious of their presence and looked up, I was suddenly aware seagulls were all around. They glided around the station aimlessly, gracefully, effortlessly, nothing particular to do, no mission on their minds. It was easy not to see them, but once you did it was impossible not to see them.

Emptying those gut drums was part of the daily routine on every fish station. Dragging the heavy barrels out of the sheds, down the dock, and onto the flat deck of the "gut boat" was the daily highlight for the birds, but definitely not for us. The only creatures as enthusiastic as the birds about the action in the sheds were the perch swimming under the docks below the sheds. The perch, unlike the seagulls, didn't have to wait for the transport to begin; their feast was quietly dropping from the end of the dock with neither fuss nor fanfare. No wonder the small pickerel hearts were attacked so vigorously when I dropped the hook into the water in the morning sun.

When those barrels came out of the sheds, the gulls knew their treat was imminent. I never missed the opportunity to be on that boat. As it pulled away from the station, the birds assembled from every direction. They were bolder now, and that meant coming closer. Excitement was building in the air. We headed out past the station to the island lying to the south, just large enough that there was lee on the far side and we could pull the boat up and dump the barrels on the rocky shore.

The birds were frenzied by that point, but they held back until it was clear we were pulling away. Then, pandemonium, squeaking and squawking reigned, the frantic birds almost colliding as they dove into the spoils. Those who might have questioned the practice of dumping on land would understand in a moment the power of nature to deal with some situations with unrivalled efficiency. The guts were gone, the birds were fed, and they turned to the heavens to wait for tomorrow. And we were on our way back to the station where the gut boat would be hosed down and readied for other tasks, like a trip to the mission across the bay later to watch a movie in the community hall.

The granite islands at the mouth of Berens River were paradise for the birds of Lake Winnipeg. Great swarms clustered on every island and rock outcropping on the ranges on the way in, and countless more filled the sky. Late every summer, the eggs covering the rocks came alive with fuzzy grey chicks bursting to track behind that gut boat as soon as nature strengthened their wings enough to fly.

As a boy, I was insatiably curious to get over to those islands and scramble around on the rocks to see the birds up close. Being out with the shore hands on the gut boat only whetted my appetite. At the same time, I was nervous about the prospect of having all those birds screeching around me when we got close to the nests. Nonetheless, my temptation grew stronger and stronger, and soon it was time to do it. Even Hitchcock's thriller, *The Birds*, which had frightened me senseless, could not deter me.

By the time I was eight I had my own rowboat that I used to move around the station. One day, Dollie's nephew Tom Bittern and I took my rowboat and headed to the nearest island. What we found was incredible: birds everywhere, eggs starting to hatch, little grey and fuzzy ones stumbling around fresh out of the egg. But the adults were above shrieking and diving closer and closer. My Hitchcock anxieties were materializing. We had to get out, now!

We had pulled the boat up onto the slippery granite. Tom jumped in and took the oars. I was supposed to push us off. In my zeal to get us going my feet slipped on the slime at the water's edge. I fell as the boat moved away from shore with me attached, but not on the inside where I desperately wanted to be. Not a strong swimmer back then, I feared I was heading for a dismal end in the deep below. I hung onto the gunwale with all my strength, and slowly hauled myself up and tumbled in. Tom was racing with the oars. Now that the birds had us on the run, they were relentless. After we got away and our breathing calmed, we agreed the trip had been well worth it.

When I was ten or eleven I was given permission to use one of the skiffs we had at the station, as if it was my own boat. It was huge for a kid like me, about 18 feet long, with a 25-horse outboard motor. That was real freedom. Now I could make the trip across the bay into the mouth of the river, past the Log Cabin Inn, and downriver half a mile to the dock alongside the Hudson's Bay store. Whenever I saw the MS *Keenora* coming by the island, I'd jump into my boat and head to the dock where she tied up. She was the big passenger ship that took people on week-long excursions and brought supplies to the settlements around the lake for decades. My mission was comparatively mundane. I was on a quest for ice cream, which the *Keenora*'s purser sold out of a booth on the main deck.

All thoughts of the excitement of the next few months were shoved aside when the *Spear* finally approached the dock. I tore up the steep stairs at the bow to the upper deck, where I could see and hear all the action and wave to Dad. There he was, trotting down the dock. As the tug pulled closer, the captain yelled from the wheelhouse to the deckhand below to toss the bowline, so he could leverage off this pivot and pull the boat alongside the dock.

The captain threw the engine into reverse, churning up a glistening turbulence and producing a thick cloud of smoke. If the weather was rough and the landing trickier, a small heaving line was attached to the main ropes below and thrown first from the upper deck. Whatever the case, Dad rushed to catch the line before it slid back into the water, and then tied it quickly to a mooring post so he could hustle down to catch the stern line. With all lines secure, the *Spear* was tight to the dock.

Even before the lines were fully cinched, my excitement got the best of me, and I catapulted onto the dock amid cries of consternation—"grab hold of that kid before he gets crushed between the boat and the dock"—from every quarter. I was a maniac. Only Major matched my enthusiasm. Upon the first sighting of land, even if it was in the form of a dock, he was determined to get there in a hurry. Given the slightest sliver of opportunity, Major would make a flying leap across the gap between boat and dock, and almost always landed four-square on Dad, knocking him back a step or two. Major's exuberance only added to the joy as the family reunited for the summer to come. And who could blame him? We were landed. We were north. When I stepped onto the dock at Berens River, I was the fourth generation of my family to do so.

CHAPTER THREE
Children Are People, Too

Kids and dogs lived free in Riverton, and that was the only way, as far as I was concerned. Adults accepted kids for who and what they were. My mom put it simply: "Children are people, too." I pushed this declaration of rights to its limits. My world was Riverton, and I believed I should be able to go anywhere, anytime—and I did, with Major beside me. Not only was he excellent company, he was my wise partner, known to pull me to the side of the road by my sleeve if I wasn't paying attention to an approaching car.

I've taken this worldview with me everywhere I've been since then, and that's a lot of places over a long time. Of course, I've had to bend a little in the cities with regard to dogs, but as long as my dog is on a leash it's with me and free. Leashes were never popular in Riverton. The only constraint on Major was having the school principal Pete Onysko chase him off school grounds at recess. Major could see us pour out onto the school grounds from his backyard, and he could never resist the temptation for some excitement with me and the other kids, even though Pete discouraged him constantly. Even Pete, who was our neighbour, seemed to understand such an irresistible urge, and the daily chase was mostly theatrics. The closest Major ever came to a leash on Lake Winnipeg was being tied at the front of the *Spear* for the trip north, but that was for his own safety. Even I could understand the logic of that.

Major and I took advantage our freedom every chance we got, and there was no better way to begin the day than by heading over to visit Amma and Afi Brynjolfson. Our first destination was the two-story warehouse—we called it a "covi"—in the backyard. The covi was thinner than it was tall, with huge, bulky doors swinging out from the front. There was so much stuff in there to grab hold of and discover what dreams your imagination might concoct for it. The smell of motors and oil and ropes was like nothing else. The floor was a rough, uneven concrete. Along one wall sat a workbench made from rugged lumber. Old wrenches and pipes lay on the bench, and below a tangle of old cables and chunks of metal. A rough-hewn bracket mounted along the wall was home to two 25-horse-power outboards—the only models of the time, an Evinrude and a Johnson.

The walls consisted of two-by-fours, with rough lumber siding on the outside. This was not a place for insulation and drywall. Rusted nails—usually crooked, because they'd been pulled out of old boards—served as hooks. Coils of rope hung on one, an old saw blade on another. And then there were those skates. Well, "skates" is stretching it. They were just rusty blades with an even rustier foot-shaped metal platform above, and leather thongs over top.

They were Afi's skates. And when I pulled them down off the wall and planted my boots on top of them he never tired of reminding me what they could do under power. He assured me that if I had the courage to challenge him, he could twist and turn, zig and zag, like I'd never seen in all my glory as a young hockey star. Afi had used the skates for many years to fly across the lake after first ice on his way to the prized first set of the nets (often the best catch of the season) when the ice was only a couple of inches thick.

Those skates also carried with them a far bigger story. Afi's nephew Helgi Jones recounted it at Afi and Amma's fiftieth anniversary celebration. Afi, his brother Beggi, and Beggi's three sons, Allan, Helgi and Binnie, set off on their usual late fall routine with hope and excitement, as fishermen always did in anticipation of another season. They crossed open water before freeze-up to their fishing grounds at Deer Island, about eight miles northwest of Hecla Island. Ice came to that spot sooner, meaning they wouldn't need to wait as long for that magic first lift.

The lake froze partially in the following days, but the ice was unpredictable and weak. Allan became gravely ill and needed medical attention. His circumstances were dire, and they had no alternative but to make the extraordinarily dangerous trip across the ice. Afi, Binnie and Helgi put a skiff on a sleigh with good runners. They bundled Allan up as much as they could and put him in the bottom of the boat. Afi and his nephews donned their skates, and with all their strength pushed the skiff across the treacherous expanse to the mainland, where they were met by the doctor. Allan was rushed to Winnipeg, but the poison from a ruptured appendix had spread throughout his body. He died shortly thereafter.

Hanging on the wall beside the memory-filled skates was a knotted clump of ragged old dog harnesses. It was the sign of an ending era. The horses already gone, the dogs were next, their work taken over by tractors. When Afi bought his first tractor in 1947, his dogs were retired from service, and I remember the last one dying in the early '50s.

One summer in the covi I pushed patience and dignity to the limit, for both Major and Afi. I don't see how Afi could have been so mad. It was, after all, he who left the paint cans in the covi. Although I suppose it's true that Major's need for a cosmetic uplift was all my idea. He really was magnificent, with the classic golden-brown markings of a Scotch collie and the rare feature of a full white collar. He had an admirable streak of independence and freedom, but hanging out with me it was easy to see how he came into that. He was a beautiful specimen. Still, everyone can use a touch-up here and there. For reasons that baffle me now, Major sat demurely as I gave him a paint job with a dirty old brush and whatever colours hadn't turned to stone in the old cans.

We met Afi when we emerged from the covi. Afi loved his own dogs and Major, too, and this was not something that Afi, usually tolerant with me beyond reason, was going to let pass. He was disgusted with me, and I was becoming more and more disgusted with myself every painful minute as Afi cut away the mess. Major emerged after several minutes, shorn and shredded and considerably less colourful. As I reflect back on that scene, I think even more than by my ill-fated choice to paint the dog, Afi was baffled at the fact that Major would let me do such a thing to him. I guess it was proof beyond measure of the bond Major and I shared.

Major's enthusiasm for life rebounded by the next day, but it took months for me to forget this transgression against my dear friend, and several more months for Major's majesty to return. I've made many mistakes in my time —usually well-intentioned—that have haunted me, but none more than that day. "Why? What were you thinking? You should be ashamed of yourself." At these moments, Major appears in my mind's eye, enthusiastic as ever and forgiving. Thank God for that.

There was no more dismal day in my young life than when Major tried to bound across the railway tracks in front of an oncoming train beside Afi and Amma's house, beckoned by a call from a bunch of kids, me included, and was sliced in two as his arthritis made him stumble at the critical moment. Telling Mom and Dad was a tough moment; burying Major in two parts was tougher still.

The next stop on my journey of memories through the covi was a little orange tractor. From as early as I can remember, I would scramble around trying to climb into its wooden cab and sit behind the steering wheel. There was a big story behind this little beast. The farm-equipment manufacturer Allis Chalmers began to build small rubber-tired tractors known as the "Model B." The ingenuity of the local blacksmiths and mechanics went to work on the Model B as they transformed machines designed for toil in the fields and readied them for service on the snow and ice. They figured out how to position and attach an "idler arm" travelling from the back axle to a point more than halfway to the front tires. Then they stretched rubber-ribbed tracks over the small tire on the idler arm and the much larger rear tires. They mounted skis on the front tires, and a fully mobile and functioning snow machine was ready to replace dogs and horses. They were light and small and ideally suited for individual fishermen. Soon they were pulling small sled-mounted cabooses across the snowdrift-covered expanse of the lake, and it was increasingly rare to encounter one of the dog teams that had long powered fishing operations on Lake Winnipeg. Afi bought his first tractor in 1947, and his beloved dogs went into retirement.

One of the days I finally rode in the tractor, it became an icon that I accept, with chagrin, into my personal history. I had been negotiating tirelessly to be taken fishing with Afi Malli and Uncle Grimsi, and the day had finally arrived. The tractor was out of the covi, and we were easing down the bank onto the ice-covered river. I was seven, but sitting on Afi's lap helping to steer, I felt manhood was just over the next snowdrift. We chugged down the middle of the river for about two miles before we travelled out onto the frozen lake.

We rode along in peaceful silence. Afi was in his element. Not many men fished every season, summer, fall and winter, but Afi did, and in some ways he preferred the winter. Something about the crisp, winter stillness captivated Afi. There was nothing cozy about it, though. It was cold, often 40 below zero or lower, but the real problem was the merciless wind insinuating its way to raw flesh no matter how many layers of clothing you wore. (Afi and Grimsi later told me that one of the most important advances ever for winter fishing was the one-piece garment developed as a snowsuit for Ski-Dooers in the late '50s.) Afi's enjoyment of winter fishing likely stemmed less from the weather and more from the fact his only son Grimsi usually fished with him in the winter season. Grimsi made his life in construction, building roads and ditches through some of the most difficult terrain imaginable. But come freeze-up he headed onto the ice, living the life he'd been born into and loved no less than his dad. This worked out nicely for both of them, because the lake is covered in ice almost six months each year. The cold autumn waters start glazing over in the last half of November, and it's not until the end of May that open water returns to the lake.

We travelled along in bitter cold. With extreme temperatures came a steady barometer, so the wind was less likely to blow that day. But when the weather system started changing the wind created a fury of swirling drifts. On those days they inched their way home using small evergreens they had cut and posted along the trail as their guide. When they lost sight of those, the only eye on which they could rely was the old compass they'd taken from the boat and placed on the floorboards beside them.

We climbed out into the frigid air when we arrived at their nets. The task at hand was to chisel out the ice that had formed over the hole since the nets

were last lifted. They had spread hay over top to cut down on new ice formation. There was still a good layer, but it took only a few minutes to get through.
Opening up a new hole was much harder. The ice was five or six feet deep by
January. It wasn't easy work, pounding the long iron bars deeper and deeper
into the ice, shovelling away the chips every couple of minutes, until finally a
bar drove through and the first sign of water sloshed up into the hole, filling it
to the brim within moments. A few years later, this operation would take but
minutes as a power auger ratcheted through the ice shield to the water below.

When the water started gurgling in the uncovered hole, Afi reached to the
corner and grabbed what looked like a plank with a metal contraption in the
middle. One of the Lake Winnipeg Icelanders had invented this tool, called a
"jigger," to run the nets under the water. This ingenious contraption consisted
of a plank about six feet long. A slot was cut into the middle of the plank and
an iron rod was placed inside and mounted to the plank with two pins so that
it pivoted. There was a weight on one end of the rod and a hook on the other.
When the plank was pushed under the ice it was attached to a thin rope used
to jiggle the plank and the rod so that it crawled along under the ice. The fishermen listened as it clunked its way under the ice, and when it had travelled
far enough away to stretch a net, they cut a second hole. The jigger popped to
the surface with the line attached and the net attached to the line. They "set"
the net in place between the two holes, stretched tight by corks on the upper
line and leads on the lower, with an anchor holding it to the bottom. The jigger was an ingeniously simple but invaluable device, which was "exported"
back to Iceland for fishing on the frozen northern lakes.

I wasn't warmed by hard work like Afi and Uncle Grimsi, and it was perhaps
15 minutes before I felt the cold crawling though my parka and boots. At the first
sign of discomfort, I was relegated back into the cab to warm up. Never one to sit
still for long, I soon wearied of pretending to steer and broke the silence to ask if I
could go back and sit in the caboose. It was a small shack around eight feet wide
and ten feet long mounted on a sleigh pulled behind the tractor. In one corner
sat a metal space heater, its chimney stretching through the ceiling into the fresh
air. The heater's fire was dying down, so I made it my business to stoke it up. As I
put the wood on the fire, I noticed the woollen mitts hanging on a line across the
corner behind the stove. Mitts were central to the lives of winter fishermen. They
needed to be flexible enough to let the men pick fish from the gill nets and thick
enough to protect their fingers from the excruciating cold. It was a tricky combination, but with the customary fisherman ingenuity, woollen mitts became the
covering of choice, with a change every half hour or so from one pair to another
as they dropped them off their hands into a pot of boiling water.

I could still feel dampness in the mitts in the caboose, and I resolved that my contribution to the morning's work would be getting the fire roaring so they would dry out in short order. I stuffed so much wood into the stove that I had to wedge the last piece in with a good kick from my boot. The damper was wide open and the heat built quickly. I checked the mitts again and again, pleased with the speedy effect my labours were having. I knew Afi and Grimsi would be impressed when they came in for coffee and were treated to cosy, dry mitts for the trip back out.

The heat pouring off the stove made reaching behind it to inspect the mitts increasingly difficult. Soon I couldn't get anywhere close to the corner, and I was broiling in my heavy parka. My apprehension rose even more rapidly than the caboose's temperature. The stove metal began turning a deep red, and it looked as if it might melt. I tried to reach the damper, hoping to close off the air, but the heat pushed me back. Suddenly my concerns took on a whole new dimension. The mitts were starting to singe, and the burning wool filling the tiny room was the smell of fear to my young nose. The singeing became a deep charring. The mitts were about to burn up before my helpless eyes.

Outside, Afi and Grimsi had finally broken through the ice. Whether they sensed something was wrong—by then the caboose was probably radiating heat—or whether they were simply coming in for the morning coffee, they were hit by a wall of heat as they opened the door and bent down to enter. Afi burst through in alarm, grabbing me with one hand and swinging me out the door in a graceful arc with the other. He went for the damper with his boot and managed to crank it around to cut off the air supply. Then he turned to the mitts, which were dangerously close to breaking into flames that could have en-gulfed the whole caboose. Afi flung them out the door, some burned to a char, others with deep burn lines, most with just a new, sickly brown hue. The reek of burnt wool was nauseating. Amid the pandemonium, I can recall nothing of what Afi or Grimsi said, but it was no doubt a fair amount, combined with gratitude that nothing more serious had happened. I can still see the horror on their faces as they charged into the caboose.

When we returned home, the smell of pönnukökurs (Icelandic pancakes) awaited us, thankfully drowning out, at least temporarily, the smell of singed wool lingering in my nostrils. The mitts episode was seared inside the crevices of my mind and retrieved every time I went into Afi and Amma's basement. Amma always hung the mitts down there to dry when the men came in from the lake. For years, some of the mitts that had escaped a fiery death with only singe marks or a ribbon of brown leered out at me accusingly. Whenever the story came up, I chuckled along with the rest of them, but I have to admit that even a couple decades later there was a hint of discomfort in my laugh. Many times over the years in the moments and days after a close call (and there have been many in a long career), thoughts of the chaos and stink inside the caboose that afternoon have wandered into my mind.

The memories of Amma's pönnukökurs, on the other hand, bring only comfort. I never saw Amma Villa use a recipe for anything, and certainly not for the pönnukökurs. Her batter ingredients were simple: flour, eggs, baking soda and a pinch of salt. I thought there must have been other, secret ingredients, but I never saw her put them in. The ingredients may have been plain, but Amma's alchemy turned them into perfect golden-brown pancakes so thin and light they were almost transparent.

Amma's wrists must have been strong. Most people used a small, light pan to make pönnukökurs, but not her; she turned to her old companion, her cast iron pan. She wielded it as if it were part of her arm. Over the stove it went, onto the elements, and then, with a mesmerizing flick of her wrist, miraculously twisting that black block of iron, Amma sent a perfectly round pancake soaring into the air, where it turned magically on its belly, then dropped straight back down snug into the pan. Then it was a quick walk to the kitchen counter for the coronation. She crowned the pancakes with a generous sprinkling of brown sugar and rolled them up like a rug. Pönnukökurs were a constant distraction.

Often when I arrived at Afi and Amma's, Afi and Uncle Grimsi would be working outside getting the nets, boats and equipment ready. Spring was the busiest time. Step one was to retrieve the nets from the attic of the covi, where they'd been hung at the end of the previous season. I'd crawl up the ladder at the back corner of the warehouse and pass through a trap door to find the nets hanging like hammocks across the open second story. I'd pass them down to Afi and Grimsi who would prepare them for action by attaching corks and leads at the top and bottom. This was just the first of many tasks. Next, the boats needed to be scraped and repaired.

Throughout it all, Afi and Grimsi worked together seamlessly, as they had all their lives, talking constantly in Icelandic, but switching effortlessly to English when I arrived. Not much got by me in those days, for I recognized most Icelandic words and always had the gist of what was being said. I never really contemplated why my own ability to speak Icelandic wasn't encouraged back then. Even Mom wasn't allowed to speak Icelandic at school in Hecla (although still today she reads, writes and speaks flawless Icelandic). Later, I came to understand that the focus on English was widespread among most people who had another living language within their family, for the priority was equipping young people for what was seen as an English-speaking world.

That I regret to this day. But any such thoughts of immigrant identity and integration were years ahead of me as I watched Afi and Grimsi work, poking around and asking questions, listening ever more absent-mindedly to their patient answers as my belly grew restless.

"Afi, maybe I should go see whether Amma has the coffee on yet?" I would offer.

He inevitably agreed it was a good idea for me to check it out, and I rushed inside. My real motive wasn't coffee of course, but the pönnukökurs, which I knew would be in the making when the men were home in the morning.

"Amma, the men want to know when they should come in for coffee," I sputtered, my eyes riveted on the fresh pancakes already sitting on the plate. My ploy was easily overwhelmed by their presence. "Amma, can I have one?"

"Yes, dear, you go ahead, and then get your Afi and Grimsi here for coffee."

Soon they were at opposite ends of the table, gazing out the window across the tracks, over the river and into the village. I pulled up in the middle. Amma was still at the stove, as usual. When she heard the water boiling she hoisted the kettle and poured it through the coffee bag, her second indispensable piece of equipment. The bag drooped from its mooring on the hand-moulded copper tubing that fit into the opening of the coffee pot. It looked like a dirty old sock, but was actually cheesecloth darkened by the countless cups of coffee that had dripped through it.

The Icelanders' love of coffee is the stuff of legend, likely an outcome of some early Viking voyages. The symbol of this part of our culture, since the days of New Iceland, has been the coffee bag. Without the bag, a true Icelandic cup of coffee can never be served. The Nobel Prize-winning Icelandic author Halldór Laxness understood how deeply entwined coffee is with Icelandic life. His characters in *Independent People* extol the virtues of the wondrous drink. At one point, the tragically stubborn Bjartur of Summerhouses demonstrates his weakness for coffee's aroma: "In such a fragrance the perversity of the world is forgotten and the soul is inspired with faith in the future...."

Amma's coffee always tasted the best. My taste for the drink, however, developed much later. In the early days I was pretty much confined to milk. Afi and Grimsi, on the other hand, woke up every morning with cups of coffee in their hands, and it was nearly bedtime before they put their cups down.

With coffee and pönnukökurs came talk, and lots of it. I loved that almost as much as the food. The topics were always the events of the day, history, or the great issues of the times. Afi wasn't one for small talk or gossip, nor were Grimsi and Amma. They hashed out the serious topics endlessly, filling the room with energy. Usually, something Afi had read in the paper the night before would get things going, and he often came armed with statistics that appeared seemingly magically to pepper his arguments. That's when things got interesting.

"Just where did you get that information from, Malli?" Amma would challenge. "You don't know anything about that."

"From an article in the *Free Press* two weeks ago," Afi would reply, swiftly and unswervingly. An article now of course long gone, so checking it wasn't an option. His premise would have to be taken upon faith, but Amma was rarely so inclined.

Then Grimsi would jump in. "Dad, who are these people producing all these statistics?"

Afi's knock-out punch was "the encyclopedia," which he rarely threw, but it meant that he was confident in the answer for it could readily checked by pulling out one of the 20 volumes of the *Book of Knowledge* that he had bought from a travelling salesman who landed in Hecla in the heart of the Depression. Mom tells me that he had spent endless hours working his way through all 20 volumes. He shared them with the young Eggertson boys next door, whose mother made a special velvet bag to carry this precious cargo between the houses protected from rain or snow. The boys went on to military service and great careers, no doubt with pieces of these books inside them. Afi was a learned man in the most ancient sense of that word notwithstanding that his formal education ended at Grade 2.

By the time I was six I was in the thick of the debate, stirring all my learned opinions into the pot. Amma defended anything I said, especially if it contradicted Afi. "Listen to Glenn, Malli," she'd chide.

That was all an obstreperous kid like me needed to hear, and I was soon going full tilt, not about to be subdued. The conversation would inevitably come round to Afi asking me what mark I got on my latest test. I would announce proudly that I had achieved a score of 100 percent on my test, and Afi would respond, "How come you didn't do better than that? I always used to get 110 percent when I was your age!" Once we got to percentages in school, I was finally onto that wily old fox.

Sometimes Grimsi took the lead in the conversation. His focus was most likely a funny situation that had occurred, or an idiosyncratic twist of some character who had struck his funny bone. Grimsi was an infectiously charming storyteller, and whether his comments were delivered with a sardonic twist or a belly laugh, the energy would inevitably build as others piped in with additional details. His stories were never mean-spirited, but rather celebrated the wonderful, curious and unpredictable ways people work and think. He excavated the humour in the improbable and the imponderable. Laughter was always part of that table.

With Afi, Amma and Grimsi, there was no doubt that kids were people, too. I loved every minute of it. I was born with a lust for learning, and thankfully so, given all that I crowded into my busy schedule from as early as I can recall. Certain topics cropped up regularly at Afi and Amma's. Afi was ever watchful of the chemical world. He always cast a careful eye when he smelled fresh bread as we came into the house. As long as it was brown bread everything was fine, but he reacted swiftly on those days when he saw the white loaves laid out on the counter. As far as Afi was concerned, the natural state of bread was brown, and anything white could only be so as a result of having had a chemical scrub of some kind. But the simple fact was that Amma made phenomenal white bread, and the taste was more than enough to compensate for any chemical intrusion into our stomachs. "Chemicals are destined to get us all" was a theme Afi explored with endless creativity. His greatest fear was that one day the fishermen on Lake Winnipeg would look back and wonder why they were never more worried about the possible effects of chemicals on the waters. This topic incited his passions more than any other. Long before it was fashionable to be an environmentalist, Afi was convinced that chemicals would prove to be the bane of our collective existence.

The talk at the kitchen table ended as quickly as it had begun, like a Lake Winnipeg squall. The men would go back to work, and calm and idle chatter over the task at hand (in Icelandic again) would replace the great topics of the day. Amma would cut the remaining pancakes in half, cover them on a dish, and into the fridge they would go until afternoon coffee, except for the ones I had in each hand as I scrambled out of the kitchen, leaving Amma to take the old pan, wipe it off, and stow it back above the stove until it was time to cook that evening's pickerel.

"Where are you going?" Afi would ask as I readied myself to leave.

"To the office!" I'd reply, and Major and I would march off down the road.

CHAPTER FOUR
My Riverton

The office of Sigurdson Fisheries, Sig Fish as everyone called it, didn't look like how you might imagine a major centre of commerce, but it was action central of the fishing world in Manitoba. An endless stream of activity poured through the front doors, which faced the main street of Riverton. The office was on a large property along the Icelandic River, just south of the "three houses" of the Sig Fish founders: my Afi Sigurdur Victor, always known as SV, Stefan Valdis, known as Steve, and Sigurdur Runberg, known as SR. The Sigurdson houses were built in the '20s on adjacent riverfront plots, and when Dad returned from the war he was able to purchase the three acres of land needed to qualify for a Veterans' Land Act loan a short way south along the river.

Behind the Sig Fish office was the "big garage" where the machinery-related work took place, with nets and equipment stored upstairs. Another sizeable building stood at the south end of the property, a grey tin oil shed where the 45-gallon gasoline drums were stored, fronted by a large loading deck where trucks delivered and received gasoline and diesel.

The office was larger inside than it looked from the street, with a warehouse at the back, a storage area upstairs, and the main open office area in front, with two solid wooden desks. A tall counter greeted you as you came in the front door and an imposing black safe dominated the far wall beside the two-way radio. The safe was always open during the day, and closed each night with a final spin of the clumsy lock once the books and business of the day were returned for safekeeping.

In the darkness of a winter morning, I sometimes accompanied Dad when he went in to open up. At first the building was dark, freezing, and not just a little bit creepy. Even worse, the sturdy brown oil heater along the main wall became grumpy from time to time, causing the nauseating smell of heating oil to permeate the office. In an elegant frame on the main wall sat a large portrait of my great-grandfather Stefan, Sigurdur's oldest son. In 1882, as a boy of 18 in Hecla, Stefan and his younger brother Johannes were amongst the first commercial fishermen on Lake Winnipeg. From the humblest of beginnings the Sigurdsson Brothers, as they were often called, became a major force in the business and life of New Iceland at the turn of the century. Often called Captain Steve, with only the credential of charisma to warrant the title, he was a larger-than-life figure known to have once exclaimed upon once missing the train: "That's the damn problem when you don't own everything yourself." (see *Train Stories from the Icelandic River*.)[3]

As you walked past the counter on the left was Afi SV's office—in today's terms, the CEO's office. It had been his space since the day the place was built, but he was almost always away in those years, running the family-owned construction business Monarch Construction at a job site somewhere in Manitoba building roads and ditches. There was always a lonely, empty feeling in the room when Afi SV wasn't there, but when he was it was a beehive, with Pal, his faithful cocker spaniel, in the middle of the action. Under the glass cover of the wooden desk that consumed much of the office were pictures of people and stations on the lake and vessels that had passed through family hands over the years, many of which had gone down in Lake Winnipeg storms.

The other fixtures in the office were my dad, at the desk closest to the counter, and Les Peaker, who sat at the back desk. Les was a remarkable man who exuded a quiet dignity and great competence. He'd been hit hard by the Great Depression. Before joining Sig Fish, Peaker was the name across many of the huge elevators in prairie grain towns, but the Great Depression brought Peaker Grain down. When that happened, Les, a widower with two boys and a new wife, was on the streets looking for work. A friend told Afi about the talents Les could bring to any business and in 1942 he went from running a grain company to the big desk in the back of the Sig Fish office. He became the financial and administrative hub of the various operations that circulated around the fishing business. It seemed that when you were in the fish business you were in every business, and Sigurdsons became the doers and dealers of everything that was needed. That meant Les was kept busy with the books and administration of the fish company, Monarch Construction, the Lake Winnipeg Fur Farm, the Gimli Hotel, North Star Oil (later to become a division of Shell), the Allis-Chalmers dealership and the Johnson Motors dealership. He later kept track of the Ski-Doos from Bombardier. When Dad joined the company, he was mentored by Les, and when Les left in the early '60s to become secretary treasurer of the newly formed Evergreen School Division, Dad took over his desk and role on top of his management responsibilities.

Everyone with any connection to fishing would at some point find their way into the Sig Fish office, for while it was ostensibly a place of business, it was also a major social centre. People would come to accomplish a task, then stay for news and gossip about the fishing world. Some people wandered in just to say hello. SR was always in peak form with an endless repertoire of stories from the old days and Steve and Victor would dart in and out ready to bark an order or serve up an order of their own gossip.

Riverton began its life as Icelandic River, the designated headquarters of New Iceland. Its personality as a community was exuberant and entrepreneurial. First was the fishing. Men and supplies came rolling and stumbling into town from every direction as a new season got underway. If you were in the business of fishing on Lake Winnipeg, you were also in the transportation business, moving fish on water and ice. Soon you were building winter ice roads and then real roads. Sometime later, the big tractor trains stole the show, with the Sigurdsons hauling endless sleighs of goldeye and tulibee to the big company warehouses along the rail line, then carrying supplies and equipment to the fishing camps up north and Ontario's Favorable Lake mine. Later, Riverton became the base camp for the Sigfusson's winter road empire across northern Manitoba. When the tractor trains arrived, Riverton became "the gateway to the North," as it was called. Soon clearing trees and building trails through frozen swamps for tractors would become building roads for trucks and cars.

When Riverton became a big construction centre, men went away for months at a time, not in pursuit of fish, but to build roads and ditches across northern Canada. In Riverton's surrounding areas, many made their living as farmers. Others lived in the bush and cut lumber and pulp. Riverton was a busy place with a frontier feel that found its way into the beer parlours at the Sandy Bar and Riverton Hotels. This was not a sleepy village; there was always "stuff happening." Some might have called it a rowdy place, but despite its rambunctious exterior, Riverton had style, spirit and talent.

Riverton is in the past for me, but the spirit of those times and the people lives on. In that sense, Riverton is, and always will be, home. Like any place, Riverton has changed over time. It's different now, but "my" Riverton remains the same. I left the village but it has never left me.

But in the muskeg of the North, roads were in many ways only an excuse to build a ditch. That's where the draglines came into the picture, essentially engines on big platforms with a long boom sticking out, rigged with cables to throw a one-and-a-half-cubic-yard scoop out into the muck to build a road an inch at a time. Then came the expansion into tractors. Monarch Construction appeared first and built roads across the province. It was also the first and largest contractor in the building of the Winnipeg Floodway. Another key player was Steinni Erickson, a mechanic who survived six hours as a sitting duck in an ocean of blood when his landing barge became stuck off the beach at Dunkirk.

He returned to build an army of machines from a base of one tree bulldozer. Erickson Construction became the pre-eminent contractor on the rebuilding of the Winnipeg Floodway 40 years later. Icelanders, many guys who I guess one would refer to as Métis, and Ukrainians worked together, along with many others, all of whom I regard as unsung and unrecognized heroes who battled incredibly difficult situations transforming swamps into farms and opening up new lands.

Many local men were part of Riverton's legacy of construction leaders, but no one would challenge the idea that Afi's name deserves a special place within those ranks. His quiet form of leadership was built on loyalty to his men, a loyalty which the men returned earnestly. They never let Afi down. Beside him were his two sons, Ralph, and Gordon, and SR's son Johnnny. Ralph would die in a tragic car crash coming home from a job site, putting Afi into profound mourning for many months. There were whole families of brothers and fathers and sons who stayed through thick and thin with him. There were the Zagozewski brothers, first trained by their dad, a skilled blacksmith from the old country. The Hokanson brothers were unequalled as equipment operators, and when the ground froze they went north on the tractor trains with the Sigfussons. Einar Palson, a key man with Afi for years, came with sons alongside; his son Ken, a kid operator like me, would become a prominent contractor in Manitoba. My schoolmate Harley Jonasson, alongside his brother and Dad, was another of the kid operators for whom Afi made sure there was a job. The Finnson Brothers, Fridjon and Wilfred, were top notch, whether sitting behind the levers or with a wrench, and in later years, Wilfred, SR's son-in-law, resurrected the Monarch name for his own company. No man was closer to Afi than Freddy Johnson, an army veteran from the Second World War. Afi relied on his leadership talents on the jobsite. The Monarch alumni are far-flung and plentiful. Everyone who was part of the company has worn his status as a "Monarch man" as a badge of honour, a membership in an august club. If a Monarch man went anywhere, it was to start his own operations, and when that happened it was with Afi's support and the Monarch badge to help him open doors.

Fishing extended its tentacles in many other ways into the life of the community. Chris Thorsteinson and his father before him had been making boats for more than 50 years, first with wood and then with steel. Riverton Boatworks developed the technology of compartmentalization in boat construction, which enabled them to build vessels in Riverton and then move them across Canada by truck to Newfoundland and the Canadian Arctic. One of their most challenging assignments was a moving exhibition of the *Nonsuch*, a replica of the Hudson's Bay Company's boat from the 1600s, 3,000 miles across North America to her final home at the Museum of Man and Nature in Winnipeg.

Sveinn Thompson was the doctor to the village and folks from miles around for more than 50 years. The centre of his domain was the Riverton Drug Store located in a small building on the main street. The floor was dark wooden planking, and on the right was a huge glass-topped counter and along the wall shelves laden with pill bottles. At the back was his office with one small examining table. When he was in, the most prominent thing you saw as you entered was the angular valise of wrinkled leather and worn handles. That was the real "office," for Doc Thompson was on the road in people's homes as often as he was ever in that room. As best as I can recall, you never made an appointment to see him in his office; you just showed up and waited.

His son Johnny was the pharmacist, sitting behind the counter hour upon hour. In one corner was a rack with magazines and comic books. Kids used to hang around there, but not for long, as maintaining a low profile in those tight quarters was impossible, and soon the awkward silence would have us back out the front door. An unlikely nerve centre for the well-being of the community and the neighbouring region, but somehow the Riverton Drug Store was perfectly suited to that place and time.

In the Icelandic way, everyone young and old knew each other by their first name, so even when I was four it was Oli, not Mr. Olafson, for example, although there may have been 60 years between us. This was true for every person except Doc or Doctor Thompson. This was the only way I ever knew him. I didn't even know his first name was Sveinn until I was well into my twenties. In his later years, as he worked away at his book, *Riverton,* he would come in to visit Afi for endless hours. Doc Thompson had been enamored by the lake and its people since boyhood. He grew up in Selkirk, then a bustling harbour and action center in the fish world. They'd relive their days together, with Doc checking and confirming facts, and reminisce about his childhood memories of running on the Selkirk dock after Afi's dad, Captain Steve, a man whom he described as his "Horatio Alger storybook hero."

Riverton's memory bank was full of Doc Thompson stories. The mention of his name was always with a quiet aura of respect. I can still see (or at least I remember hearing the story so often) Doc in his office squinting at a bottle handed him by my anguished mother. Scrutinizing the red liquid inside, he said, "This isn't blood. This is food dye. Has he eaten something?" The jig was up on my illicit snack. Mom discovered an empty bottle of maraschino cherries when we returned home, and the diagnosis was confirmed. Doc was an acknowledged master of diagnosis. He knew everyone in the community, their mother and father, and grandmother and grandfather. He knew family dispositions and traits, so when he made a referral to the famous Thorlakson Clinic, now known as the Winnipeg Clinic, any tentative diagnosis reached by Doc Thompson was embraced with respect. From three onwards Dr. Thompson called me the "little boy with the big words" as I made my rounds about the village talking to anyone and everyone.

Next to people, I believe Doc Thompson's next greatest passion was trees. In this, he had a narrow lead on Kris Thorarinson, who ran a general store and a lumber business based on a mill he operated at Hecla; most of the trees in the community were planted by one or the other. Doc also exercised his devotion to the people and community wearing many other hats, including as an MLA (member of the legislative assembly) and, in his last years, as a historian of the area.

Doc Thompson was our hero, and we shared him with the surrounding area. He had a special relationship with the people from Hecla. Afi Malli was often his chauffeur, taking him by dog team in winter or boat the rest of the year. However, it wasn't Afi behind the sleigh the night of December 17, 1927. For my mother, only five-and-a-half years old, the day began shrouded in mystery, but it remains indelibly implanted in her memory. Still in their first home, a "shanty" on the wind-whipped shores of Hecla Island, there was an air of expectation that soon turned into apprehension and tension. Kristjana, my mother's cousin, arrived to look after Mom and distract her from questions about what was going on. Mom became all the more mystified when the woman who sometimes helped with washing in the house arrived on the scene and began carrying hot water and towels into her bedroom. "Was she now washing people as well as clothes?" she wondered. It was getting dark, the wind was howling, and Afi was pacing the floor. Suddenly, they heard the scraping of sleigh runners, and dogs yelping. The back door opened and Dr. Thompson burst through. He threw off his heavy coat and rushed into the bedroom. It was less than an hour later that my mother's only sister arrived safe and sound. A couple of years later he insisted on making the same five-hour trip for Solveig bouncing in a cariole (a toboggan with canvas sides) to cover the 25 miles from Riverton in near blizzard conditions to ensure she not grow up disfigured as a result of a bad cut. Enroute, the sleigh broke through the ice and tragedy was narrowly averted.

Nothing epitomized Riverton better than its ice rink, and the efforts to build it. "Now is the time. Let's go boys, it's now or never!" someone shouted. And another shout: "There is no better time!" And so, in the late fall of 1949 the decision to make a final push to complete an enclosed ice-rink in Riverton was made. Afi SV, the first mayor of Riverton, recounted the details upon the opening of the Riverton Skating Rink on January 7, 1950. That night, the Riverton Skating Rink joined the railway station, the community hall and the big school as the places where the soul of the community resided. As Afi SV said back then: "In Riverton, as in all towns of its size and economic conditions, a project such as this can be successful only when everyone in the community is behind the effort. It can truly be said that this is a successful community effort because every organization and every home in the community has in one way or another taken a part in the work. The fundamental reason for such wonderful co-operation and success is the hope and faith that we are doing something worthwhile for the youth of our community; that good clean sport will build better citizens for tomorrow."

Doc Thompson conceived of the project of a closed-in rink around 1947. Building a better future for the youth of the community was top of his agenda. Financial contributions started rolling in, but completing the task wouldn't be possible without substantial commitments of volunteer time and talent. Local crews sourced tamarack stands and Chris Thorsteinson's Riverton Boatworks transformed them into huge arches. Foundations were poured under the direction of a local contractor, Kalli Vopni. School principal Peter Onysko stood alongside his senior students, helping with the work. Frost was coming and it looked like the project would need to be postponed, but the cry for the big final push rang out. A volunteer force of carpenters, fishermen and farmers was mobilized under the leadership of Oli Olafson, who drove the project to completion, except for the wiring. The young electricians Benedictson, Collins and Johnson "came to the rescue," completing the enormous amount of wiring needed for a building that size.

Building the rink was a remarkable achievement for a community of Riverton's size. The grand opening was made an even greater success by the presence of skaters from the Winnipeg Winter Club. They became involved through the leadership of Solli Thorvaldson, then a prominent Winnipeg lawyer and soon to become a well-known senator, but first and foremost a son of Riverton, whose father Sveinn Thorvaldson had long been a cornerstone of the community. That night began a long relationship between the Riverton Ice Club and the Winnipeg Winter Club, which provided the skating instructors and guest performers for the annual carnivals. When my Afi opened the fourth carnival on February 27, 1953, he was able to report that the rink had now been further developed with the addition of a time clock and bleachers and the completion of the upstairs club rooms with hardwood floors and drapes. The club rooms were soon the home of everything from the international organization of country women known as the Women's Institute, to the social hub of the big bonspiels when the ice became a curling rink for three days each year.

No childhood memory is more vivid for me than the endless hours I spent in that rink, starting as a little boy waiting on the bench for my skates to be tied tight by Walter Kornick, the first caretaker. Those were the days when the term "caretaker" was tantamount to "caregiver," and in Walter's wake came Dori and Margaret Bjornson, who were like surrogate parents to most of the kids in the village. Hockey was huge in Riverton, and had been since the 1930s. When the Riverton Lions Senior A team roared across the Interlake region, competitive passions were especially fired up as they entered the arenas of the neighbouring towns of Arborg and Gimli. My hockey obsession had me coaching the peewees after school, practising every night from seven to eleven, playing concurrently at three levels: Midget, Juvenile, and the Lions. Your ability to skate and handle the puck was the condition of entry, not age, and with the Riverton Lions I was playing games every Friday and Sunday with guys as old as 35. With games on Friday and Sunday night, the Lake Winnipeg Hockey League was the NHL of those days for kids like me. When the Riverton Lions won the championship in 1962 there was a motorcade over a mile long that made its way to Beausejour where the victory was secured before 1,200 fans. My big chance was the next year when I got to take a seat on the Lions bench.

No one escaped the clutches of the Riverton Figure Skating Club and the women (like my mom) who ran it, especially not the aspiring young hockey players. I proudly made my debut as Gus Gus the Mouse in Cinderella in the carnival of 1954. Figure skating taught us to skate erect, not crouched in the typical hockey bend, and so gave us better stick control. The rise to NHL superstar status of our own Reggie Leach gave the village a new brand: "Home of the Riverton Rifle." Those of us who played with him in the early days attach ourselves by association to a little corner of his success. At a "Legacy of the Lions" tribute on September 21, 2013 with 300 people in attendance, honouring the players and fans alike over the generations, former Philadelphia Flyer Reggie was there, as he has always been, supporting the community which had always been his greatest source of support. Perhaps Reggie would never have shot down the ice with those smooth and mighty strides, driving the puck to the net from just over the blue line, as he did in winning the NHL scoring championships, and the Conn Smythe Trophy, without the inspiration of the figures skaters.

Like the presence of the rink and the inspiration it created, music was part of everyone's life. Nothing better epitomized the "mustang" spirit just below the surface in the community than the remarkable New Year's Eve dance. The hall would fill well beyond capacity as it accommodated our entire village, along with the Ukrainian settlers at Shorncliffffe and Ledwyn, and even some Hecla Islanders. The New Year's parties were going strong by the time midnight arrived. Johnny and His Musical Mates, the local band, were reaching a climax as Johnny, with his brother Chris and other Johanneson family members beside him, waltzed and polkaed the community across the floor. Johnny and Chris seemed timeless, and the band was refreshed regularly by succeeding generations of the family. This was "a night in the old town" for old-style dancing—no holds barred—and usually that meant a tussle or a scrap of one kind or another as frustrations and booze washed out the old year and rambunctious energy ushered in the new. But no sooner had a scuffle started than it ended, either with the protagonists thrown outside to do whatever they were determined to do, or with the exuberance of the dance floor simply swirling the scuffle into the frenzy of feet below.

The community also whooped it up to The Whisky Jacks, under the leadership of my cousin Solli Sigurdson, a PhD in one hand and a guitar in the other. They were part of the birth of a decade of Hootenannies and sold-out halls. Their signature pieces were Solli's songs of the lake, ballads that sung of the people and the times. The tunes were captured forever in an album, "The Lake Winnipeg Fishermen," that had a spot in every home in the Interlake with any connection to the fishery.

The Riverton spirit moved down the road to Gimli during the Icelandic Celebration, a tradition of 120 years. Johnny and His Musical Mates were an institution at the Monday night dance, and you could also find the Whisky Jacks in full flight warbling and roaring to a packed house. The Fine Country Folk followed soon after, and in their wake the Fine Country Kids. Performing on the main stage, the Kids (anchored again by the Johanneson prodigies) enamoured themselves to the Icelanders in the audience and soon found themselves performing in Reykjavik.

Music was the voice of Riverton. In 1994, the Hootenanny celebrated its 30th anniversary with a celebration of music in the life of the community and a testimonial to the musicians who had left the ranks of its great musicians far too early. Roddy Palson, Riverton's own Ed Sullivan, was at the podium, with performers from across the generations taking the stage. Premier Gary Filmon and his wife Janice were among the throngs in the sold-out hall. On the cover notes of the live recording, Janice shared:

> Only on a Saturday night in a small Manitoba community could you
> be treated to such a special brand of entertainment ... Only in Riverton

could you experience the universal language of love through this musical showcase of the musical legacy... an inspiration to see young and old on stage performing together ... speaking the same language, even though their ages were years apart.

The Sig Fish families worked hard and played hard together. Everyone came together as one indivisible unit at family gatherings and brought into their midst what seemed like half the population of Riverton. The gatherings were never more vibrant than at Christmas. As soon as the river froze over and the skating rink appeared on the river, I knew Christmas was around the corner. About two weeks before Christmas the festivities began to take shape with the Sig Fish tradition of chocolates, mandarin oranges and nuts for each of the partners. And turkeys, endless turkeys for every house and employee and person with whom they'd done business over the year. Afi SV ran around Winnipeg in his massive fur coat delivering turkeys to every business associate he could think of. Christmas was the one time the purse strings loosened at Sig Fish.

For children of fishing families, Christmas meant all the usual excitement, but it also meant time spent with fathers and brothers and grandfathers back from the winter fishing stations. Kids were the centre of attention, and Santa Claus appeared each year without fail. My only problem was that Santa terrified me as he ho-hoed and stomped around the room handing out goodies. Without fail, I burst into tears, but I stuck around long enough to claim my gift. I found out later that our Santa was SR. Once Santa had belly-laughed his way out again, my trauma had ended for another year, and the party roared into action. The keys on the piano were soon dancing, the crowd gathered, and the singing began, with SR in the lead. SR's great joy was singing, and he was passionate when he got going. The sound of his voice was a sure signal that the party was starting to roll. In the grip of some particularly heart-tugging rendition, it didn't take long for the tears to well up in his eyes. He had a repertoire of hundreds of old-time songs from every genre, with a specialty in good old schmaltzy Western tunes. Then the chairs were pushed to the walls and Steve would start up. He knew all the Al Jolson masterpieces, and could sing every one complete with theatrical gestures. "SwannnEEEEE," and off he went, on his knees singing before the ladies, and peering down into the kids' eyes, which were almost popping out of our heads.

Afi SV invariably became inspired at some point, and the strains of "The Face on the Barroom Floor" burst out in his rich baritone. Each line of this dramatic poem twists you toward the agony and uncertainty of the next, and Afi's emotions rose with every stanza. There was a hush as the climax neared:

"With a fearful shriek, he leaped and fell across the picture ... dead." After the last gasp, SR was back to the piano and on went the singing. We kids were taken home, eventually, but the party lived on. The next morning you could see stragglers' cars still at the house.

Kids did kids' stuff, but we never sat in the family room eating supper in front of the TV. Young or old, you were at the table and in the conversation, learning to talk and to listen. That was the Icelandic way, and it became Riverton's way, whatever your background. There were few secrets. You knew the good news and the bad, from family finances to arguments. Early in life, you became aware of who you were and what you were a part of. I was free to live in my childhood world, but it overlapped with that of the grown-ups, and with the adult world came responsibility and accountability.

Riverton, maybe even more than most small places, didn't like to be pushed around. In the 1960s, the women and children stood as one when the rural-centralization ethos of the ARDA (Agriculture Rehabilitation Development Act) program became twinned with "school consolidation." Henceforth, the children of Riverton were to be bussed to Gimli or Arborg. Riverton was not a typical farming community. Fishing and construction were its lifeblood and that took the men away for months at a time. It was the women of the village who bore the brunt as community leaders and caregivers. The school and the achievements of the students were a source of great pride. They understood one thing very clearly. If the schools were lost so was the village, because the schools were a big part of the glue holding the place together. Without them, people would migrate to other places. So the moms fought back, with my mom in the lead. If they were to go down, it would be fighting. They painstakingly composed a brief—every word carefully selected and backed by statistics of academic achievement—no doubt borrowing a page from Afi's book of tricks. It framed the school as the centre of gravity of the rich history of the community. The kids were no less engaged, especially senior high students like me.

The moms argued their case with passion and impeccable logic. With the instincts of trial lawyers, they put the choice starkly: if the school was lost, so was the community. A commission was struck to make the decision. There were strong and mixed feelings. Voices emerged from other communities to stand beside the moms. It would be Dr. Ingimundson, a long-time dentist in Gimli, who cast the final vote with his conscience: the integrity of the community of Riverton trumped school rationalization. He would not vote against Riverton. The moms had their school and their community.

Much of my career has taken place in the hot zone between communities, companies and governments in collision, and amid clashes in values, often triggered when the social engineers come marching in to reshape the lives of others in their own image. Seventy years later, when Mom recounts these events, her voice, steady but not as strong, still rings with intensity, and reminds me once more what a pivotal moment this was in giving me a visceral understanding of the power of resistance and determination when a community fights for its right to be. The school was much bigger than a building with a bunch of classrooms and desks; it was the heart and soul of the community.

In my Riverton, everyone was expected to stand on his own two feet. There was no expectation that someone else would pave the way or solve your problems. What's clear to me now is that Riverton was full of self-starters, and from that came many success stories in business and academics. Whether the path led to nets or plows, Caterpillars or lecture theatres, staying home or going away, this was the DNA that connected them. And no one epitomized the deep independent undercurrent of the community more than the great farmer poet Gutti Guttormsson.

"Gutti," as young and old knew him (to this day in the Icelandic community, "Gutti" is enough to identify who you mean, like Cher or Madonna), immortalized Sandy Bar in his poem of the same name. It's a lonely place, the sort of spot that just might inspire a poet. Everybody knew of Sandy Bar, but almost no one ever went there, except kids on a bike adventure or old guys from Riverton in the mood for reminiscing. I can't remember a time when I didn't know of this sliver of sand threading its way between the lake and the marshland, south from the mouth of the Icelandic River. Like an outstretched hand it reaches northward across the bay toward Hecla Island. Moving and moody like the sky it meets effortlessly, it shuffles and shifts with the ebb and flow of the swampy waters behind it and the crashing waves of the lake in front. Sandy Bar has an iconic place in Riverton's history and identity. It was a bit out of the way, so it wasn't a place one went every day. There were two ways to get there. By road, it was the kind of trip that meant getting your bike and stuff ready before you left, an expedition. Or, you could travel there by boat. But almost no one went by boat, except the odd fisherman and my friend Brian Oleson and I. We'd take a skiff with an 18-horsepower motor and water-ski the three miles down the river, past Gutti Guttormsson's farm and the Big Bend out onto the lake and to Sandy Bar.

Gutti's "Sandy Bar" was a poetic vision of the pioneering immigration from Iceland to Canada in 1875. From Gutti's humble farm home, he could look over the marsh grass onto the thin strip of sand beyond. People from Winnipeg and Gimli often talked about Sandy Bar, and when they said the name they did so with the rhythmical emphasis on the "Bar," as if they knew it. I knew that most of them had no clue where it was. Seeing another person, much less a car, on that narrow, muddy road made by the draglines through the swamp, was a big deal. I knew those from outside Riverton had just heard the name from Gutti's poem. Gutti had never set foot in Iceland, yet wrote in the Icelandic language with an elegance that immortalized him as a giant of Icelandic litera- ture. He was first recognized as such with Iceland's highest honour, The Order of the Falcon, in the 1930s. One of his most beloved poems was the "Winnipeg Icelander," in which he poked fun at the insidious anglicization of the Icelandic language among the Big City Icelanders. He was a great humorist and also a musician with a renowned band. He was a favourite after-dinner speaker, called into service at endless community events, weddings and golden anniversaries.

Gutti was a humble, understated man, beneath whose covers was har- boured a legacy of generations of Icelandic values and the storytelling that kept them alive in modern times. His granddaughter, Heather Ireland, nee Sigurdson (on her father's side my cousin), has been the Counsel General of Iceland in Vancouver for many years. She herself was an accomplished vocalist, and trans- formed Gutti's poetry into music, which she has performed to great applause for national audiences in Iceland. She also had his poetry translated into English in the publication *Aurora*. Gutti was our icon. He was the soul of Riverton.

Many have tried to translate "Sandy Bar" into English and have been per- plexed by the skillful rhyming and the powerful portrayal of the agony the im- migrants faced and the ecstasy they longed for. Against the backdrop of a fierce thunderstorm, Gutti composed "Sandy Bar" as he stood amidst the settlers' graves on that sliver of barren beach. The lives of those "buried deep at Sandy Bar" were inside his soul, and with his words he entered into their long-sleep- ing souls. He immortalized their legacy with the revelation that, "More than flesh and all its grandeur lives today at Sandy Bar." And he wrote, "Broad and definite tracks will lead to the world from Sandy Bar." So it was, and is. As I grew older, I discovered what those words meant to me, whether or not Gutti had intended them in this way.

By the time I began school, Riverton counted among its graduate's engi- neers, mathematicians, lawyers, doctors, and even a senator. PhDs were common. Riverton had two Rhodes scholars in the 1950s, and in the early 1960s Riverton students stood near the top in the national mathematics exam. In my own fam- ily, Elaine would become a clinical psychologist, and a management and human resources consultant. My brother Eric, after completing an MBA and then a CA, would go on to a prominent career as a businessman and entrepreneur.

My friend Brian and several of his brothers earned PhDs and went on to distinguished careers in academia and government. Riverton always embraced the concept of provincial exams; they were proof that Riverton kids could stand up to any others, whether in small towns or Winnipeg. In Grade Eleven, I was awarded one of Manitoba's Isbister Scholarships funded by Alexander Kennedy Isbister who left the bulk of his estate to fund this scholarship program. He was a renowned headmaster in London who honoured Manitoba, where he had been born. Throughout his life he was a great supporter of the Red River settlers, and these scholarships were to be based on merit only, to be given without distinction of race, creed, nationality, or gender. Nobody in my day could say that any of our aspirations were beyond reach just because we were "country kids from Riverton." We knew we could do and be what we wanted. Feeling sorry for one's lot in life just wasn't on in Riverton.

I still remember Bill Valgardson's comment about the students not long after he arrived as a young teacher: "In Riverton, everyone seems to aim for 100 percent. In Gimli, getting over 50 percent was the goal." Bill went on to prominence as one of Canada's most distinguished writers, and the head of creative writing at the University of Victoria. He has taught many others to become successful at the craft over which he has such mastery. He was starting his writing career in those years. He was also a tough marker. Anything over 68 percent was an "A" in Bill's mind, and getting beyond that was no easy task. To add some inspiration to any of us who might want to become writers, he made this point: "Before I finish any piece, I have written at least 30 drafts." More recently, when working on a book he commented that "he had left blood on every page."

Another teacher, Russ Gourluck (who wrote several wonderful books on Winnipeg's history after his retirement) had us complete so many précis that I still never write without that discipline flowing back into my brain. Bill and Russ were only two of many very solid teachers who drilled discipline and insight into us under the remarkable leadership of our principal, Peter Onysko. He was there on my first day in school, as he was my last day.

Pete was a gifted mathematics teacher, and so much more. French was required to enter university, and it was almost impossible to get French teachers in the rural areas. So Pete took over teaching French as well, attending summer school for several years to increase his proficiency. Pete was the ultimate pragmatist, and while he couldn't utter a word that any French-speaking person would understand, he knew the name of the game was a written exam, and he taught accordingly. No way was Pete going to have his students, strong in every other respect, deterred by that hurdle. In my own case, I secured 85 percent on the provincial finals although "parlez-vous français?" was about the only comprehensible thing I could say. Pete had used Coles Notes to great effect. He was a good man, with great dignity, who enjoyed great respect. He gave quiet and stable leadership not just to the school but to the community of which he was such an integral part for 25 years.

"Is history bunk?" With that provocative question, Wally Johannson, who spent years boarding with my Afi Malli, Amma, and Grimsi, challenged his Grade Nine students to think deeply about history. I cannot remember my answer (although I'm confident that a keen sense of self-interest caused me to virulently disagree with the proposition), but the question stayed with me. Wally was a special teacher who transferred his passion for history to many of us who studied under him for all four years of high school, as I did. Now, I might be inclined to ask, "Is history everything?" I could never have anticipated the ways I would revisit that question and continue to deepen my understanding of the answer over my life. History is a story, but a story with a difference. We own this story. History is glue. It is as important to a group as memory is to a person. History expresses what we share and how we differ. History is alive. It shapes the lens through which we see the world. History is identity.

PART TWO

HISTORY IS WHO WE ARE

CHAPTER FIVE

Are We Traitors?

My great-great-grandfather, Sigurdur Erlendson, left a short diary containing the story of his most momentous decision. He wrote of his immigration from Iceland, the great island in the North Atlantic, to the area around Lake Winnipeg. The diary reveals precious little about the state of mind that propelled his remarkable journey. This may not be surprising, for shortly after arriving in Canada he lost the notes he made during the trip. He wrote the diary decades later, probably when he was in his eighties.

I begin Sigurdur's tale as he did, with the names and places of his origin, as was the way in the Icelandic sagas. Sigurdur was born on New Year's Day, 1830, on a farm in Hoskuldsstadir, in the most northerly part of Iceland, a remote region of fjords and rivers known as Thingeyjarsyslu. His father was Erlunder Eyjolfson, the son of Eyjolfur Saemundsson, who lived and farmed for a long life at Thvera in Laxardalur. Sigurdur's mother was Ragnhildur Jonsdottir, the daughter of Ingibjorg Andresottir and sister of old Arngrimur of Sigridarstadir in Bjosavatnskar. Sigurdur had three sisters: Anna, Ingibjorg and Hildur. He was the only son.

Sigurdur was born into a world that had seen the Icelanders brutalized by relentless waves of misfortune for more than 150 years. Smallpox had eliminated 15,000 people, almost one-third of the population, from 1703 to 1707. The country had been under oppressive Danish rule since 1397, worsened by an overbearing trade monopoly in the latter half of the seventeenth century. Trade was only allowed with Danish firms operating under royal fiat and later was extended to Danish citizens. Trade directly between Icelanders, even the sale of a few fish between peasants, was punishable by years of hard labour. It was not until the middle of the next century, when Sigurdur was a boy, that the trade monopoly was finally dissolved.

Then came the great volcanic eruptions of Mount Hecla (1776) and Mount Lakki (1783), which unleashed gases that devastated Iceland and wreaked havoc across Europe for decades. Poisonous ash turned the landscape dead grey and the hoofs of the sheep into raw sores, filling the nostrils of man and beast with noxious dust, and destroying the water. Up to 25 percent of the population of Iceland died in famines that followed the loss of four-fifths of the sheep and half the cattle and horses.

The sulfur dioxide dumped into the atmosphere, more than three times the annual output of industrial Europe in 2006, poured over Europe in a thick haze, impervious to the sun, causing respiratory distress and thousands of deaths. Weather patterns and soil fertility were affected, with economic consequences rippling for decades. Smallpox returned, but this time the availability of vaccination thanks to previous outbreaks of a close counterpart, cowpox, gave the population reprieve and contained the march of the disease to the south.

Iceland of this time was a land of farmers trapped in a feudal system. Only 10 percent of the population lived in fishing and trading villages.[4] Over 80 percent of the farmers were sheepherders tending flocks on lands they occupied as tenants, not landholders, who signed an annual contract and were allowed to change farms only one day each year. They were destined to no luxury beyond sod huts they shared with their animals through the long winters.

Sigurdur was a "bondi," a main farmer who engaged other working men. At every farm, Sigurdur signed the obligatory contract with the landowner. The contracts were carefully recorded in registries kept now in Iceland's Husavik Museum. He moved to the farm at Thvera at age two, was confirmed at 14 at Helgastadir, and worked his first real job at Breidamyri at 16. Sigurdur lived with his parents until he was 18, then left to find work wherever he might be useful. He married Gudrun Eiriksdottir in 1853 when he was 23 and she 27. She was a farm girl from Svalbarddtrond, daughter of Eirikur Halldorsson and Gudrun Hallssdottir from Eyjafjordur. Gudrun's lineage was notable as granddaughter of the great sorcerer Thorgeir. This connected her deeply with the tradition of Norse mythology, from which Tolkien drew inspiration for his great works. It was Thorgeir who conjured up Thorgeir's Boli in the 1700s. The apparition, a bull calf half-flayed and bloody, is reputed to appear on moonlit nights, dragging its hide behind and bellowing into the night.[5]

Sigurdur and Gudrun began their life together farming at Storulauger in Reykjadl. Their first child, Sigridir, was born within a year, at Narfastadir. After moving around between farms in the area—Storulaugar, Hallbjarnarstadir, Midhvammur—they moved to Klumbrumin Grenjadarstada in Thingeyjarsysla in 1866. It was from this farm that they left for Canada in 1876. He was 46 years old.

The north of the country was especially inhospitable in those years. Young Sigurdur began the farming life amidst a livestock epidemic in the 1860s that killed 200,000 Icelandic sheep. A tapeworm parasite, *Echinococcus granulosus*, caused cysts in sheep, as well as cattle, pigs and dogs, and also infected humans, causing cysts that spread to almost half the population.

The disease was brought under control in humans and animals starting in 1864, thanks to a public information campaign on avoiding contamination. Literacy helped defeat the insidious parasites. A Danish parasitologist saw that his booklet on the illness was delivered to every household. The Icelanders were hungry for any literature in their language and most families read it aloud every winter.[6]

How, in the face of centuries of assault by nature and man had these hapless souls on an isolated North Atlantic island become literate? Vikings had begun the settlement of Iceland with the arrival of the Norwegian chieftain Ingolfur Arnason in 874 at what he referred to as Smoky Bay, now the site of the capital, Reykjavik. They brought with them their ancient language, now known as Icelandic.

By 930, what is said to be the world's first parliament, the Althingi, had been established and a legal code developed. In the year 1000, the entire country converted to Christianity. Then came the sagas, the great classics of medieval literature. Fighting amongst rival chieftains brought about the demise of the country's independence, and by 1283 it had fallen under the domination of the Norwegian Crown, and by the end of the next century the Danish Crown. Throughout the difficult centuries ahead, stories and poetry sustained these impoverished souls and kept their collective soul alive. Undoubtedly, it was this legacy that inspired a literacy rate reaching 90 percent in the early nineteenth century.[7]

In the 1870s, the best of the grazing and farming land—coasts, lowlands and valleys—was becoming overcrowded. Young families began taking chances on mountainous regions in the north and west, areas too barren to attract settlers otherwise. These farms subsisted when the climate cooperated, but bitter cold spells pelted the 1870s and 1880s. Adding to the desperation, starting in 1875 volcanic eruptions spewed ash and poisonous gas over enormous swathes of vulnerable territory crucial to farmers.[8]

Uprooted families could either split apart or hope for humble servitude on farms, no matter how distant from one another, or they could search for a better life in a new land. Departures to North America began, displaced farmers joined by peasant and tenant farmers whose leases on shoddy land were useless in the harsh weather.

The northern Icelanders were desperately poor people in a remote part of one of the world's most isolated places. It's impossible to know what the harder choice was at the time—staying or leaving. Being independent Icelanders was the ultimate goal for some. This meant never admitting defeat and never leaving their own soil. Like Nobel Prize-winning Icelander Halldór Laxness' stubborn character in *Independent People*, Bjartur of Summerhouses, they would rather barely cling to life than abandon their homestead. For others, hope simply sprung eternal.

Departure was far from easy for those choosing this path, and a cause of great suffering for the families and friends determined to remain in Iceland. Leaving tore families apart. Those who chose to look for a future elsewhere couldn't help but have a sense of guilt. They left behind a feeling of abandonment and resentment. During times of scarcity, sticking together as a family was extremely important. Every family member was someone who might have a little hay or grain to share at the end of a long winter. And each decision to leave was an insult to those left behind, an unspoken accusation that people couldn't make it in Iceland.

Finally, Sigurdur could no longer bear his family's bleak existence. The lava, dust, difficult winters, and crushing poverty added up to a powerful—maybe the most powerful—vision of why he must leave: the hope that he could give his children a better life.

Many things pushed Sigurdur away, but without something pulling him he may never have made the journey's first step. The pull came in the form of a promise: the Icelanders would not only be travelling to a new land in Canada, but to a place where they could have their own land, to escape what was little more than indentured servitude in a feudal system.

Sigurdur had no land to sell. He had always lived in the sod houses provided on the farms. To finance the trip, he sold his only possession of value, the herd of sheep he had slowly built up. After making an initial payment, unscrupulous merchants refused him the final sum. Sigurdur may never have been able to leave were it not for two stalwart locals who loaned him the sum he was owed. But, to add another heart-wrenching dimension to his decision, Sigurdur still didn't have enough to take Sigridur, his oldest daughter, still living at home. When they collected the balance of the funds, she would follow them to Canada two years later. Sigrun was already married and remained in Iceland. Sigurdur left nothing behind to return to if his journey went wrong. The family's only possessions fit in a couple of trunks.

Under the leadership of Sygtryggur Jonasson, a number of Icelandic immigrants had made their way to Kinmount, Ontario, lured by promises of free land and abundant jobs. Unhappy with what they found there, they made a visit to Manitoba in the summer of 1875 and returned persuaded that the location along Lake Winnipeg was ideally suited for a colony. They were particularly impressed with the area around the Icelandic River, where they believed there to be black soil, stretches of hay land and abundant forests. The area also offered close proximity to fishing, and any native people they encountered there were friendly.

In Canada, the serious business of nation-building had begun. Ensconced in the new capital, Ottawa, the first prime minister, John A. Macdonald, was determined to secure his dominion from coast to coast. He wanted bodies, not pelts, railways not traplines. He was skittish about potential incursion by Americans into the vast plains area, seeing American troops engaged in "Indian Wars" on the western plains. The Red River Colony had developed its own mixed-race identity, and under Louis Riel was becoming irksome. The government saw it as critical to colonize the area and establish stable relations with tribal interests. Over the next decade they entered into the so-called "numbered treaties" with tribes across the region.

Bringing in the likes of Icelanders and Mennonites was also a Macdonald government priority. Within a month of Treaty Five being signed at Norway House covering the Indians around the top of Lake Winnipeg, the government had designated land for the Icelanders, complete with an Icelandic agent, in the District of Keewatin, which was later to become part of an expanded Manitoba. The land promised was legally the "Icelandic Reserve," but was known by the settlers as Nyja (New) Iceland, the Republic of New Iceland. On October 8, 1875, a parliamentary order-in-council granted Icelandic immigrants exclusive settlement rights along Lake Winnipeg from the northern border of then Manitoba (just beyond Selkirk at Boundary Creek), 80 miles north to Hecla Island, and inland to the west a distance of 36 miles. (Legislation for the settlement was passed by the Parliament of Canada in 1879. The Act was to come into force on proclamation, but as circumstances unfolded it was never proclaimed. The settlers were granted exclusive rights to settle in the area, and a prohibition against non-Icelanders moving into the area was not lifted until 1897.) The New Icelanders described Manitoba as the "neighbouring province." South of them, within the province, the Mennonites were also given a reserve.

The country was only eight years old, and then tiny Manitoba only five. The British and French had entered this land mass 250 years before. 'The Governor and Company of Adventurers of England Trading into Hudson's Bay' (HBC) was there for fur, not settlement. The company needed beavers, and the Indians wanted kettles and guns. Traders and trappers, Indians and British, living together in a vast territory: the seeds of what would become Canada. New Iceland was part of a huge region in formation, the heartland of a continent. Manitoba had joined the Canadian Confederation in 1870, but it was a mere "postage stamp" of a province, including the land south of Winnipeg to the border and north 25 miles to include the town of Selkirk. Selkirk and beyond was part of the Northwest Territories, a federal jurisdiction of the Dominion of Canada. Writing the story of Canada had just begun, and an unlikely group from Iceland was there to help to write it.

Together with John Taylor, a federally appointed Icelandic agent, Sygtryggur travelled to Ottawa. Obtaining government funding to assist the settlers in moving to Manitoba that fall and securing winter supplies was critical. The idea of such support for immigrants already in the country met with considerable resistance, but before he left Ottawa, Sygtryggur had a government loan as a result of support from unexpected champion

The first group of settlers arrived late in 1875. On October 21, the MS *Colville*, towed three 32-foot barges with 285 passengers onto Lake Winnipeg. Their intended destination was a settlement site known as Lundi, beside what became the Icelandic River, about three miles from where it empties into Lake Winnipeg. The settlement there is now known as Riverton, the village where I grew up.

A storm reared its head 30 miles from their destination. The wary captain was towing three small barges loaded with people. If he continued north, he would need to navigate a much more difficult channel to enter the mouth of the river from the lake, and then make a three-mile trip upriver. The more prudent choice was to cut the barges loose as close to the shore as he could navigate.

They were about to receive help from their Viking past. The MS *Colville* was accompanied by a single York boat (the legendary workboats of the Hudson's Bay Company) very similar to those used by the Vikings almost a millennium earlier to establish trade with Constantinople and the Orient.[9]

Eight rowers boarded the York boat and managed to tow the barges over a kilometre to shore as the storm closed in. They made land at Willow Island, just south of what is now Gimli. Ice was already forming along the shore, a harbinger of one of the coldest Manitoban winters on record. They cut logs to build shelters, but stoves were limited. Food supplies were exhausted by Christmas, and cases of scurvy developed. Some of the group made the 60-mile trek back to Winnipeg hoping to find employment, but most of the settlers endured until spring. It wasn't thanks to any luck, though; the weather continued to torment them, with heavy rains and flooding and unseasonably late snow. It wasn't the bleakness of the present, but rather optimism for the future that led them to call this place "Gimli," a name at the heart of Norse mythology. *Völuspá*, or Sibyl's Prophecy, describes the origin of the earth and the lives of the gods. In the heavens, Gimli was the eternal home of the righteous, the fairest of all houses, with a roof of gold.

Sygtryggur Jonasson was appointed as an agent of the Dominion of Canada to encourage further immigration from devastated northern Iceland. He returned to Iceland that winter, but now, in addition to land and opportunity, he could offer the promise of a new homeland, a New Iceland on Lake Winnipeg. The first group of settlers could only dream that such a colony would materialize; they had had no assurance. The dream became reality in the fall of 1875, with the establishment of the Icelandic Reserve. Like the aspirations of so many others who had left their old country for the new, they would leave a place behind but take their identity with them. They would build a place of prosperity, while holding true to their values and strengthening the Icelandic spirit that had so long sustained them.

Sigurdur became part of the next contingent bound for New Iceland, called the "large group," totalling some 1,200 people. With him were his wife and children, Jakobina (16), Stefan (12), Johannes (8), Kristjana (5) and baby Sigfus ("Fusi"), who was 18 months. They began their journey on June 27, 1875. The first leg led from their home in Klombrum to Akureyri, where they would board the ship for Scotland. Sigurdur hired a horse and a guide. There were many rivers to cross, starting with the Lax and Reykjadalsa. They travelled as the road lies from Flotsheioi to Skjlafandafljot, ferrying everything across the river and swimming the horses. They stayed overnight there with a well-to-do farmer, Skuli Kristjanson, whose hospitality was familiar to travellers and who asked nothing in return. By the time they arrived, two other men had already stopped at the farm for the evening, Benedikt Sveinsson, the local county sheriff, and Jon Sigurdson, Sigurdur's cousin and a member of the Icelandic legislature, the Althing.

These men accused Sigurdur of cowardly abandonment of his homeland. "They called me a disgrace to my family and a traitor to my country," Sigurdur wrote. It hurt him deeply, but he said little; he knew he would regret leaving with the taste of angry words on his tongue. When they parted the next morning a more subdued Jon earnestly wished them success. Sigurdur knew there was space left in Jon's heart for him, and it eased the agony of departing.

After ferrying across Fnjosk River and traversing the Vadlaheidi heath, they ferried across the bay to Akureyri. With a few hundred inhabitants, Akureyri was the largest village in northern Iceland, and must have felt bustling. Their ship—the *Verona*—arrived the next day. They paid the fares and went aboard, the bile surely rising in Sigurdur's throat as he thought of how dishonest dealings meant a child left behind. Home was already far behind, but leaving the shore of Iceland was another thing altogether.

The crossing to Scotland took them to Leith, the borough adjacent to Edinburgh. These feudal peasant sheep farmers were dropped into the new industrial age in a huge harbour in a great city. They would have loaded their few belongings onto a horse-drawn cart and clunked along the cobbled streets, meeting the belching steam engines of trains thundering down the tracks. For the boys, Johannes and Stefan, it was a glimpse of a modern world. No one where they were going would have seen such sights.

During a week waiting in Glasgow they were processed for departure to Canada. Glasgow too must have been wondrous, and daunting, with its stone buildings and cobbled streets. Sigurdur's memory of the trip had dimmed by the time he wrote the diary. Nothing of Scotland's wonder was mentioned, but he never forgot how the immigration official yanked open baby Fusi's mouth to check inside, like a man might check a horse.

The diary is then bare until their arrival in Quebec City, from where they were taken to Montreal. Others who made the journey reported that cargo ships carried them from Iceland to Scotland. They were cramped into damp holds usually filled with livestock, fish, wool and other goods. They survived on the meagre supplies they were able to bring with them. In rough weather the hatches were closed; many became seasick.

The ships that took them from Scotland to the New World were ostensibly passenger vessels, but still crowded with 600 people, of which 500 were third class. They kept the holds and benches as clean as they could. They were given breakfasts of coffee and bread, a heartier bowl of cabbage soup for lunch, and tea with a slice of bread and a biscuit for dinner.[10] Even with a doctor aboard, the combination of poor health and a difficult crossing meant many deaths and burials at sea.[11]

After arriving in Quebec City, they were fed all they could eat. They soon left for Toronto, where they stayed a week before some of the group departed for Collingwood. Sigurdur's group made the trip from Sarnia to Duluth on a paddle wheeler packed with humans and livestock. The ship fought powerful winds, and Sigurdur hustled his family back and forth across the deck while the crew rolled barrels around to keep the boat on an even keel. Stomach problems from the drinking water soon hit many of the travellers.

From Duluth they travelled by rail across Minnesota. They were unloaded on the bald prairie to swelter in tents for two or three days before another train took them to a village on the Red River, where steamboats and barges were ready for the long, slow trip down the river. Finally, exhausted and disoriented, they arrived in Winnipeg. It was at best a small town, with a few thousand people and one simple brick building, two poorly constructed brick-faced buildings, three or four hotels, and many log houses. They only had sixty miles left to travel, but their difficulties were far from over.

The authorities had sent men to Winnipeg to build scows for the trip to New Iceland. Two oar-powered, flat-bottomed boats, 16 feet wide and 32 feet long, were constructed for the colonists. The settlers loaded their belongings into these box-like vessels and smaller, unmanned boats, and began drifting down the Red River toward Lake Winnipeg, steering with rudders fore and aft. The Icelanders referred to their awkward, square-ended scows very unflatteringly as "dallar." The descendants of the Vikings, some of history's greatest shipbuilders, drifted toward their new land in floating boxes. Stefan, Johannes, Kristjana and Sigfus settled in for the ride, but Jakobina stayed behind, as she had found work with a farmer outside Winnipeg.

Some of the unwieldy boats ground to a halt on rocks in the rapids just before Selkirk, and the men waded ashore with ropes to drag the boats against a strong northerly wind forcing the current upstream from the mouth of the lake. Ten to twelve men strained on each rope, soaked to their waists in the marshy river banks. When they finally reached Lake Winnipeg, the sea was too heavy to proceed until the third day.

They rowed the "dallar" along the shoreline, reaching the pond behind what is now called Willow Point, a long sand bar with a marshy estuary behind, just south of present-day Gimli. A heavy thunderstorm struck, sending them scrambling to beach the boats. They walked to town in the rain. They found a draughty shack with a flat roof and a door. It was meagre accommodation for weary, drenched travellers, but it served for a few days' recuperation.

There was no rest in sight for Sigurdur. They had left a hefty chest of his wife's clothing at the estuary at the river's mouth. That alone may not have tempted Sigurdur into immediate action, but other baggage also contained coffee and chewing tobacco he had brought from Iceland and hidden in a roll of bedding during inspection in Scotland. Sigurdur and one other man struck off again. A powerful northeast wind forced them to land several miles from their destination. They tried to finish the journey on foot, but they encountered creeks too deep to wade and so spent a hungry night under the stars. With fair weather the next morning, they reached the estuary, found their possessions and some food, and turned back to Gimli.

There was little to do but wander around town for the next few days. With his last cents, Sigurdur bought bread, milk and fish to supplement the flour, potatoes, tea and sugar they had from Winnipeg. He conferred with Helgi Tomasson, another Icelander in the group, and they decided to continue onward together and settle on Mikley, the island eventually known as Hecla. They also decided to purchase a cow for life-giving milk.

They hauled everything back into the cursed dallar and started out. The cow travelled first-class on a raft built just for her. They spent a sleepless night on the riverbank 15 miles south of Gimli, being devoured by mosquitoes. Since Iceland has no mosquitoes, the Icelanders had no immunity, and the bites caused welts and sores. Even after all they'd been through, Sigurdur thought "a night spent in hell could hardly have been more uncomfortable."

The next day they floated with a heavy south wind toward Breiduvik. The boat filled with water, but Sigurdur got his wife and children safely to shore. The day turned sunny and the wind dried their clothes. The families started for Mikley Island again the next morning. The wind still blasted from the south, making it impossible to travel around the south corner of the island, so they were forced to land north of the sand bar on the west side. This is when they discovered the cow had disappeared from her raft.

That night, they were startled awake by crashing in nearby bushes. They recoiled in fear as a shape plunged into their midst with a heart-rending roar. Their cow! She must have swum to shore and made her way toward their fire. Her milk went on to serve five families.[12] They woke again in the middle of the night to a serious blow from the north. As waves crashed in they rushed through the darkness to higher ground.

They made their way around the south corner of the island the next day, but another strong wind forced them to stay on shore for the night. Like most of the Icelanders, Sigurdur was a farmer, not a fisherman, but he had brought a short net from Iceland. The net wasn't quite suited for Lake Winnipeg, but the next morning there was plenty of fish for breakfast. A small ration of fish for dinner became their salvation throughout their first dismal months in their new home.[13]

They floated north along the shoreline and finally walked ashore about midpoint on the island. "This is where I will live," Helgi said. That place has been called "Helgavatn," Helgi's Bay, ever since. Sigurdur went half a mile north and built a hut, but it was little protection from the wind and rain. He cut trees for a log cabin, but decided instead to go north to Mylnuvik (Mill Bay), where a Scotsman, Thomas Halcrow, ran a sawmill. The Icelanders nicknamed the Scot "Bad-tempered Tom," because he had little sympathy for the destitute newcomers, but that well may have changed once he had fallen in love with and married an Icelandic girl.[14] Regardless, he lent Sigurdur a ramshackle hut with a clay stove but no chimney. It was almost unbearably smoky, but they were lucky to have somewhere to spend the winter.

Sigurdur and another recent arrival, Benedikt Peturson, rowed back to Gimli to retrieve the trunks they had left. Sigurdur's diary entry was characteristically understated: "I found it a long distance to row, more than forty miles each way. I had lost a lot of energy because of stomach trouble. This trip took a week." Not long after, he was sent to the island again to procure flour, cured pork and sugar. Fall weather was already upon them and they had precious little time before the cold set in.

The Icelanders had fled oppression, hunger, volcanoes and smallpox in an odyssey of imponderable obstacles, and their reward was a Lake Winnipeg snowstorm unlike anything Sigurdur would see again in 35 years. Some faced the bitter winter in make-shift wooden huts, others in tents. All the land offered was the leaves of a small bush from which they steeped "Indian tea." Most of the early snow melted, but the winter snow followed quickly, and the temperature dropped with each passing day. The expanse of the lake and its winds can be frightening and brutal, the cold's penetrating grip turning flesh to stone in moments.

It was now September 15. Around 30 people, mostly children, had died since the group left Iceland on June 30. And yet, an even more serious threat appeared when smallpox reached the settlement in the summer. By the end of November, 19 had succumbed. Sigurdur was convinced that God saved his and other lucky families from the disease. Perhaps the answer was more medical than divine, however, as many Icelanders had received the cowpox inoculation after smallpox ravaged their homeland.

The end of the year was indeed bleak. Sigurdur wondered constantly if his decision to leave Iceland had doomed them. Sigurdur and Stefan waded through deep snow into the woods most days to find dry firewood. It warmed them just a little in the clay fireplace, and they choked on the smoke. They were freezing cold, surrounded by smallpox and on the edge of starvation. Much of what they had spent a lifetime learning in Iceland meant nothing on Lake Winnipeg. Sigurdur's worsening stomach troubles haunted him. "I was beginning to think that every day would be my last," he wrote, "and I worried constantly about what would become of my wife and four children." His one consolation was watching how his boys were shaping up. Sigurdur believed they would be successful if they lived, that his dream of building a better future for his children would be realised. The only thing he was truly certain of, though, was that it would not be sheep farming that would sustain the family on Lake Winnipeg.

Sigurdur's health began to improve in January 1877, a few months after arrival. He attributed it to the coffee he had brought along. To Icelanders, coffee is the nectar of the gods. Whether the coffee had restorative powers or not, Sigurdur believed it did, and that alone may have made a difference. He was soon strong enough to make a much bigger fishing net than the one he had brought from Iceland. With the first bearable weather in the New Year, Sigurdur and Stefan ventured out onto the Lake Winnipeg ice. After two days the net was in the water.

They were energetic men, but with no tools or clothes to protect them from the cold. How they broke open a large enough hole through five to six feet of ice is unclear. Sigurdur must have learned from the Indians how to set the nets using poles cut from the forest. The Indians slid long lines attached to poles under the ice, watching the progress if clear and thin ice allowed, otherwise estimating where to cut the hole to anchor the other end of the net. However he did it, Sigurdur rejoiced to pull three plump whitefish from the deep. They wrapped them in canvas and rushed back to show Gudrun.

Sigurdur had located and fixed a broken stove and a pot. Later, with a belly fuller than it had been in a long time, Sigurdur wrote that "those who have experienced hunger will understand how much we relished the first meal after the whitefish was cooked." From then on, they had fish to bake or fry, even enough to share with those less fortunate. They finally had a glimmer of hope that things would work out for them.

In April, Sigurdur chose land one mile north of their shack and built a log cabin. He called the house "Skogar," for "heavily wooded." Sigurdur was proud of his boys:

> Stefan was my main helper, and assisted me in all the work although he was only twelve years old. My younger son, Johannes, then eight years of age, brought the dinner to us daily, fried whitefish. I thought he did well...to walk all that distance against a cold north wind and no road along the lake. We enjoyed good times together then, my boys and I.

They cleared land near the shore for potatoes and planted a few rows full of optimism, but the weather was relentless. The rains came and the bushel of potatoes Sigurdur had seeded floated away. It was "a hard loss for a pioneer." The one piece of good news was he was able to secure a cow from those attained through the government loan.

Before the government lifted the smallpox quarantine on June 20, 1877, Sigurdur noted the procedure of moving through quarantine boundaries: "At Gimli people from the government were bathing all of the settlers from smallpox," he wrote. "It put me in mind of immersing lousy sheep." From there they could go to Selkirk, holding a "purification" certificate.

Smallpox had an unexpected consequence. The bones of many Indians and Icelanders went to a common grave, and nothing connects people like adversity. Take the story of John Ramsay. Ramsay was the first Indian the New

Icelanders encountered, in the summer of 1876. The settlers remained unaware of the Indians their first winter because the Indians hunted north of the settlement. But Ramsay lived not far from the mouth of the Icelandic River, where settler Olafur Olafsson started building his home. The settlers first glimpsed him when they crossed to the north side of the river to work on the house. Ramsay refused to let them land, pushing their boat away each time it neared.[15] He left after one of the settlers brandished his axe, only to reappear later with armed Indian men including one English-speaker who informed them they were on Indian Territory.

They waited to settle the dispute until Sygtryggur Jonasson and the large group of Icelandic immigrants arrived, accompanied by a government representative who explained to the Indians that New Iceland did, indeed, claim land north of the Icelandic River. Olafsson allowed Ramsay's garden and teepee to remain on his land, and Ramsay became a most excellent neighbour, single-handedly supplying the settlers with game and making generous trades of produce.[16]

Along with one of the settlers, Ramsay accompanied a Dr. Baldwin to inoculate the 196 residents of Norway House. Afterward they stopped at Sandy River, near the northern tip of Hecla Island, home to 200 Ojibway people. Ramsay had news for his many relatives there of the loss of his wife and two sons to smallpox.

They could see no smoke as they approached, and they arrived to grim silence. Every soul was dead and frozen in their bunk. In profound agony, the three men set the village ablaze to provide the dignity of a final resting ground. The fire also prevented passersby from stealing smallpox-infected Hudson's Bay Company furs and spreading the disease to unwary buyers. The men themselves nearly met their end during a fierce snowstorm on the trip home. Sheltered behind an ice wall formed by a massive crack in the ice, they could only say their prayers as they waited for the storm to abate.[17]

Ramsay's wife and sons were buried alongside Icelandic colonists at Sandy Bar. He took his daughter Mary, badly pockmarked by smallpox, to Matheson Island. Ramsay ordered a marble headstone to honour the grave. The clerk misunderstood the name as "Rumsey." Being illiterate, Ramsay was unaware of the error. His family's is the only marked grave at that location, standing inside the white picket fence he built around it. It is now a Manitoba Municipal Heritage Site.

CHAPTER SIX
Friends in High Places with Fond Memories

The seeds of the epic journey my great-great grandfather Sigurdur took with his family were planted in 1855 during a great story of human bonding. A young Irishman, Fredrick Hamilton-Temple-Blackwood, the Earl of Clandeboye (later to become Lord Dufferin), made a fateful trip to the northern latitudes accompanied by Sigurdr, an Icelandic law student (not "Sigurdur," my great-great-grandfather, but "Sigurdr").

The future Lord Dufferin shared his journey in *Letters from High Latitudes*. The book is part travel guide, part adventure tale, but at heart it is a story of human connection. Dufferin and Sigurdr's profound human encounter led eventually to a home for Icelanders coming to Canada.

The trip to Iceland was a heavy crossing, and Dufferin was often ill. Sigurdr fared considerably better. This fortitude could not have escaped the Irishman's eye. After spending the evening playing chess on the deck with Sigurdr, Dufferin wrote his mother: "Already I feel much stronger, and before I return I trust to have laid in a stock of health sufficient to last the family for several generations."

His enthusiasm soon blossomed further. Dufferin fell in love with Iceland at first glimpse. Perhaps it reminded him of Scotland's west coast, only more dramatic—hills loftier and gaunter; glittering peaks of ice and snow piercing an azure sky. Upon making land, Dufferin admired the Icelandic people, too. He loved their energy, their hospitality, the nights of revelry, games of chess over endless coffee, and the women's full kisses. He was especially entranced by their intellectual energy, unexpected in such a secluded community. Perhaps, he thought, "it was this very seclusion which stimulated into almost miraculous exuberance the mental powers already innate in the people...devoting the long leisure of their winter nights to intellectual occupations."[18]

Letters from High Latitudes overflows with praise: "I have invariably found the gentlemen to whom I have been presented persons of education and refinement, combined with a happy, healthy, jovial temperament that invests their conversation with a peculiar charm."[19] Dufferin wrote that his short trip to Iceland resulted in "friends who could not have been kinder had they known us all their lives."

He described the site of the modest capital, Reykjavik, as "determined by auspices not less divine than those of Rome or Athens." Inland at Thingvalla, the site of the Althing parliament, he observed that, "long ago at a period when futile despotism was the only government known throughout Europe, free Parliaments used to sit in peace and regulate the affairs of the young republic." He marvelled at the genius of the Icelandic scholars and the fact that a printing press had been introduced as early as 1330.[20]

Of his companion, Sigurdr, Dufferin had this to say as the trip drew to a close:

> To-morrow I leave...my good Sigurdr...I take away with me a most affectionate memory of his frank and kindly nature, his ready sympathy, and his imperturbable good humour. From the day on which I shipped him—an entire stranger—until this eve of our separation—as friends, through scenes of occasional discomfort, and circumstances which might sometimes have tried both temper and spirits...there has never been the shadow of a cloud between us; henceforth, the words "an Icelander" can convey no cold or ungenial associations to my ears, and however much my imagination has hitherto delighted in the past history of that singular island, its People will always claim a deeper and warmer interest from me, for Sigurdr's sake.[21]

Had these two men not bonded so deeply, and had Dufferin not bonded through Sigrdur to the Icelandic people who reciprocated with unhindered honesty and energy, the genes inside my story would almost certainly never have journeyed to Lake Winnipeg.

The charismatic thirty-year-old Irish Lord became one of Britain's most distinguished and gifted diplomats. Within twenty years of his trip with Sigrdur, he visited the Icelanders again in a new land to which Queen Victoria had appointed him governor general in 1872—Canada. He and Lady Dufferin and their daughter visited every province. Lady Dufferin herself wrote weekly letters to her mother in Ireland, published as *My Canadian Journal*.

When he arrived in Gimli, the Icelanders' newspaper published Lord Dufferin's claim that "he had left his home in Ottawa with the firm intention of letting nothing stand in the way of visiting our colony."[22] Dufferin's family had indeed made a remarkable journey to reach them. He followed the same route as the colonists had to Winnipeg. He then visited the newly created Mennonite reserve south of Winnipeg almost to the US border. They returned to Winnipeg and visited northwestern Ontario before canoeing for days down the Winnipeg River. Upon reaching Fort Alexander, east of where the Winnipeg River meets Lake Winnipeg (my friend Phil Fontaine's home community), they were windbound for six days as the *Colville* tried unsuccessfully to enter the river to pick them up. Finally aboard, they left to visit the North End of the lake and Grand Rapids, but on the return journey a ferocious storm prevented landing in Gimli, so they continued up the lake into the Red River to Selkirk. Lady Dufferin and their daughter were exhausted, but Dufferin was undeterred. The next morning the *Colville* departed once again for Gimli.

Meticulous preparations were made for the visit. A large area lined with pine boughs surrounding a central platform had been prepared along the sandy shore of the lake. Dufferin toured Gimli and the area for hours, inquiring about families' living conditions and hopes for the future.[23] Dufferin's speech expressed his optimism for the Icelanders' future based on his expectation that they would accomplish much as loggers and farmers due to their innate intelligence, "which is the essence and foundation of all superiority."

Dufferin was impressed by the presence of books in even the humblest huts. Indeed, in the trunks the Icelanders had packed for their journey, alongside the meagre assortment of clothes and household necessities, were their precious books. Books were part of life on the farms where most had grown up, and in every household children learned to read for religious purposes and for entertainment.[24] Education was monitored to ensure that no child of any circumstance would miss the opportunity to learn to read.[25] The deep history in literature stretching back to the time of the sagas was part of their Viking soul, and near universal literacy served these newcomers well.

Dufferin offered these concluding words: "nor in becoming Englishmen and subjects of Queen Victoria need you forget your own time-honored customs or the picturesque annals of your forefathers. On the contrary, I trust you will continue to cherish for all time the heart-stirring literature of your nation, and that from generation to generation your little ones will continue to learn in your ancient Sagas that industry, energy, fortitude, perseverance, and stubborn endurance have ever been the characteristics of the noble Icelandic race."[26]

Had Dufferin not secured desperately needed funding from Prime Minister Macdonald on behalf of the Icelanders, the colony may never have become a reality. Macdonald's government frowned upon the interventionist exuberance of the second governor general as they struggled to assert parliamentary independence in the new dominion. On that, Dufferin had only this to say in his speech: "I have pledged my personal credit to my Canadian friends on the successful development of your settlement."[27]

Never underestimate the power of human connection. Who could have fore-seen that the brief friendship between two young men, an Irish Lord and an Icelandic law student, would play a role 20 years later in the creation of New Iceland? Interpersonal chemistry is a fragile foundation upon which to build enduring relationships between groups and organizations. How, in the absence of the magic of the unlikely, can you make such connections likely? This query is at the core of my work. History is fragile, and so too, in the world of taking people from fighting to talking, are human relationships, all the more so when you strap to their back the organizational luggage they often carry in the situations where I meet them.

The *Framfari* newspaper's accounts of Dufferin's visit gushed with grati-tude. Dufferin's earnest demeanour, voice, noble gaze, humour and clothing were praised. Not even the proportions of his lower face and the size of his eyebrows escaped mention.[28] But Dufferin's boost of the settlers' pride and resolve was short-lived. The government loan was exhausted by the winter of 1878, and the situation became dire. As prescient as Dufferin was, he had not foreseen that fishing, not farming, would be the salvation of his beloved Icelandic colony.

If there was to be a future, the demands of the present needed to be an-swered with nets, not ploughs. The potential importance of fish to the col-ony was recognized on Sygtryggur's first exploratory visit, in the summer of 1875. He noted that Lake Winnipeg was teeming with fish species and that the Indians fished year round and lived off their catch. He even foresaw the value of fish for trade.[29]

When the Icelanders arrived, the Indian people living around Lake Winnipeg—invariably situated near the mouths of the great rivers rushing into the lake—had relied on fish for millennia. The Métis referred to the lakes and rivers as "the storehouse of the good god."[30] They harvested almost exclusively within the riv-ers and at shore fisheries within the river estuaries. The fall whitefish catch was the most important—large fish, plump and round with a hump marking them as distinctive to Lake Winnipeg. The importance of fish for food was accentuated with the growth of permanent settlements as fur trade posts were established. Like furs, fish meant trading power for the goods on which the Indians were be-coming dependent: flour, tea, tobacco, twine, clothing and additional income.

Men from Winnipeg tried as early as 1872 to commercialise a fishery to serve the growing city, but their initiative failed, perhaps because of the limited market and competition from localized production.[31] The Métis already used the prized whitefish and other species for limited trade. With the commercial-ization of the industry and the development of export markets beginning in the 1880s, the Métis maintained an expanding role.[32]

The settlers should have focused on fishing from day one, but this group of sheep farmers saw their situation through sheep farmers' eyes. Fish was always an important food source, but securing an adequate supply appears to have been the result of individual efforts rather than an organized group effort that recognized fish as critical to sustaining the community. Within two years, the importance of fish seems to have begun to sink in, but by then circumstances were desperate.

In the third winter the fish debate heated up in dauntingly prescient letters and articles in *Framfari*. An early letter advanced the case: it was obvious that trading fish would generate cash income much sooner than farming crops. The letter encouraged a leadership group to form a company to salt and ice fish, construct boats to transport it to Winnipeg, and build storage facilities for the winter production.[33]

The next month another *Framfari* writer emphasized the need for effective fish transport routines with the neighbouring province, Manitoba, and trade as the means to self-sufficiency. "In every land inhabited by civilized men," he wrote, "trade is as essential as breathing is for the body." He identified the only item capable of generating trade in the near future as fish. He encouraged the production of all species known to be plentiful (especially goldeye) and suggested the possibility of smoking species like catfish. He noted the role a fish plant could play, and promoted icehouse construction, all to meet demand from the 8,000 people then living in Winnipeg.[34]

Within these same pages another conversation raged. Should the settlers look outward to the wider world for opportunities or focus on building up the colony? Johann Briem—editor of *Framfari* and Sygtryggur Jonasson's brother-in-law—argued for isolation along with most of the others. On the other side was Reverend Jon Bjarnason, of the Lutheran State Church of Iceland, who had been persuaded to leave a position in Minnesota to serve in the colony. The immigrants' momentous choice to come to Canada was stimulated by a quest for opportunities, he wrote, and opportunities would only appear by reaching out and becoming active participants in the country taking shape. Bjarnason was pessimistic about the colony's prospects for self-sufficiency and feared that unseized opportunities would slip away.

Bjarnason punctuated his arguments with a powerful indictment:

> The only occupation here in the colony which can at the moment provide an abundant revenue is fishing. But because the residents of the colony are for the most part so dreadfully poor, no one has the strength or pluck to get a regular trade in fish under way... People obtain their food from

the fish, but nothing else. If, in addition to Icelanders, there were also as many Americans or Canadians living here, it is certain that the trade in fish and other commodities which are now in short supply, but are actually indispensable [sic], would come into being here, while as things stand now there is little likelihood of that happening.[35]

Briem saw in this philosophy the dangerous potential that Icelandic values and identity would be lost if the centre of gravity moved outside of the colony. Bjarnason saw it differently: imprisonment by poverty was no basis on which to protect and preserve identity. Economic opportunity was central to both perspectives: standing on their own two feet required building an economy. Although they had very different perspectives, both men sought the best path to preserving the integrity of the Icelandic identity within this new land.

The *Framfari* debate also split out in other directions. Should people other than Icelandic immigrants be allowed to settle in New Iceland? And if the experiment of an independent colony were to fail, would it destroy opportunities for others who wished to do likewise? And yet another, much deeper, chasm was opening. Tensions arose between the fundamentalist Lutheran doctrine espoused by the Norwegian Synod, as articulated by Reverend Pall Thorlaksson, and the more liberal views of the Icelandic State Church, expressed through Reverend Bjarnason. This was an ironic twist, as these two men were friends, had both found themselves in America after theology studies in Iceland, and had both been drawn to New Iceland from parishes in the United States.

Soon, fish also entered this fray, as subsistence and religion locked horns. In February 1878 (in what *Framfari* editor Briem called the "begging letter"), Reverend Thorlaksson wrote to the US Norwegian Synod asking unabashedly for help for his parishioners. He said that without assistance the colonists may starve. The loan extended by the Government of Canada to assist in the transition to a new country had been exhausted, and difficulty finding and catching fish through the Lake Winnipeg ice, combined with illness and lack of clothing, thwarted fishing efforts.

Briem called this assertion "sensationalist." He wrote that a good catch was possible for those devoted to it, and that while many families were short or devoid of provisions, the members of Reverend Thorlaksson's congregation were no worse off than anyone else in the colony. Any money contributed should be redirected to Iceland, Briem asserted, where no fish had been caught in almost two years in the southern districts and people were far worse off than the New Icelanders.

In the years immediately following, many colonists followed Reverend Thorlaksson to a settlement in North Dakota. Impassioned *Framfari* debates were not the only reason for the exodus; many who sought the farming life saw more opportunities elsewhere. Too much of New Iceland was soggy, sandy or rocky. And dismal economic possibilities caused many others to relocate to seek wage employment, most to Winnipeg, where anyone who could drive a straight nail could make a few dollars. The departure of so many struck the colony a harsh blow. Amongst those who left were Reverend Bjarnason and Reverend Thorlaksson, back to the United States, and Sygtryggur Jonasson to Selkirk (then known as Taylors Crossing). Johann Briem returned to Iceland.[36]

On Hecla Island, circumstances facing Sigurdur and the other islanders were grave, although there were small blessings. The mill on the island continued, with repeated ups and downs and ownership changes, to provide wages for some men. The government loan had made purchasing a second cow possible, and their belief in the life-giving quality of milk probably gave them a spiritual and physical boost. More cows followed to Hecla, and throughout New Iceland, and no doubt each was soon named as a Sigga or Gudrun, Helga or Villa, as was the tradition in Iceland where cows were treated as family.

The settlers continued to survive on fish in the winter by keeping holes open in the ice. Sigurdur's diary notes that he was able to trade 56 whitefish to an Indian man for a bag of flour. The next year he was able to sell a whole whitefish for seven cents. Sigurdur had had his first encounters with the business side of fishing, and soon scraped together a little extra money. He and two of his neighbours bought an ox to haul hay for the cows. Gardens were planted. A few new souls arrived, like Jon Jonsson, whose family Sigurdur invited into his home for their first winter. Jon later became his neighbour.

In 1880, a new threat appeared. Heavy rains flooded low-lying hay lands that year (and two years previous). Even away from the shore, much of the land was so wet it was almost impassable. Much of the hay for the cows was destroyed. It was a devastating turn for people living at the margins of survival. Adding insult to injury, extra groundwater meant massive insect breeding. Tormented by mosquitoes, they were forced to build "smudges" using green wood, but while the smoke helped keep mosquitoes away, it also filled their tiny shacks.

Many families, alarmed by prospects of losing their cows and other animals, and envisioning another year at the brink of starvation, left over the winter and spring, most to Winnipeg or North Dakota. At one point only six families remained on Hecla Island. If it weren't for the fishing, every last settler may have left Hecla, and most from the rest of the colony, too.[37] Some were so poor they didn't even have the money to leave and their kids had next to no clothing.

While chances of making a living from the land seemed to shrink, a new industry took its fledgling steps. In Sigurdur's fourth winter (1879), he set out for Winnipeg with the ox and a bag of fish. Interest was low in his 160 tulibees, but he finally sold them for one dollar. He received more for 22 whitefish, although not enough to remember the sum when he wrote his diary. The trip was a success, and he brought home more provisions than they had had since leaving Iceland. Sigurdur walked often like this in the wintertime, even though the roads were difficult and he was often close to freezing.

That same winter, more than 40 men from Gimli and Icelandic River travelled north over the ice from Hecla to fish off Reindeer Island and Little Grindstone Point. The extreme cold froze their hands and inhibited an otherwise good catch. A few men made camp and persisted, using three horse teams to haul the fish into Gimli and Winnipeg. Two Indians fished alongside.

The importance for survival of catching and transporting fish had become clear. In the summer of 1880, Sigurdur partnered with Helgi Tomasson to have the first big sailboat on the island constructed. It was painted blue and named the *Bluenose*. They intended to use her to transport goods and fish to and from Selkirk and Winnipeg for themselves and other islanders.

Around that time, word arrived of opportunities for work in Selkirk, at a new sawmill and quarry. Several men from Mikley went on the *Bluenose* to investigate. Some found work they liked, but Sigurdur and others returned to Hecla. Measles broke out immediately upon their return. Concern that they had brought measles with them was likely unfounded, for measles was rife in Iceland at this time, and probably found its way to the island through a new arrival. Two pregnant women and three children died, including Jon's youngest daughter.

The colony was all but finished. In *Icelanders in North America: The First Settlers* historian Jonas Thor notes that only about 250 settlers remained in 1881. Eighty homes in the Gimli area at the end of 1879 had become 12 and a mere five of 31 remained in Arnes. There were nine left on Hecla.[38] Sytriggur Jonasson had started a sawmill in Riverton, and that was giving much needed wage employment to many. But lumber and mills in this part of the world would never be a sufficient base on which to build an economy. The simple fact is that the settlers should have focused on fish much earlier, rather than being distracted by religious debates and futile strategies like farming which would take years to develop.

Fishing was the only flicker of hope. Fish had saved these sheep farmers from starvation, but they had not yet understood it as their ticket to self-sufficiency. From the Indians and through trial and error they were learning the ways of the lake. By 1879, there were already 129 boats, mostly flat-bottomed, square-bowed punts only safe close to shore, but they got the job done along with skiffs and sailboats. Selkirk and Winnipeg represented markets for fish, and trade was starting to materialize. Imminent rail connections to Chicago and New York opened prospects of a far bigger commercial world.

The future arrived with a sailboat that made its way to shore at Hecla. The boat was owned by Reid and Clarke Co., commercial fishermen from Lake Simcoe in Ontario who saw potential in the waters of Lake Winnipeg, and so moved to Selkirk to found Lake Winnipeg's first commercial fishing venture. With one sailboat Daniel Reid and James Clarke supplied the expanding Winnipeg market, then around 25,000 people strong.

They expanded to Hecla the following year with a second sailboat. The day after arriving they set the nets off the north shore. The nets came up full, and the islanders were given a good share. A bond forged between these two Scotsmen from Ontario and the Hecla Icelanders. Stefan and Johannes saw their future and never looked back.

Stefan and Johannes Sigurdson understood that when a window of opportunity opens you must scramble through. Timing is everything. The brothers knew their time had come, even though they were little more than big kids. Perhaps their brief time in Glasgow helped them imagine the worlds and markets of New York and Chicago. Unlike the other settlers, they had been given a glimpse of how the bigger world worked, and it was certain to have stuck in their minds as they imagined their futures.

Reid and Clarke set up operations at Mill Bay. In the fall, they constructed an icehouse, its thick walls filled with sawdust. After freeze-up, they cut lake ice and filled the icehouse for the summer season. Reid and Clarke recognized that the best fishing would likely be in the deeper and colder waters to the north, and over the next couple of years built basic camps with rustic bunkhouses, cook shacks and simple docks at Swampy Island (Berens River) and Little Saskatchewan River (Dauphin River).

They put a small steamer into service the next year, and a steady stream of fish flowed from Hecla to Selkirk. Suddenly the young men of Hecla, Sigurdur's sons among them, were at the heart of a blossoming industry loaded with potential.

The fish secured the Icelander's toehold as a distinct community in the centre of Canada. "Better news" stories reached the homeland and brought new arrivals. Salome Thorkellsdottir, Speaker of the Icelandic Parliament, brought with her 1994 visit to Manitoba's Icelandic Festival this observation:

> The people back in Iceland were closely observing how their brothers and sisters in the West were doing. It gave them added confidence in their own

struggle for home rule and independence when the Icelandic communities in "Vesturheimi" [western home] began to prosper. They felt proud when they received good news from their relatives across the ocean.

(Salome personally embodied this story, for two of her closest living relatives were sons Sigurdur had later in life, my uncles SR and Steve.)

New settlers arrived at established locations and new locations within the Interlake, the area between Lake Winnipeg and its smaller sisters to the west, Lake Manitoba and Lake Winnipegosis. No longer concentrated from the north of Iceland, they came from across the country, from very different circumstances. Ironically, it was far from home that Icelanders from every corner of a big island with a small population would be "cross-pollinated." The community in New Iceland (and most strikingly the marriages) crossed classes and regions, joining people who otherwise would almost certainly never have laid eyes upon each other.

About 30 families came to Hecla around that time, amongst them my mother's family. If Dad's family, through Sigurdur, typified the first arrivals, Mom's typified immigration to follow.

My mother's grandparents, Brynjolfur Jonsson and Katrin Magnusdottir came from impoverishment in southeast Iceland, known today as home to volcanoes that periodically spit their lava and poisonous ash, clogging air travel across the Atlantic and smothering Europe. This was part of the reason they left. They emigrated from Storulag in Nesjum, Austur Skaftafellsyla in 1889 to Mikley (Hecla Island), leaving behind their parents (Jon Brynjolfsson and Ingibjorg Kettilsdottir, both from Thorisdallur in Loni). Their optimism for a new future for their children was soon pierced with despair. Two little boys died on the voyage and were buried at sea. Four girls survived the journey: Ingibjorg, Gudrun (Gertie), Gudny (Winnie) and Jorunn (Josie). Katrin's trauma was so overwhelming that she lost her hair. She disdained wigs, so wore a dustcap the rest of her days, a constant reminder of those dark burials at sea. She rarely left her house. Nonetheless, it was a place of spontaneity and humour, for she kept her mind occupied and her spirit alive with books, propping them beside her spinning wheel, her daily companion. Three more children were born to the couple in Canada: Thorbergur (Beggi), with whom she was pregnant during the voyage; Magnusina (Maggie); and finally my Afi, Marus (Malli).

Youngest of a family of twelve, the main burden of caring for his bedridden father and elderly mother fell upon Afi. In 1910, he began his life as a fisherman working for his future wife's uncle, Johannes Grimolfson, and this boy-man was working as an engineer on steam freighters by age 18. He would give up his bunk on trips south for medical attention for those stricken by the Spanish flu, a terror far deeper than the poverty he had known throughout his young life. Miraculously, he didn't become ill, but the family did not fare as well. Afi arrived home in the fall of 1919 to news that his oldest sister and her son were at death's door, leaving her husband behind to raise twin girls. So great was the dread of the disease that no one dared attend the funeral.

His older sisters went to Winnipeg to find work. Like many young Icelanders in those early years, they adopted a new name. The Jonsson girls became Jones, and with them the rest of the family. Afi took a different course that reflected his deep sense of identity. He became Brynjolfson. According to the ways of his forbears in a land he had never known, he took his father's first name Brynjolfur and adding "son." I always knew he was the Brynjolfson amongst the Jones's, but I never heard him speak of why he made that decision. Knowing him, you knew why. On rare occasions I heard him referred to as Malli Jones, but only by Cree and Ojibway fishermen on Lake Winnipeg who found Jones easier to roll off their tongues.

The family on Mom's mother's side was living in Snaefellnes, near Reykjavik, when they left in 1893. Her grandfather, Grimolfur Olafsson, was born in Raudamel, Kolbeinnstadahreppa, and then moved to Stadarfelli, Bardarstrandasyslu, and lived there for 15 years looking onto Mount Esja. He served as hreppstjori (justice of the peace) for 27 years in the district of Neshrepp. The family then moved to Mafahlif (Gull Shelter), where Mom's Amma Solveig was born.

Most remarkable about Grimolfur's story is the age at which he made this move. He was 66, and with him and his wife Steinun came four adult children: Johannes, Hildur, Groa and Oliver. He was successful in Iceland, powerful and distinguished in demeanour and better educated than the average person of the day. In ten years, Grimolfur would be dead. A poem written on his death, "Hetjan er fallin," ("the hero has fallen") indicates the esteem in which he was held. Johannes stayed in Hecla, married Gudrun, and raised a family of 12. Hildur and Groa both left the island, Hildur to the United States, and Groa to Selkirk. Olafur went to the West Coast. Mom's great-grandmother, of whom she has only the faintest recollection, very old and blind, but still knitting woolen underwear for the men in her family, died in the 20s.[39]

What prompted Grimolfur to make this move even though he was successful in Iceland has always been a mystery to Mother. He must have been searching for even greater opportunities for his family and escaping severe circumstances at home before they could steal away what he had built. Mom's amma and afi followed her parents to Hecla seven years later, in 1900. Solveig had spent two years in Iceland training as a midwife. She used her much-needed talents to serve Hecla Island for almost 20 years as the midwife, retiring around the time the legendary Doc Thompson arrived in Riverton.

Jon Hoffman, Mom's afi, had roots reaching back to Jutland through his grandfather, Hans Petur Hoffman, who immigrated to Iceland in 1842. His father was Jon Jonsson, from Selvellir, his mother Elinborg Hansdottir from Budarsofn, granddaughter of the family patriarch. They had three children born to them: Jon, Kristjana and Ingunn. Jon added to his father's first name to become Jon Jonsson. He was from a mercantile family with businesses in Reykjavik, but with a temporary downturn in the family business, Solveig's determination to join her family in New Iceland carried the day. When he arrived, he found too many "Jon Jonssons" in Hecla so he adopted "Hoffman," his mother's family name.

As unlikely as it was for a people whose lives in the North Atlantic were intimately interconnected with the sea and fish, their future in this new land would be similarly entwined with fish on a lake inside an ocean of prairie, a prairie ocean. New Iceland would resurrect from despair, and the New Icelanders would begin to play their part in writing the story of Canada.

CHAPTER SEVEN

The "King of the Icelanders" and His Queen

An eye injury spun Valgerdur's life in an unexpected direction. A family friend, Eirikur Magnusson, a scholar at the University of Cambridge in England, returned home to visit Iceland. Confident that physicians in England could treat Valgerdur's impairment, he invited her to return with him and his wife. Valgerdur spent over five years—starting in 1874 at the age of 18—living with this distinguished couple.

She had gone from isolated Iceland to Cambridge, a great centre of learning and culture. One eye was replaced with glass, but the sight in her other was restored enough for her to attend school, where she became proficient in English and did teacher's training. She returned to Iceland and taught for three years until England lured her back for another three. And then letters from her brother, Sigurdur's close friend Jon Jonsson, changed her life forever. Had he not sent news of the optimism in New Iceland toward the end of the 1880s, and word of other Icelanders joining the settlement, she may never have made the move that took her life in dizzyingly triumphant and tragic directions.

Whatever additional motivations Stefan had for studying with Valgerdur in the winter of 1887, he and Johannes were deeply respectful of the learning they lacked. Stefan had been schooled until age 12, when they left Iceland. Johannes's opportunities were limited growing up in New Iceland in desperate early years. Education or not, no item in my dad's archives rivals a letter in Stefan's hand-written Icelandic from 1886. Finely penned along lines straight as arrows, it bespeaks the work of a man of letters.

Stefan's worldview was shaped in Hecla, Valgerdur's in Cambridge. She was quietly elegant; he radiated exuberance and charm. Differences aside, they were equally compelling personalities, and much tied them together. They were strong-willed and determined, independent and smart. Becoming soulmates was perhaps inevitable, notwithstanding their difference in age: she was 31 and he 24 when they married.

Valgerdur, no less than Stefan, made her mark in New Iceland. Perhaps her most practical gift to the brothers was her skill with the English language. Stefan and Johannes had picked up some English at the mill and later from Reid and Clarke, but Valgerdur undoubtedly enhanced their fluency. Many New Icelanders weren't so lucky.

Soon the Sigurdson and Jonsson families became even more intertwined. Jon's daughter and Valgerdur's beloved niece, Thorbjerg, caught Johannes's eye, and soon they were married. Jon was pleased with his niece and sister's choices. He had developed a close friendship with Sigurdur and his boys over years struggling on Hecla as others departed. His diary reflects his esteem in their ambition. Living in the "tail end of the world" and lacking education would never restrain those men, he wrote. "They were unlike in most ways except for getting ahead, each with his own way of accomplishing this."

Whether in affairs of the heart or business, when opportunity appeared Stefan and Johannes seized it. A prosperous last half of the 1880s meant the world around them was changing quickly. Winnipeg—"Chicago North"—was bursting out at the confluence of the Red and Assiniboine Rivers. The arrival of the first riverboat had brought with it dreams for a network of river highways across the prairies with Lake Winnipeg the epicentre. Steam freighters had made their Lake Winnipeg debut with the *Colville* in 1875, and each year saw more boats constructed. Fish and lumber out, freight and equipment in, with people always on the move—Lake Winnipeg was hub and Selkirk was a big port. By the turn of the century Winnipeg was positioning itself as the next Chicago, and it was a powerful combination of boats and trains that powered this new era. Stefan, drawn like a bee to honey, was back home in the centre of the action. Rail expansion beyond Winnipeg and Selkirk was inevitable, but it was equally clear that no line would ever extend to Hecla Island. Stefan and Johannes pondered relocating to the mainland.

They had deepened their understanding of the fish business. By the time they were ready to move, Jon had already closed his small operation. He had no difficulty securing fish, for he paid the same prices as the fish companies, but the vagaries of the market taught him a lesson. After the second year, the price of frozen fish fell, and the risk was not worth the small profit.[40] The fish business was not for the faint of heart, for uncertainty and risk shadowed every step between lake and plate.

Stefan and Johannes understood the value of powerful friends, and Booth Fisheries of Chicago topped their list. This American goliath was the first and biggest to establish a presence on Lake Winnipeg. It takes little imagination to appreciate why the confident and audacious Stefan sought "The Booth" as his partner; he wasn't afraid of being gobbled up. He would match his strengths with people and the lake with Booth's skills in the world of markets and money.

~   The US fish giants, led by Booth Fisheries, worked through intermediaries, financing anyone able to operate in the north. Their goal was to secure fish to sell, not to take risks in remote locations. Many lined up for the opportunity to do so, asking for only the credit to make it possible. Several companies began operating out of Selkirk with marketing and financing arrangements in Chicago and New York. Production challenges and price fluctuations kept many fledgling operations in peril and under the control of the purse strings held by the big US operators. Many did not survive.

Icelandic names soon appeared on the mastheads of many commercial operations on Lake Winnipeg, first the Hanneson Brothers in Gimli, followed quickly by the Sigurdson Brothers, as they were then known. Many of the fishing families who personified the Lake Winnipeg fishery for decades trace their roots to that period. The money men in Chicago and New York sniffed out the fact that these young Icelanders were tough, smart and aggressive and understood the lake and the people.

Almost immediately, the power imbalance between those with the money and those who produced the fish was exacerbated by apparent disparities between prices paid on the lake and prices in the markets in the south. This led to ill-fated efforts to organize a Fishermen's Protective Union as early as 1889. The hurly-burly of the fish business had reached New Iceland and fuelled endless dock talk. Secure in their arrangements with "The Booth," the Sigurdson Brothers stood aside.

The major open water fishery was that of the whitefish at the North End of the lake. Selkirk Whites become renowned in Chicago and New York. In 1894, the Inspector of Fisheries for Manitoba expressed great optimism for the future of Lake Winnipeg fishing. The total catch of all species, he noted, had increased from 1,924,224 pounds in 1889 to 3,873,281 in 1893, the number of steam vessels from 8 to 13, and the number of men engaged in commercial fishing from 68 to 136. He also stressed the value of the "famed Manitoba whitefish" and urged utmost care in preventing its depletion.

Heavy harvesting of fish within the burgeoning commercial fishery alarmed the Indian fishermen, who saw large volumes of fish taken in the open waters of the lake before beginning their annual journey up into the rivers. Indian agents of the day referred often to concerns about the excessive harvest and the wastage inherent in selecting only the best for southern export, leaving less valuable species or coarse fish to the waste heap. This led to the appointment of Samuel Wilmot in 1890 to conduct the first of many investigations of the

Lake Winnipeg fishery. Wilmot agreed with the concerns and closed several locations to commercial exploitation in the fall season.

Wilmot's investigation also revealed a mounting imbalance between the Indians' subsistence fishing practices and the capital-intensive technologies of the commercial fishery. But Wilmot resisted providing special grounds for Indian commercial exploitation or special access to capital, arguing that if the Indians desired to fish outside the waters set apart for them, they ought to compete unaided with other fishermen. Commercialization proceeded, and the chance of the Indians to be central players was gradually eroded by their inability to compete on a capital-intensive basis.

Four Royal Commissions in succeeding generations (1910, 1933, 1954 and 1966) examined the fishery primarily along two dimensions: the biological mysteries of the stocks and control of the market by large US buyers. The heart of the problem was that fish are both elusive in the wild and perishable when captured. These factors tilted the marketplace in favour of those at the purchasing counters, not those on the skiffs. There was some safety working the middle, but the tides could turn against you quickly. Stefan and Johannes were determined to cover all bases.[41]

After many difficult years and the departure of so many who simply could no longer survive there, prospects for Hecla were improving dramatically with the growing fish economy. The excellent harbour at Hecla's north tip, known as Gull Harbour, made the island a strategic location for operations always moving northward, for it was already clear that Lake Winnipeg fish were a moody lot whose presence shifted from location to location, year to year, and the body of water to the north was all that much larger and seemingly more productive.

The family's relationship with Booth continued for 80 years. Neither needed the other, but working together was better than the alternative. Stefan knew the importance of being, and being seen to be, independent and self-sufficient. He was prepared to stand alongside but not beneath another. That core value grounded the family's business relationships from that point onward.

The brothers could see the future. Trains and commerce were transforming Winnipeg into a major city. Hecla was isolated. It was time to move to the mainland. Gimli and Riverton already had other family operations established there. Building a distinct identity required a distinct location. Several families resided in the area six miles south of Riverton and eighteen miles north of Gimli, known as Hnausa; here is where they would establish operations. Stefan and Valgerdur, married three years and with an infant son Johannes, established their home on a quarter-mile of shoreline with a quarter section of land behind. Sigurdur and Gudrun—and young Fusi—remained in Hecla.

Stefan and Johannes opened business as Sigurdson Brothers, Merchants and Fish Dealers at a location that came to be known as Braedrahofn ("Brothers Harbour"). Their store became an area supply centre. They also produced fish and bought and sold the fish of others. Business expanded rapidly. They began, as they were always wont to do, to move northward, extending operations into the Channel area and beyond to Berens River. Their presence in Selkirk and Winnipeg was growing, and they strengthened their position in the Chicago and New York markets. Their business and their reputations flourished. Young Icelanders competing with the big companies was a source of community pride, and Stefan and Johannes were emissaries of a growing sense of confidence in this adopted land.

Stefan entered politics in 1892, becoming the first reeve (equivalent to mayor) of the newly created Municipality of Bifrost. He was re-elected in 1894. A key problem for fishing operations on the west shore of Lake Winnipeg, both at Hnausa and Gimli, was the absence of a natural harbour, and the construction of a wharf and breakwater was essential. The night Stefan was elected, a resolution passed to ask the federal government for two wharfs, one at Gimli, the other at Hnausa. Stefan lobbied the Conservative government aggressively, and arranged for his ally and friend George Bradbury, a strong Conservative, to visit Ottawa on the communities' behalf. Bradbury secured approval for both wharfs.

The first government dock on Lake Winnipeg went up in front of the Sigurdson store in Hnausa. There was a practical reason for this. Reaching the needed depth of 12 feet required only 600 feet of wharf at Hnausa, but 1200 feet at Gimli. Construction of the smaller dock could begin within the available budget, but the larger required additional appropriations. Therefore, Hnausa's dock was completed in 1895, and Gimli's in 1900.

The decision to build first at Hnausa came at a political cost to Stefan. Many within the electorate concluded that he had used political connections to his own advantage. Stefan lost the next election by one vote. Not one to take allegations about his integrity lightly, he withdrew from politics, except for a stint as reeve of Bifrost when the Municipality of Gimli was divided into northern and southern halves.[42]

Increasingly, Johannes emerged as the political face of the brothers. Whether it was their astute sense of covering all bases, or genuine differences in philosophies, or perhaps both, Johannes and his family for decades following were staunch Liberals. Johannes' low-key style engendered less passion, but it also provoked fewer enemies, and he drew support across the political spectrum. He was elected reeve of the Rural Municipality of Gimli in 1897, 1898, 1899, 1901 and finally in 1920.[43]

It was time to consider expanding the fleet. The growing relationship between Sigurdson Brothers and Booth Fisheries enabled them to obtain financing for a major freighter and passenger vessel, which they christened *Lady of the Lake*. She was the largest boat owned by Icelanders to be built on Lake Winnipeg to that point. The *Lady* was built of BC fir in Selkirk for $15,000. She was 100 feet long, with an upper and lower deck, and drew six feet of water without a cargo. She carried up to 750 boxes of fish with room to sleep 20 passengers. Her launch was lauded in *Heimskringla* ("Around the World," founded in 1886), one of *Framfari's* successors, on April 19, 1897 as "a fair summer gift indeed, given to the Icelanders in America by the Sigurdson Brothers, merchants of Hnausa."

Selkirk was becoming a major port. Stefan must have pinched himself as the *Lady* launched. He had travelled past this very spot, then a humble settlement, 20 years before. A few miles up the Red River, he had struggled to help his father and Helgi Tomasson pull the clumsy, flat-bottomed boats through the rapids to get to New Iceland.

The Selkirk dock had not existed then, nor the buildings stretching alongside, where the burgeoning Lake Winnipeg fish companies had receiving and shipping offices. Selkirk had been barely a hint of the bustling town now looming on the plateau above. No one could tell at a glance that Selkirk's expectation of becoming the rail centre of the west had been usurped by Winnipeg, there at the meeting point of the Red and Assiniboine. Many had believed that to be a serious mistake; the danger of prairie floods was well known, and Winnipeg didn't have steep banks like those protecting Selkirk. The locks that would make the river navigable from Selkirk to Winnipeg were years away, and Winnipeg was defenceless against the ravaging Red during the prairie run-off each spring. Rail hub or not, the growing fishing industry had centred in Selkirk, and its epicentre was the Selkirk docks. This was Stefan Sigurdson's domain.

The path his sons were on was beyond anything Sigurdur could have imagined when he made the fateful decision to sell his only asset, his sheep, and leave for Canada. As the *Lady* started down the shipway, there could be no doubt in his mind that he had done the right thing. It was incomprehensible that Stefan and Johannes would have been blessed with this destiny in Iceland. In Canada, anything was possible, and where the future might lead him, Sigurdur, now 67, couldn't imagine.

Stefan and Johannes had become successful men in their adopted country, thriving merchants and fish dealers. With the *Lady of the Lake*, they entered the transportation business, both freight and passengers. One can only imagine the excitement of the *Lady's* first trips, Stefan's exuberance filling the ship. The *Lady* set out for Winnipeg, where she acquired thirty passengers, including Icelanders from North Dakota en route to visit family in New Iceland.[44]

Stefan and Johannes were players in the fishery as suppliers and buyers, and the *Lady of the Lake* provided the transportation to move much of their own and others' fish to market. They were also active in the Berens River area, where they maintained a station from as early as 1895 targeting the area's plentiful sturgeon. Transporting the fish was the biggest challenge in operating this far afield. They lacked the freighting capacity for the volumes being caught. Around the turn of the century, an ingenious technique was developed for freezing the whitefish upon catch. Large freezer buildings were built and insulated with two-foot-thick walls of sawdust. Drums inside were refilled regularly with a coolant combination of ice, dry ice and salt, allowing the temperature to drop below freezing. Galvanized steel shelves charged with the same potent cooling combination ran across the room, and the fish were laid out on pans. Facilities like this were built all around Lake Winnipeg.[45] Once frozen the fish were packed into wooden boxes, and big steamers like the *Wolverine* or *Lady* came with their own freezers to transport them to storage in Winnipeg, awaiting sale into the markets when the price was favourable.

To many, the Sigurdson brothers were symbols of what could be accomplished with hard work and opportunity. Everything seemed to be going well—perhaps too well. Stefan, friend to everyone, was loose with credit. One can imagine the irritation that caused cautious Johannes. Stefan was flamboyant, and his predilection for parties no doubt irked his brother. Then, misfortune struck. In 1898, fire destroyed the prosperous store at Hnausa and much of its largely uninsured inventory. The brothers weathered the storm, rebuilding and restocking the store within months, likely thanks to Booth's line of credit.

The US fish markets were volatile in those years and the squeeze was felt in the middle, by the intermediaries who took the risks day in and day out. Stefan wasn't a man who liked to say no, especially to fishermen in hard times, so his credit practices loosened even further. Nonetheless, Sigurdson Brothers was prospering at the turn of the century. In June 1901, in one of his many letters to *Heimskringla*, Stefan reported that they had over 70 people on the payroll, making Sigurdson Brothers North America's largest Icelandic-owned business at the time.[46]

It was a shock when Stefan and Johannes announced the dissolution of their partnership later in 1901 in the *Logberg* (another of *Framfari's* successors, founded in 1888). Their differences as partners (not as brothers) had overcome their bonds. Little is known of what triggered the break-up. Perhaps their contrasting impulsive and cautious natures could no longer be reconciled. They sold the major assets, including the *Lady of the Lake*.

Together the brothers had accomplished what neither could have done alone. They had a deep relationship and were also bonded profoundly as a family. Johannes' wife was Valgerdur's beloved niece, and Valgerdur would never have allowed partnership dissolution to affect this family relationship. Valgerdur must have understood better than anyone the joys and rewards of being part of Stefan's life, but would also have seen the challenges and agonies he represented for his brother. This much is clear: Stefan and Johannes went their separate ways in business matters with dignity, and they and their families remained close for the rest of their lives.

Johannes continued his record of success in business affairs and civic life. He was a man of stature in the community, no less so than his brother. He moved to Selkirk after the partnership ended. He stayed in the fishing business and established a partnership with Sveinn Thorvaldsson as Sigurdsson Thorvaldsson for the operation of a number of stores, including in Riverton and Gimli. (The partnership continued long after Johannes' untimely death at age 56 in 1924, until Sveinn Thorvaldsson died in 1949.)

Johannes' and his family returned to Gimli from Selkirk, where he would soon become Gimli's first mayor, a position he held from 1908 until 1911. He was widely travelled in Europe and the US (including the 1892 Chicago World Fair) and an astute observer of municipal government and town planning. He contributed many ideas when Gimli was laid out as a town, and much of that original design remains intact. He also helped energize Gimli's economic life and status and raised its profile within the business community in Winnipeg, whether it was helping bring the train into Gimli and Riverton, securing banking services, or having mitts and socks knit in the community sold in the Winnipeg wholesale houses.[47]

Stefan continued to operate the store and fish business from Hnausa. He bought a small steamer, the 65-foot *Viking*, which lacked the power and glamour of his *Lady*, but enabled him to start a freight and passenger service around the South End. Gold had been discovered on the east shore across from Hecla, and the *Viking* began transporting boatloads of miners and all the booze they could carry.

It was now 1904. The *Viking* was a shuttle for Lake Winnipeg commerce, travelling around the South Basin moving men and supplies and fish. Stefan's personality was ever flamboyant, and as the legendary captain Ed Nelson wrote, the "unexpected [was] always expected" when the *Viking* was in town.[48] Stefan made his rounds in the townsite up the bank from the docks. He called first at every general store, filling grocery orders from people up and down the lake. Then he'd visit one of the taverns—in those days going strong at seven in the morning—and then follow up with a trip to one or two wholesale liquor stores, where beer kegs or bottles of hard liquor were available to all except treaty Indians. Once the *Viking* was loaded, she departed while there was still enough light to make her way up the river and out onto the lake. There was always a keg of beer tapped on the main deck as the self styled "King of the Icelanders" boarded.[49]

Two years later Stefan acquired the *Fern* and had her enlarged to work as a freighter on the fishing grounds, leaving the *Viking* for the lucrative passenger service. By 1906, Stefan's financial status allowed him to build a two-and-a-half-storey home in Hnausa. Some described it as a mansion. It had a striking turret and bay window, a large porch with pillars supporting a sundeck above, steam heating, gaslights and full plumbing, all the convenience of any home in Winnipeg. Finishing the house in 1906 had a special meaning; it was 30 years after Stefan's first winter in the shack at Hecla.

Valgerdur was critical to the success of the home. Her practicality and high standards were matched by high expectations, directed first to herself and then to others. She was a gracious and elegant woman with a strong impact in the community. She became a sought-after public speaker, but her busy home life took precedence. She was beside Stefan throughout each of his ups and downs.

They entertained often, with great joviality and hospitality. One memorable gathering was the reception for Premier Rodmond Roblin on January 3, 1901, his first visit to New Iceland. Hnausa was not to be outdone by the premier's Gimli visit earlier that day. They planted evergreens in the snow from the highway to the palatial home and Roblin was greeted at the door with a spray of spruce cuttings spelling out, "Here you are at home."

After a feast, an honour parade of 60 accompanied Roblin to the Hnausa schoolhouse for the meeting. Icelandic national songs flowed into the crisp night air. As they approached, the procession divided into two lines in military style, and the premier walked down the centre and across the threshold to cheers. A spruce bough shaped like a crown adorned the front of the room, with the name R.P. Roblin below, a touch not seen in Gimli.

The premier's enthusiasm for this rousing welcome and the preparations co-coordinated so ably by Gestur Oddleifson, the chair for the evening, can best be measured by the fact that he spoke uninterrupted for one-and-a-half hours. He remarked that he had never seen a finer group of men and women. Three hours later, all returned to Stefan and Valgerdur's, where the reception continued until the wee hours.

In 1910, Stefan was financially stable enough to re-enter the big leagues of the northern whitefishery. He bought the *Mikado*, a freighter 150 feet long with a carrying capacity of more than 1,000 boxes of fish. She was extremely successful in her first year, both with freight and 20 staterooms for passengers, but crisis struck again that fall. The *Mikado* sheltered in Swampy Harbour, on the large island outside Berens River, and was driven from her position in a northeast gale that shattered her rudder and stranded her on nearby shallows. The *Wolverine*, another legendary Lake Winnipeg vessel also running from a brutal storm, struck a reef and broke her rudder in the same harbour. The gale continued, and soon the boats were ice-locked for the winter, the men conscripted to hastily constructed shore camps. It wasn't until spring that the ships could be rescued and towed to Selkirk for repair.[50] The *Mikado* was rebuilt in later years and returned to service on Lake Winnipeg by Booth Fisheries as the *Grand Rapids*.

Fishermen used sailboats on the lake, typically 32 to 34 feet with fore and aft masts, open except for a six-foot deck at the prow, under which the foremen and two crew could seek a crowded cover when circumstances required.[51] Each grouping of sailboats travelled with a small tug, usually steam-powered, which shepherded them to the fishing grounds, catered to their needs, and provided rescue and support in heavy seas. There were the *Douglas M.*, *Purvis*, *Betty Lou*, *Barney Thomas* and the *Frank Burton* (rebuilt and renamed many times, finally becoming the Sig Fish freighter the *Goldfield*), to name a few.

Disaster haunted Stefan and Valgerdur. In 1911, the store in Hnausa once more burned to the ground, destroying the stock. Stefan needed to rebuild again. This time he had two sons beside him, Solberg (Solli), born in 1893, and Sigurdur (SV, my grandfather), born in 1895. As Sigurdsson Fisheries Co., (one "s" was eventually dropped from the historic spelling) wholesale and retail fish merchants, they operated at Grindstone, Bloodvein, Pidgeon and Berens River. They supported and supplied fishermen, and in return had the right to acquire their catch.

Ledger records from this period show a broad base of relationships within the Berens River and Fisher River communities. Friendships between the Icelanders and the Indians of Fisher River should not be surprising. They had much in common. Each had come to essentially the same place to build a better life. Both hoped to farm, but found the land inhospitable, and so turned to the water in order to survive. Soon they would also be bonded by the devastation of smallpox.

Much of the fish production in those years occurred in the winter. As the rail moved northward along the western side of Lake Winnipeg, the first railhead was established at Hodgson in 1914. Boats, dogs, horses and now iron horses transported winter fish production from Fisher Bay and regions north. Stefan established a store in Hodgson and located SV and Solli there for the winter to buy fish. The fishing effort expanded north from the prime grounds for tulibee and goldeye in Fisher Bay to the whitefish-filled waters around Reindeer Island. With a Sigurdson Fisheries station at Warpath, the fish would be moved over land to Gypsumville, which would become, like Riverton, the end of the line.

Area settlers, often recent Ukrainian immigrants, were hired to haul the fish to the railhead using horses and sleighs. Securing the extension of the rail line from Gimli north to Riverton and Hnausa was another of Stefan's dreams. Approval wasn't secured until 1911, after a lobbying trip he and other delegates made to Ottawa. In 1916, the line finally reached Riverton, six miles from Hnausa. With the rail terminus in their backyard, Riverton became the centre of family operations. The establishment of the three partners and the incorporation of Sig Fish (as the company had become known) cemented the decision.

These were good years for Stefan, but there was no sweeter day than in 1915 when he reacquired the *Lady of the Lake* from the Government of Canada, to whom she had been sold some years before. As the government vessel, she had been used by federal officials, fish inspectors and agents of the Department of Indian Affairs. No doubt one of her finest moments was in the summer of 1910, when she carried Prime Minister Sir Wilfrid Laurier down the Red River from Winnipeg to Selkirk. The *Lady* had become available for purchase when a new government vessel, the MS *Bradbury*, named after Stefan's good friend George Bradbury, was put into service.[52]

Just before the end of the Great War, tragedy struck at home. Business had been challenging, but Stefan had held his own. In May of 1917, he suffered a stroke and within days was dead. It was a powerful blow at a difficult time.

Solli (23) and SV (21) operated the business that fall. It was rough going. SV, unmarried, was under pressure to join the war effort. As a former student at Winnipeg's Kelvin High School, he was entitled to enter the officer core. Early in 1918 he enlisted as a member of Canada's fledgling air force. With the sudden capitulation of Germany that fall, he was discharged from active duty as a second lieutenant while still in training.

The business wasn't able to sustain itself in the months following Stefan's death. SV was away and Solli wasn't strong enough to run it on his own. Most of the assets were liquidated, including the *Lady of the Lake* once again. She survived on the lake for a few more years, but eventually tied up in Selkirk during the Depression. She was broken up for firewood around 1934.

My great-grandfather Stefan personified the triumphs and disasters waiting in this new land where the Icelanders hoped to make a better life for their children. Through success and failure, hard work and hard partying, his spirit and determination were relentless. He lived a full life in too few years. He reached out with confidence as to what was achievable. He overextended credit and fell down. His aspirations were remarkable given his humble origin. He was charismatic, enthusiastic, and free of grudges or enemies, qualities he used in wielding his determination on any project. He was a born leader. But all of this was not necessarily conducive to success at business.

Stefan's death affected his family profoundly and shook the Icelandic community. The family lost its centre of gravity and the community lost a leader. He was a man of successes and excesses, whose triumphs and tragedies were a mirror in which many saw their own lives, as they were or as they aspired them to be.

One can only imagine Sigurdur's pain. His oldest son Stefan was beside him as partner, friend and son through the agony of deciding to leave Iceland, and stood beside him at the ship's railing as they left Akureyri in 1876 to face an uncertain future. On March 1918, just before the end of the Great War and within a year of Stefan's death, Sigurdur died at his daughter's home in Gimli, to which he had retired a few years before. Johannes died in 1924 after struggling with cancer. Sigurdur, Stefan and Johannes rest together along the shore of Lake Winnipeg, about one mile north of the Big House at Hnausa.

Sigurdur's life had not stood still in the years since he watched the *Lady of the Lake* slide into the Red River. Gudrun had passed away. And Thorunn Maria Magnusdottir, a 31-year-old woman from desperate conditions in Iceland arrived in Canada in 1900. She became Sigurdur's housekeeper one year and wife the next. He soon brought three more children into the world: Sigurdur Runberg (SR) in 1901, Stefan Valdis (who would become known as Steve) in 1903, and Gudrun Margaret (Runa) in 1908. Their home was on Hecla, next door to Solveig and Jon Hoffman's. Thorunn was a meticulous housekeeper, but the pioneering life proved too much for her. In 1909, she succumbed to a disabling mental illness and was institutionalized for the remainder of her life.

Sigurdur, now an old man, was in no position to care for the young family. Steve and Runa went to the "Big House" in Hnausa to be with their much older brother, Stefan. SR went to Stefan's sister in North Dakota but was soon back where he felt he belonged. Valgerdur mothered them all. That was for most of the next 20 years. Both young men learned the fishing business early. SR started as a cook on the *Misk* when he was but a boy, and then moved to the *Lady of the Lake* in 1915. By 15, he was an engineer on the boats. Later, he went with SV and Solli to work the store in Hodgson. Young Steve started as a cook on the *Husk* when he was only 12.

Valgerdur had ridden waves of triumph and tragedy since stepping off the *Victoria* onto the dock at Hecla. The business turmoil paled beside the brutal reality arising from the children they had brought into the world. Her first child, Johannes Helgi, was born when she was 32. Her next child, Einar, entered the world just over one year later, stillborn. Within a year Jorunn, her first daughter, was born, and two years later Solberg. My grandfather, Sigurdur Victor, arrived in 1895. Valgerdur had now had four surviving children in six years, and was 38. In the next three years she brought two more children into the world, Gudrun, born in 1896, and Stefan in 1898. Young Stefan died in 1901 at the age of three. Gudrun died three years later, at eight, and Johannes in 1905 at age 17. Jorunn was next, in 1914 at age 23. Valgerdur had borne eight children in little more than a decade. She buried six of them, and one who had already reached adulthood. Only my grandfather SV survived, and after the loss of her husband, Valgerdur saw her only remaining child depart for a war taking lives by the millions.

There can be no doubt that Valgerdur was ambitious and determined. From a remote island in the North Atlantic and close to blind as a young woman, from the time she was 18 to 22, she had lived in the refinement and elegance of Cambridge. She then joined the pioneer lifestyle of Hecla and Hnausa. Stefan must have been quite the young man to engage the attention of a woman of such calibre and drive.

Throughout their marriage her husband built and lost what were fortunes in those days, and their lives were wracked as tuberculosis took the children one after the other. The family seemed vulnerable to TB, like the Indians with whom they so closely associated. Any of countless fearful stories illustrates the desperation they and so many others experienced. There was the night that one of Valgerdur and Stefan's children fell ill. They were in Hnausa. It was spring, and travel on the thawing lake ice had become dangerous, but Stefan risked sending two men with a team of horses 20 miles to Gimli for the doctor. They collected him safely and returned by the same route, but with eight miles left the horses plunged through the ice. The men escaped, but the horses floated dead the following morning.[53] Everyone survived that day, but the death bell tolled mercilessly. Eventually, the only survivor, my afi, was also struck with TB, but sensed its onset in Berens River in 1919 and took to bed for six months, determined to beat the disease with rest and sturgeon oil administered daily by Lisa Berens. He pulled through with no damage aside from a lingering spot on his chest x-ray.

As his own life drew to a close, Sigurdur had every reason to believe he had made the right decision in bringing the family to New Iceland. They endured many dark days in a freezing shack on Hecla Island, and future challenges were inevitable, but there is little doubt he went to his grave knowing he had made a better life for his children.

Stefan and Johannes had emerged as remarkable men in New Iceland, and then in Manitoba—leaders in business and the community. His daughters lived secure and fulfilled lives. Kristjana was married to Bergthor Thordarson, Gimli's third mayor, and they were leading citizens. A few miles north in Selkirk, Jakobina was married to Johannes Helgason, one of the lake's first sea captains. Sigrun, who had arrived two years later, lived and worked in Winnipeg. In the 1930s she met her husband Mr. Foote, of Pincher Creek, Alberta, where she moved and came to be known as Lady Sarah. His oldest daughter Sigridur, already married when Sigurdur left Iceland, along with her husband Albert Hanson, had also immigrated and lived across the border in Mountain, North Dakota.

Over on Lake Manitoba, young Sigfus had married a Riverton woman, Sigurlaug, daughter of Jon Frimann Kristjansson and Kristin Jonsdottir, who had immigrated to Canada in 1889. Fusi and Sigurlaug struck off on their own and homesteaded near Shoal Lake, where he made his way as a farmer, fisherman and family man. Sigurdur's many grandchildren enriched his life. Stefan's boys Solli and Siggi (as Afi was often called within the family) were actively engaged in running the business.

For Afi SV, the sudden loss of his dynamic father must have been a mighty blow. He inherited the leadership of the family at a time when everything seemed to have dwindled back to ashes, with the business lost and the painful loss of all but one of his siblings in the decade before. The family needed to start over, and the burden fell to him. It was 1919, and he went north to Berens River, a prime spot for whitefish. The family was known in the area, and SV expected it would be a good place to start his fishing life in earnest. His brother Solli, along with SR and Steve, joined this fledgling venture. The next generation of Sigurdsons was starting over, but not without a rich legacy left by Stefan and Johannes, a web of relationships on the lake, connections in the markets, skill and will. Stefan had taught SV and Solli fishing and the business of fishing since boyhood. Steve and SR were kids already working as men. "My uncles by heredity, my brothers by adoption, and my partners by free choice," was how Afi SV explained on the occasion of Steve's 25th wedding anniversary his intricate relationships with SR and Steve since they started Sigurdson Fisheries in 1921.

The years following Stefan's death were not easy for Valgerdur. The home abuzz with children, a daughter-in-law preoccupied with attending to them, and a son almost as energetic (and certainly as determined) as his father, may have only intensified her feeling of isolation. She had endured the ebb and flow of her husband's fortunes and the ceaseless tolling of the bell. Valgerdur endured, but one can only imagine her loneliness.

Valgerdur's dignified aura filled every room, but she was also deeply empathetic, probably an attribute arising from her own struggles. Her deep religious faith enabled her to bear the brutal blows that struck her life. Valgerdur became blind in the last years of her life. When she lost her ability to read, she spent hours reciting poetry. She was always able to find new life in the mind, drawing on the resilience of the Icelandic forbears who had done no less in grinding poverty for centuries.

The love and respect of those who knew Valgerdur was clear in the condolences that poured in from the community when she died, praising her as one of the last of the early pioneers who had contributed invaluable leadership with the highest of ideals. Einar Jonsson, the editor of *Logberg*, wrote a lengthy memorial, drawing on conversations with Valgerdur in the last years of her life on her annual trip to Hecla Island. My mom's first book, *Thora's Island Home*, is about two Icelandic girls growing up on Hecla. She recalls Valgerdur's visits and deep attachment to the island.

I was only three when she died. I have vague memories of running to the end of the hall and peering into the small room at the back of the house. I can see her sitting on the side of the bed. Beyond that, everything is dim.

The "King" of the Icelanders and his Queen, Stefan and Valgedur Sigurdsson.

The *Lady of the Lake*

The "Big House" alongside "Big Business"

1915: Sail boats at ease awaiting a white capped sea—fishing at Warren Landing.

1931: Horses pulling Frozen Gold; next stop—Chicago

1934: *Tullibee Jubilee*—the US embargo would soon end the tullibee bonanza. Afi, Sr and Steve.

1930s: The *Grand Rapids*, (once the *Mikado* owned by Stefan in 1915) heading into the Big Lake.

1946: From wedding bells to Catfish Creek and tomato sandwiches each night

1944: Sigurdson Families, crews and shorehands, and Dave Sayers, mate, standing tall

1946: Dori the Mechanic's shop with his "helpers." (LEFT TO RIGHT) Sylvia, Dori Benjaminson, Elmer and Kay Briem

1950: Glenn and his pal, Peter Boushie.

1950s: The *Keenora* steaming past the Berens River Station southbound with a load of passengers.

1954: The Berens River Station

1955: "Have you got my gang on Board, Over? Roger Roger." Elaine, Eric, and Glenn climbing, climbing ...

1956: Catfish Creek late October loading the *Spear* southbound

(LEFT) 1950s: Senior Captain Gusti Helgason: his mate Victor Sigurdson
(RIGHT) 1950s: Afi SV—a big coat for doing big business in Winnipeg in the 50s

1950s: Tree dozing a winter road first, draglines in the summer. Leslie Olafson on a Monarch Caterpillar.

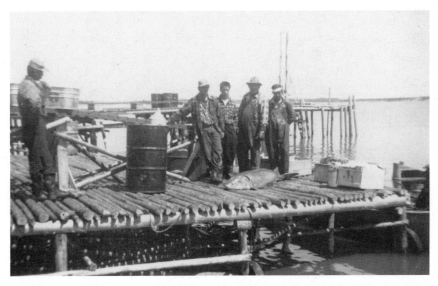

1957: 130 pound sturgeon caught by "Oli Knee High" arriving at the Berens Station

With high water comes sandbags and more sandbags. Berens River Crew organized by Harrison Boulanger saving the Catfish Ice House.

All hands on board: Saving the Catfish Station. Tom Bittern and Dad Stefan nailing the plastic on; sandbags next.

1950s: Afi Malli on his gas boat loading up in the river at home to Go North.

Late 40s: The *JR Spear*: Loading up at a North end fish Station.

1957 : The *Jr Spear* beached at Grindstone Point

Jr Spear pulling the *Goldfield* down the Winnipeg River to Selkirk Drydock

Dori Benjaminson: "Dad's man" till the end.

Sigurdson Station at Spider Island 20 miles south of the Northern end of the lake.

Captain Steve (LEFT), "the bear in that lair" and Arni Goodman, a "man with a big history."

1960s: *Jr Spear* in the Icelandic River to freeze in, with whitefish boats on the shore with their winter crutches

1972: The Office would go within hours, and The Freshwater Fish Agency Building would remain.

1970s : The *Goldfield* loading the Riverton Transfer at the End of the Road.

Uncle Grimsi (Brynjolfson) having lunch after a morning lifting nets.

1980: Hecla, Net House with the Lutheran Church behind, looking out onto the lake.

PART THREE

BORN IN A WARP OF TIME

CHAPTER EIGHT
Twins: A Man and a Company

D ad and the newly incorporated Sigurdson Fisheries were like twins. Born in 1921, they grew up and got old together. Dad's first recollections are of his father and SR and Steve spending endless hours debating, discussing and deciding. Those were critical years for the Sigurdsons and their fishing business. They were starting over with just their hands and their ingenuity. Their most important asset was a rich web of relationships in the industry and the community, inherited from Stefan and Johannes. But they had no money; they could not afford to make a mistake. Before they made a move, they left no detail unturned as they covered off all the possibilities that could go for or against them. The boy, Stefan, listened eagerly to the conversations until the moment he was invited to join them. He didn't have to wait long. You became a man early in our family.

The last days of school were tough. Stefan could think of nothing else but boarding the *Grand Rapids* to go north to his dad at Berens Station. He left his Winnipeg house running to catch the 7:00 a.m. train to Selkirk as soon as school was out. He and the company had just turned eight, and for the first time he was considered sufficiently independent (surprising even back then) to make the trip alone.

A couple of hours later, Stefan climbed down from the train and made his way to the Selkirk docks. There was no small amount of importance in his step as he marched along the docks packed with men, nets, boxes, drums and every other imaginable item needed to supply the fishing operations. But the real thrill wasn't the chaos on the docks. It was the great ships alongside. They were fish freighters, but to young Stefan they were ocean liners. The freighters were 50 to 100 feet typically, carrying upwards of 100 tons, with a load of up to 1200 boxes of Lake Winnipeg product. In Selkirk, the boxes were loaded onto railcars, which arrived a day later in the great fish markets of Chicago and New York.

Soon Stefan spotted Captain Hugh Cochrane. Stefan was already a familiar face to him, and he welcomed SV's son aboard as if he were his own son, then took him to his bunk to stow his stuff while the men finished loading the supplies. Stefan had already made the trip to Berens several times in his short life, but he felt a special pride taking this first trip by himself. He felt at home on the *Grand Rapids*. He was already steeped in the family's history on the lake. When his Afi Stefan had owned this boat she had been known as the *Mikado* (she was rebuilt and renamed). Stefan never knew his Afi, but he carried his name and his story as if he had.

Stefan had made his decision. He was part of the family business. This was the life he wanted. There was no time to hang out on the bunk. He dropped his stuff and returned to the dock to find a way to make himself useful. Usually that meant pushing boxes down the big rollers stretching across the dock from the supply sheds to the freighters as the endless stream of supplies was taken aboard and then down into the hold on the elevator. Everything went down those rollers.

It was nearly eight o'clock on the evening of June 25, 1930. The tug would soon be off. Captain Hugh wanted to be down the river and onto the lake while it was still daylight. The endless paperwork he had to review had cost him an extra hour, and he needed to pull out immediately. Stefan heard the captain's familiar voice hollering to the deckhands below: "Let the bowline go! Tighten the spring line!" With engines revving, the captain levered the bow into the river while his men pulled the last lines aboard.

Berens River was 20 hours away. Stefan's mind was full of the small island where he would arrive in the morning and stay the summer. He ran to the galley for supper, anxious to arrive before anyone else so he could wolf down his food and race back to the wheelhouse and the captain.

The river meandered its way through the vast Netley Marsh. By ten o'clock they had entered the South Basin, just as the sun was dropping over the horizon. They would steam north through the night. Captain Hugh was on the wheel, conferring with his wheelsman about the weather ahead. The dropping barometer signalled an impending shift in the wind and the potential for heavy seas in the North Basin. They were deep in conversation and soon forgot Stefan was there. He lay on the wheelhouse bunk watching the captain direct the men and adjust course with a glance at the compass. The steady rhythm of the engines lulled Stefan to sleep.

"Stefan, time to get you into your bunk, my boy." Captain Hugh walked him down the upper deck to his own cabin and helped him into the upper bunk. When he woke the next morning, they were in the Channel with the shorelines of the narrow pass between the Dog Heads visible on either side.

He gulped his breakfast in the galley at the stern on the main deck. Normally the galley looked like any ordinary kitchen, but when the water was rough the tables were covered with wet tablecloths so the plates and utensils wouldn't slide. The cooks were never short of food or stories, and they could fill a young boy's stomach and imagination at the same time.

Stefan headed back to the wheelhouse. Captain Hugh had decided to pull into Pine Dock to replenish the cordwood that fired the steam boilers driving the rhythmical thumping of the giant engines below. As the captain swiftly manoeuvred the *Grand Rapids* alongside the small dock, Stefan could see Bill Selkirk striding down the hill from his log house on the bank above. A couple of young fellows followed, pushing a small boxcar loaded with short logs down a rail track from the shore onto the dock.

Bill was a Scotsman who had come to the area in the early 1900s to set up his cordwood business. It had expanded into a small settlement where he ran a trading post and fish station. All along the lake were small operators who had set up camp to supply steamers with cordwood. Hanny Hannesson was nearby at Little Bullhead Bay, and on the other side of the lake, about ten miles north, the Andersons ran an operation at Rabbit Point. The *Wolverine*, the *Grand Rapids*, the *Keenora*, the *Granite Rock*, the *Phyliss Williams*, all the great steamers of those days, had their favourite stops to take aboard additional fuel depending on the length of the trip and, as always, the weather.

The loading took only a few minutes, and then the whistle sounded and the engineer down in the bowels of the ship threw the engines into reverse as the ship arched its way back out from the dock. The second whistle from the wheelhouse signaled the engineer to let the clutch out and set the engines to their forward position.

Captain Hugh told Stefan a "big head sea" was ahead as they passed between the Dog Heads with Black Bear light at the northeast tip of Black Bear Island now in sight. The wind was blowing straight from the north but the captain, eyes on the barometer, predicted it would soon shift northwest. When they reached the light the winds were indeed norwesterly, gusting 30 to 40 knots. Captain Hugh set the course for Cox Reef, the next major navigational aid on Lake Winnipeg. It was at least five hours away.

At Cox Reef Light, they turned east onto the ranges on course into Berens River. As Sigurdson Island came into view, Stefan rushed to the bow to wave to his dad, who was already waving back. When Stefan's feet touched the planks of the dock, his dad greeted him with a hug. There was no time to waste. Stefan's first task was to find his bunk and get it set up for the summer.

Sigurdson Island was a lively place in the early '30s, the centre of activity in the community when the fishing season was underway. Tents were everywhere on the island. Many of the Indian fishermen preferred the convenience of staying close to the fishing grounds rather than travelling all the way from their home upriver in the morning. Usually, their families were there with them. In the summer, some of the Icelandic fishermen's families joined them from down south. The island was bustling day and night. In addition to the fishermen picking up ice in the morning and bringing in their catch at night, there was a big crew on shore—weighmen, shore hands, cooks, bookkeepers and mechanics. There were frequent line-ups to get into the little building that served as a store and office, Grand Central Station on Sigurdson Island.

In those days, when the big whitefish fleets were also operating out of Berens River, the boats left for the fishing grounds at four in the morning. Breakfast in the cookhouse was served to 60 or 70 men at three o'clock. Each day they travelled out 15 -25 miles to lift their nets, and then returned to the station around two in the afternoon, hauling the catch into the packing sheds where the fish was dressed. Then they'd find a spot on the rocks behind the station to work on their nets, or hit their bunks for a rest before supper. At six sharp, Stefan would pick up the iron rod to bang the same battered propeller I too would use years later to summon everyone to the cookhouse.

Life was mostly work, but that doesn't mean there wasn't fun. A humble square dance platform—no bigger than 24 by 30 feet—stood beside the ice slide. SR was one of the great square dance callers of his day, booming out: "Promenade right, promenade left, and circle 'round, and do-si-do!" His energy breathed life into the dancers whirling around the platform under the light of the stars. On those long summer nights, the dancing often carried on until breakfast was served and the men headed back onto the water.

Stefan established his own island work routine. When the first fishermen returned from lifting their nets each day, he would rush to the sheds to discover the size of the lift, as that would signal whether the fish were running or not. After that, his headquarters was the store, working alongside his dad recording the fish receipts brought in after the catch had been weighed. And he served customers with groceries, candy bars and Cokes.

Meanwhile, people from the community, mostly fishermen and their families, stood by the gutting tables pulling fat away from the plump innards of the whitefish. The fat would be rendered down for use in the winter as part of their medicinal arsenal, and the rich fish livers became dinner. Most often they made their way up to the store at some point to buy supplies or review the status of their accounts. As the end of the season approached, people from the community often made major purchases to stock up for the months ahead. Although interlopers in some sense of the word, for the fishing operations only lasted a few months each year, they were as much a part of the flow of life and the economy as the Hudson's Bay Company or John Alex, a Lebanese trader who had established a trading post at the turn of the century on the small island up the river where Stefan had first established his operations in 1895.

Stefan was often in the store when Mrs. Alex Bear came in. His dad had a special link with her husband Alex, forged in a brush with disaster. In 1919, Afi had been under sail north off Swampy Island near Barrel Rock. A fifteen-year-old Alex Bear was with him on the boat. It was a heavy sea, and in a struggle with the mast, Afi was struck and went overboard. In a masterful piece of seamanship, the boy brought the boat around and rescued him. Afi owed his life to him, and he never forgot it. Year after year, he refused to let his wife leave the store without a gift of food and money, as did Dad in his days.

When he wasn't helping at the store or in the sheds, or tending to his own business nailing boxes, Stefan spent hours watching and talking with the men working on their nets. The cotton nets could deteriorate rapidly in the water, and back then they relied upon a substance called bluestone to protect them. Every six days, all the gangs of net set over the days prior were brought into the station. The men laboured for hours picking out moss and debris, patching holes, and then spreading the nets over the rocks for a good coating of bluestone. Spreading the cotton nets (the more manageable linen thread was introduced in the 1940s) was especially painstaking when a big blow had rolled them into a twisted bundle commingled with twigs and moss, but with good humour, patience and conversation the hours passed until the job was done.

As he grew older, Stefan was charged with organizing the "seaming on" of the nets, which took place in the winter months in Riverton. When the cotton nets arrived in bundles from Scotland, they were still a long way from fishable. "Seaming on" meant attaching the net's webbing to a thin cord called a sideline. It was a laborious process, but experienced hands became quite adept. Often a mother and her younger children seamed on as a source of household income. Stefan's job was to deliver the bundles of twine to the families doing the seaming on, and then to pick up the finished nets. The fishermen then outfitted them with corks on the top line and leads on the bottom to enable them to spread out in the water.

The first major Sig Fish expansion was the establishment of a fall station at Black Bear, just north of the present-day settlement on tree-covered Matheson Island. Black Bear is a perfect harbour, insulated from wind in every direction. Its strategic location northwest of the Dog Heads means access to the prime fishing grounds to the south in the Channel area, north to Moose Island and west to Fisher Bay. The fishing business, like real estate, has always been about "location, location, location."

Their next big step was acquiring the *Husk*, a small fishing freighter that gave them much greater flexibility to move the fishing efforts to wherever the fish, with their mysterious ways, were moving. It would be impossible to calculate the hours of intrigue spent amongst fishermen reading and speculating on the "signs" that might tell them where the fish would appear next. With an extra freighter, the Sig Fish team weren't any more accurate in their predictions, but they were more mobile.

Summer fishing season typically ran from the beginning of June to early August. In addition to buying from other fishermen, Sig Fish ran its own fishing operation. Two gasboats were the mainstay of operations in those early days—the *Leading Star* run by SR, and the *Whoopee* by Arni Goodman. Arni was a young man who had come under my great-grandfather Stefan's magnetism and worked at the store in Hnausa. Arni also became a top fisherman. He and SR were a formidable team, each hauling four or five flat-bottomed boats or skiffs filled with fishermen heading out to work. Steve, often with Dad tagging along, was on the *Husk*, carrying ice north and south and returning with fish. SV operated the station at Berens River.

The cornerstone on which the business was rebuilt throughout the 1920s was winter fishing goldeyes and tulibees in the Channel area. Winter fishing was more accessible to the little guy—you didn't need fishing stations and big freighters. You just needed sleds and a dog team and a small outpost camp. Location was everything in the winter, too. The first step was getting men to where they could catch fish, and this meant building camps as close as possible to the bountiful zones. A few men, often fathers, sons and brothers, usually banded together to "freeze out" after fall fishing in one of the remote locations sprinkled around the lake. They'd wait three or four weeks with their dogs and horses for the ice to form. They'd need at least two inches, but three was preferable. That usually came around the third week in November. The fishing was typically heavy in the six weeks from mid-November freeze-up to Christmas. The men usually made the journey home for Christmas. Those who had not caught their entitled limits by then made the return journey in January and continued fishing.

They packed the fish frozen in 150-pound wooden boxes to await pickup by horse-drawn sleds at the end of the season. It was taken to Riverton and received by whatever company had made arrangements with the individual fishermen. At certain times of year, fresh fish sold for a premium, and a snow house and small coal-oil lamp could keep fish from freezing for several days.

The Lake Winnipeg fishery was under the control of the vagaries of the fish markets in Chicago and New York. Companies based in those cities had been supporting, and often financing, young men who wanted to enter the fishery to supply them with product. The few buyers in these centres also controlled the price. For much of the winter the fish sold for two or three cents a pound frozen. But around certain holidays, particularly the Jewish holidays, it shot up to seven or eight cents. Increasingly, from January 15 to March 30, the goal was to take the fish off the lake fresh and ship it immediately by rail to the big markets in the south, for fresh fish always commanded a premium price.

Riverton, the terminus of the Northern rail line, became the epicentre of winter fishing operations on Lake Winnipeg. As Stefan and Johannes had moved from Hecla to Hnausa for better access to markets and opportunities, the Sig Fish partners now made the smaller but important move from Hnausa to Riverton. In the late 1920s, they acquired four contiguous properties along the Icelandic River, three for their homes and a larger lot for the business.

Their initial relocation to Riverton was to a rental home behind the busy Riverton Hotel. It was here that Stefan started to become acquainted with one of the fundamental truths of the fishing business. Successful fishing enterprises only begin with pulling fish out of the water or through a hole in the ice. There's no point in having a net full of fish if there's no market for them, or no way to get them to the market. Success in the fish business required mastering the even tougher business of transportation. The biggest hurdle wasn't the 800 miles from Winnipeg to Chicago; it was moving the product on Lake Winnipeg. Transporting men and supplies one direction and fish the other was no small feat given the lake's often punishing physical environment and climate. The Sigurdsons had fishing in their blood, but an entirely different set of skills was required to succeed in the transportation business. Boats were key in the summer, and in the winter it was dogs and horses, then tractors and tractor trains, and, many years later, Bombardiers and Ski-Doos. The young Stefan definitely knew the boats, and he was about to become familiar with the dogs.

Every day he wandered over to the Riverton Hotel to see the dog teams tethered to a line of hitching posts as the men arrived off the lake and headed inside to the beer parlour to thaw out after the cold and strenuous trip south. Some of the big players, like Walter Bessasson and JB Johnson often arrived and then left their dog teams for a couple of days while they took the train into Winnipeg for business. The dogs needed to be fed, and JB put Stefan in charge of handing over their unappetizing but nourishing daily feed of two frozen tulibees. He was also told to give the dogs a daily workout, so he hitched them four-at-a-time to his toboggan and took off down the streets of the village. He looked like a big shot to his buddies, and it was good fun until all hell broke loose. The dogs spotted a flock of turkeys in a farmer's yard and went wild.

Forget frozen fish! Four dead turkeys soon lay on the ground, fresh, and juicy and devoured before Stefan could react. The big shot was reduced to tears while receiving an unsolicited lesson in Ukrainian slang as the farmer shouted at him and the bloody-snouted dogs.

The dogs of Lake Winnipeg were famous. Typically, a team of five or six could pull loads of 300 to 500 pounds on the ice. No man's teams enjoyed greater notoriety than JB Johnson's. JB was a legendary figure who had been producing and buying fish on the North End for over two decades. One of JB's teams reputedly pulled over 1200 pounds on his 12-foot steel-tracked sled. When explorer Ernest Shackleton asked the Hudson's Bay Company to help him select dogs to take to the South Pole, they turned to the likes of JB Johnson and Sigurjon Isfeld, both from Gimli. JB and Sigurjon chose 99 of the toughest-working dogs on Lake Winnipeg. They were well looked after and highly prized, typically mixed breeds including huskies, Saint Bernards and Newfoundlanders.

JB and Sigurjon travelled by train to Montreal and then by ship to London in 1914 to deliver the dogs personally. Shackleton encouraged at least one of them to accompany him to the pole to oversee the dogs. They telegrammed home advising of the invitation for a further voyage. The return message was a succinct "Come Home," no doubt providing a ready excuse to decline Shackleton's entreaties. While neither saw the wonders of the pole, they each received an engraved gold watch in appreciation of their contribution to the expedition. The dogs were critical to the survival of the expedition, but none of the dogs made it home.

Big changes were coming in the transportation realm. Gasoline and diesel replaced hay and pulpwood. In the 1920s, horse-drawn snowploughs were the winter transportation staple on the lake, taking the men up to the remote camps and bringing the fish back south. John McNab from Clandeboye had the biggest horse-based hauling operation. He made one major trip a year, close to the end of the winter season, to haul fish from the small camps across the North End. He had about sixty teams of horses, cabooses and sleighs. Alongside each five-foot caboose were canvas flaps that became makeshift barns each night when the horses were bedded down. John's last trip, in the early '30s, landed him in very difficult weather—heavy snow and slush. Many of the horses didn't survive.

The fish business was competitive. To succeed, you had to adapt. Adopting and improvising new technologies was a key factor in their success. When Sig Fish saw the potential of tractors, they jumped. In the winter of 1933, SV and Hadli Bjornson (one of the Bjornson brothers from Riverton, with whom they had a long and close association) learned of the availability of a crawler tractor, the Model M, with a 35-horse-power engine that could reputedly hit six miles an hour. SV and Hadli travelled to the Winnipeg offices of the Allis-Chalmers Rumley Corporation and bought two.

The tractors weren't the only deal made that day. Afi SV saw an opportunity and returned home as an Allis-Chalmers dealer. When you need something, others must, too. Tractor dealing became another pillar of their business model, and a string of dealerships followed in the wake of the growing fish businesses on the lake.

The Model M's failed to deliver on their promise, reaching speeds of only four-and-a-half miles per hour, not six. They arranged for a special mechanic to visit Riverton and work with them to solve the problem. They suspected the Model M's gearing system was to blame, but soon realised the problem was most likely the solid tracks. They were clumping with snow and slowing the machine down. The solution wasn't clear at first, but an answer soon emerged. They could increase the grip on the highways of ice and snow by cutting round holes in each piece of track. After that creative re-jigging, the Model M's lived up to their promise. They were still going strong when I was a boy.

The partners' romance with engines, tracks and ice had been fertilized a few years earlier by the scent of gold. Tales of gold first surfaced in 1929 in the Poplar River area 20 miles north of Berens River. This excited the interest of many, but none more than the Sig Fish partners. They busied themselves that winter inventing an unwieldy machine that may have been one of the earliest tracked snow machines, and which they reasoned would enable them to haul in supplies and take out ore before anyone else. When the awkward-looking beast, the "Iron Horse" as it was soon called, arrived in Poplar River in the dead of winter, it was met with bewilderment by the people in the small community. As for the gold, that was destined to the halls of myth, and the Iron Horse to rust.

Another critical piece of technology was the plough, without which the "snow trains" would not have been possible. Whether drawn by horse or tractor, they left a precious pathway for the sleighs. The first ploughs on Lake Winnipeg were made by Sandy Vance of Selkirk as early as 1913. The introduction of the plough made horse-drawn transport more prevalent. The ploughs were pulled by a powerful team, with 8 to 12 sleds behind, and a caboose where the men ate and slept. There were places along the lake where men and horses could stop for the night, often exhausted by the gruelling cold and grinding winds, and the horses could be fed and watered.[54]

When tractors came on the scene, they needed no sleep and didn't care about the weather, but they still weren't equipped to push a mountain of snow in front of them. The challenge was to design a blade a tractor could push, not pull. The blade would need to be designed in such a way that the snow would be thrown up and over the snow banks that would inevitably grow alongside a route.

With some whiskey and beer and late nights to ignite the creative process, the partners spent long hours discussing how this technical challenge could be met, with a young Stefan listening to every word. They soon enlisted the great blacksmiths of the day, Mike Magnusson and Helgi Stefanson. Finally, plans and drawings were in place. In 1935, Helgi built a plough with two huge winged blades towering over the tractor, swooping steeply upward in a long arch to a sharp peak at the front. The snow would travel up the blade and then be thrown to each side, leaving two banks of snow and a road behind. This huge plough was soon crossing the frozen expanse of Lake Winnipeg, hauling up to three sleighs and a caboose, no longer bumping and grinding over the drifts and outcroppings but on a smooth glide as they made their way north.

Tractors pulling long trains of sleighs great distances over ice in frigid weather are a dangerous business. Only the tough and tough-minded could do this work. Much of the history of the early days of the tractor trains was seared into SR's memory, for he was the lead player in those operations, and in later years, a much younger Victor with him.

Tractors broke down and needed to be repaired in the dead of winter. Even for a finely-tuned tractor, the ice is full of invisible and insidious threats. The deep layer of ice heaves in the bitter cold, opening deep cracks beneath the uneven cover of drifts. Once opened, it continues to open. Then ice re-forms over the open water, first a thin layer, but enough to capture the snow blowing across the drifts. Soon, the crack comes under full cover of a white blanket, hiding below a shallow covering of ice slow to freeze under the snowy insulation. It's the perfect trap.

But the trains ground relentlessly onward day and night, shifts changing as men took turns driving, sleeping and eating. Without the tractors there would be no fish. Crawling along over the ice and drifts hour after hour, day after day, the shadowy warning signs of slush could easily be missed. And when they were, the tractor would plunge into the water, pulling the sleighs down behind it. Every tractor cab had an escape hatch on the roof so that if the tractor went down the driver could scramble out from what would otherwise be a water-bound casket.

In the 1920s, Fisher Bay was the epicentre of the goldeye production. Tulibees were also prolific but more broadly dispersed across the Channel area. Close to the base of the bay Sig Fish built a big shed out of which they operated each winter. The Fisher Bay operation had begun in the early 1900s. At the base of the long, swooping bay was located the community of Fisher River, with whom Sig Fish formed strong relationships that lasted decades. My great-grandfather Stefan's fish receipts and accounting records indicate that he was doing business with many men from Fisher River in 1917, and their interactions most likely started many years before that.

Driven by the winter fishing operations, especially goldeye and tulibee, Riverton became the gateway to the north, and the train station was the centre of the action. The station was the stately red classic of the old-time movies, with an elegant high-pitched roof and broad eaves stretching across the commanding platform. The inside was basic, planked wooden floors, benches along the walls, and a windowed ticket booth. Typically, the train chugged in around nine in the evening, and the frenzy began. First the freight, often drums of heating oil and piles of cordwood, was unloaded from the baggage cars for storage in the warehouses. The big canvas mailbags came off, too, causing a stir. Half the people in the village milled about the station waiting for the postmaster to sort the mail, which would have taken half as long if the din of conversation weren't driving him crazy. Young paper carriers waited to receive their bundles and made their deliveries in the cold of night, down to 40 degrees below in the winter. After everything was unloaded, the fish was packed onto the cars, and at 5:30 a.m. the train departed for Winnipeg, only to return back to Riverton again that night.

Five huge sheds, with a rail spur running alongside, were the symbol of Riverton's stature as transportation hub. Each shed was built by a different fish company to hold fish during the winter months. With the spring thaw, the fish would be shipped to Winnipeg or directly south to the US, depending on market conditions.

The largest, most northerly shed, painted bright yellow, was owned by Booth Fisheries and operated by Sigurdson Fisheries on their behalf. The Stefansons, the Monkmans, the Kristjanssons and Leifi Hallgrimson were all players in the Booth world who brought their fish through that shed. Armstrong Gimli (later known as BC Packers) had another of the sheds. That company was built by JB Johnson, renowned for his sled dogs. Sigurdson Thorvaldson, the outfit that Johannes and Sveinn Thorvaldson operated, had another shed. Northern Lakes, owned by Jack Maybank and Louis Bland of Winnipeg, worked out of another.

SV toiled throughout the winters in the Booth Fisheries shed, weighing fish and preparing bills of lading, young Stefan working beside him on the books and then with the loading onto the railcars. Meanwhile, SR and Steve were out on the fishing grounds producing for Sig Fish on their own account.

The sheds lay along the Icelandic River, and its frozen winter expanse became a busy highway as the horse-drawn sleds loaded with fish arrived from
up north and set camp pending delivery into the sheds and a chance to acquire
provisions for the return trip. A constant stream of sleds and cabooses shuttled
men, supplies and fish between the railhead and the fishing grounds. Attached
to each caboose into the early '30s were makeshift lean-to shacks where the
horses bedded down for the night and the dogs were tied to their posts and
curled up for the night on their mattress of snow. Open fires and coal-oil lan-
terns set the entire area alight in the bitterly cold, but crisp and clear night air.

Once the tractors came into operation, more and more production started
moving directly down the lake, through the Narrows, south to Riverton and
Gimli. Operations on the east side were confined mainly to frozen fish, shipped
in 150-pound boxes on sleighs pulled by tractor train. Each sleigh could hold
over 200 boxes and each tractor could haul two sleighs as well as the caboose,
which served as sleeping and eating quarters. The tractors ground their way
relentlessly over an endless expanse of ice toward Riverton. On arrival, the fish
was held in a storage shed and then loaded for shipment south by rail.

The demand for Lake Winnipeg fish continued to grow, particularly in New
York and Chicago. The markets were built on the early fame of the goldeye. Many
other species, like the tulibee and the whitefish, gained renown. The fish markets
were part of the rhythm of life for religious communities, especially for Jewish
holidays like Passover. Many of the big fish buyers were Jewish. Unlike other
meats, Jews consider scaled fish a religiously neutral food, so it's kosher for them
to eat fish with dairy products. The Jewish staple gefilte fish, made from whitefish, also created demand on Lake Winnipeg. Soaked in brine, it didn't need to be
cooked, so Jewish families could enjoy it without turning on their electricity or
making a fire, which were forbidden on the Sabbath. Catholics were also a force
in the fish markets, because many observed a tradition of eating fish on Fridays.

The increasingly popular pickerel (walleye) were usually served as fillets,
which made an attractive plate. The less attractive chunk or steak of whitefish
usually couldn't compete with other fish varieties. But they were a smoker's
delight, especially the big hump-backed Selkirks from the North End. Plump
and fat and softly smoked, they were a delicacy.

The Lake Winnipeg goldeye found in the great dining rooms of the day, in
Chicago and New York, and in first-class rail compartments, had an unlikely
route to fame. The flesh is soft and unappealing when fresh, but Aboriginal
people had discovered that goldeye became much more palatable after smoking over fires of local oak and willow. It had long been used as a domestic food,
and as a trade commodity to provision the trading posts.

An Englishman who had emigrated from Hull to Winnipeg would unlock goldeye's true gastronomic secret. In 1886, Bob Firth bought some of the fresh goldeye which he smoked himself to feed his family. One day, he accidentally smoked it too long and found that he had cooked the fish. Too poor not to eat it, he soon realised he had transformed it into something truly special. Firth's accident became the smoker's secret, and instead of the traditional twigs, vegetable dies were added. That story was shared in the menu of one of Winnipeg's great dining rooms of the era, the Rib Room at the Charterhouse Hotel.

With the rising popularity of the goldeye came demand for its fraternal twin, the tulibee. The two species are similar, but easily distinguishable to the discerning eye. Goldeyes have a mouthful of teeth; the tulibees are toothless. Tulibees are not as delicate, but are nearly indistinguishable when smoked. Goldeyes and tulibees are both usually served whole, with butter and lemon. To take the fish from the smoking room to the table, you just heat it until the skin turns a rich brown and begins to pull away from the red-tinged flesh. Roughly one pound in weight, goldeyes and tulibees presented perfectly on the finest gourmet tables of the times.

Trouble was lurking around the corner for the tulibee. As unlikely as it may seem, it was a New York City courtroom where the tulibee would face its greatest challenge, not in the frigid waters under the ice-bound lake that was its home. *Sigurdson Fisheries Ltd. versus The People* pitted the partners against the US Government. The case was highlighted in *The New Yorker* on January 28, 1933:

Tullibee Jubilee

Government agents seized two cases of smoked tullibee and brought about unusual doings in the Federal Court last week. The tullibee is a kind of whitefish suspected of carrying a parasite deleterious to health and of being therefore inadmissible to the country. The action before the court, entitled, respectively, "USD vs 288 Boxes of Tullibee (Sigurdson Fisheries Claimant)." Judge Coleman presided. Assistant District Attorney de Koven represented the U.S. Mr. J.J. Weinblatt represented the tullibee (Sigurdson Fisheries, Claimant). The two actions were tried together. There was wide interest in the proceedings because when the tullibee were seized the entire fish importing industry arose as one man, or as five thousand men, and protested vociferously.

The trial proceeded conventionally until the court interrupted one of the witnesses to ask him an important question. The witness was, at the moment, in the midst of an impassioned speech on the harmlessness of the tullibee.

What the court asked was this: "Would you eat one of these yourself?" The witness didn't answer this orally, but instead made a motion to Mr. Weinblatt, who hurriedly passed up a tullibee weighing two pounds. The witness seized this and ate several hearty mouthfuls, handing the fish back to counsel.

The Court (to the recording secretary): Make a note that the witness did not eat the whole fish.

At this, the witness recovered the fish and proceeded to devour it all, except the bones and the tail, which he returned to counsel.

The Court: Make a note that the witness is unwilling to eat the tail.

Mr. Weinblatt, who had sat down, smiling happily and confidently leaped to and gave the remains back to his witness, who proceeded to eat the tail. Mr. Weinblatt then went into a long oration in which he said that the tullibee, even fresh, was harmless. The court interrupted to ask if the witness would consider eating a raw fish. Counsel submitted, with feeling, that his witness never ate raw fish, that it was unheard of in a civilized country, that only cannibals ate raw fish.

The Court: Make a note that the witness seems unwilling to eat raw fish.

Counsel looked baffled. The witness looked anguished. The spectators all looked hopeful. After a few seconds of desperate consideration, counsel picked up a raw fish from among the exhibits and firmly handed it to the witness. The witness squared his shoulders. At that point compassion descended upon the bench. "Make a note," said the Court, "that the witness is willing to eat the fish, even when raw."

The witness was allowed to descend from the stand, filled with fish and pride. The Court reserved decision.

The decision came down that the embargo on all Lake Winnipeg tulibee entering the US was confirmed. The tulibee fishery on Lake Winnipeg was finished in a stroke. Sigurdson Fisheries achieved some infamy, to be sure, but it wasn't concern for the fate of the Lake Winnipeg fishermen that attracted the editors' interest. Rather, it was the appearance on the stand of a particularly flamboyant witness, Hadli Bjornson. The Bjornson Brothers operated out of Riverton and had a long family and business relationship with the Sigurdsons. One can only presume that Hadli was thought most likely to speak persuasively in the legal war pitting the "People" against Riverton, and there can be little doubt that he applied his full energies to the task.

Having eaten and thrived on tulibee for years, most fishermen found talk of a full cross-border embargo because of fears of parasites[55] dubious at best. Substantial winter inventories were at risk, and the market was replete with rumours.

Sigurdson Fisheries had wind of the possible embargo, likely tipped off due to their relationship with Booth Fisheries in Chicago. They were not prepared to risk being stuck with their inventory. They dropped the price of their massive frozen tulibee inventory by two cents a pound and sold every last fish just before the embargo went into effect. Had Sig Fish not acted boldly, the fledgling business they had worked so hard to develop would have suffered an almost insurmountable setback, especially coming, as it would have, in the heart of the Depression. After the embargo was put in place, all existing tulibee inventories were died blue and turned into animal meal. For many, the loss was devastating. "If we had not sold the tulibees we would have been wiped out." Speaking at his seventy-fifth birthday, that was how Steve described their narrow escape from financial ruin in the winter of 1933. That decision, he added, was one of the three most important business decisions they ever made.

The tulibee crisis had been averted, but dark clouds were gathering on another front. The threat to the goldeye had nothing to do with parasites, but rather arose from the goldeye lifecycle. Unlike tulibee, they don't spawn annually, but follow a different rhythm, captured eloquently by Frances Russell in *Mistehay Sakahegan: The Great Lake.*

> Goldeye, like Lake Sturgeon, is a mysterious fish and, like sturgeon, only infrequently interested in propagating its species. This leaves both goldeye and sturgeon vulnerable to extinction through overfishing. Even today, experts haven't fathomed the goldeye's love life, except that it prefers turbid to clear water. Males mature in their third year, females in their fourth or fifth. A mature female may contain from 5,000 to 25,000 eggs, an average being 14,000. Goldeye spawn in the very early spring, at night. The eggs do not sink to the bottom as each one contains a globule of oil that makes it float a few inches under the surface of the water. There, the relatively high temperature causes early hatching.

> Within the first year, a young goldeye may attain a length of 15 centimetres. At spawning, the fish averages about 31 centimetres. Goldeyes rarely grow large. A one-kilogram fish is considered exceptional. The oldest goldeye on record attained 16 years. Despite its age, its size was not remarkable.[56]

Expanding fishing operations caused a serious reversal of the goldeye's fortunes. In its heyday in the late 1920s more than one million pounds of goldeye came out of Lake Winnipeg annually. Soon it was near extinct. To this day gold-eye fishing is neither viable nor permitted on Lake Winnipeg.[57]

Young Stefan watched his dad's world turn upside down. The consequences of the embargo on the tulibee fishery and the decline of the goldeyes were far-reaching. The search for replacement fisheries found a new target in sauger. It became increasingly evident that sauger were abundant across the lake. They were smaller than pickerel, but otherwise almost indistinguishable, except for swimming at deeper depths—they were fished about a fathom off the bottom. They were typically fished with a three-inch mesh size, which may have con-tributed to the continuing decline of the goldeyes, which had been fished with three-and-three-quarter inch mesh.

There was deep foreboding everywhere on the lake as to where the future would lie. But once again the lake revealed its magic with bountiful catches of pickerel and sauger. Perhaps necessity was the mother of invention in this case. The tulibee had always been caught close to the surface, so the nets were set just below the ice or the waterline. Pickerel were most accessible along the shorelines, and sauger swam much closer to the bottom. It didn't take long for the fishermen to figure out that repositioning their nets along the shore as well as dropping them closer to the bottom tapped into a bountiful catch below. Pickerel and sauger be-came the new production focus. In fact, they were easier to catch and could be fished much farther south. In contrast, the whitefish were elusive. They moved over great distances, requiring frequent relocations of nets, a not inconsequential aspect of which was pounding through five or six feet of ice without an ice pick.

Fishing had been good to the Sig Fish partners throughout the '20s, largely thanks to tulibee exports to the US. Had they made a misstep with the tulibees they would have been finished, but they escaped that disaster by the narrow-est of margins. By the early 1930s, they were ready to take a number of critical steps. They needed to continue evolving to stay ahead. They'd been struggling before the Depression, and that didn't change much when the economy plunged. If anything, it made them more determined. The demand for fish continued through the Depression. People had to eat. The fishermen of Lake Winnipeg worked away during those years, insulated from much of the economic mael-strom around them. The business survived, and even grew.

The drive was always to fish further north, and this was all the more im-portant in the quest for pickerel and sauger. Big norwesterlies were the prevail-ing winds on Lake Winnipeg, and with the water they pushed ahead of them were the fish. Being at the most northerly point was seen as the key strategic play. The closer to the northern extremity of the "line" established by the licens-ing authorities, the better the prospects for a full net. But fishing in the North

Basin had other implications. Fewer fishermen worked up there, and tug traffic was sparse. In addition to a station, they needed a tug, and to justify both they needed more boats and more production.

Booth Fisheries had word that a hull built out of exceptional elm timber on Lake Manitoba might be available. This marked the beginning of the second half of the life of the *JR Spear*. She was built originally to work as a freighter on Lake Manitoba, supplying the gypsum mines discovered at the turn of the century. Her work there was finished by the early '30s. Moving her from Lake Manitoba to Lake Winnipeg was no small feat. The waterways connected via Lake St. Martin and the Dauphin River. Crossing the lake was no problem, but the river was a different story. Except for a few weeks during the spring runoff, the river was inaccessible for a hull of her size. She had a narrow berth, but a deep draft, drawing eight to nine feet when fully loaded. For the next three springs they persevered in their efforts to use the high spring waters to get her through the swollen rapids and down the river. In the spring of 1933, she finally reached Lake Winnipeg. There, she was strapped to the government vessel *Bradbury* and brought to Selkirk. The *Bradbury* was also used to access Indian communities around the lake and deliver equipment, medical supplies and other necessities.

The *Spear's* future was secured when Sig Fish heard the hull was in Selkirk and up for sale. Booth accepted their offer of five thousand dollars. She would need to be outfitted for work on Lake Winnipeg. The major shipyards and boat builders were located in Selkirk and Captain Ed Nelson and his crew were among the best. He agreed to rebuild the tug to ready her for life as a Lake Winnipeg freighter. Steve worked alongside him. The height of the hull was increased by 18 inches, and then the main deck was put in place, followed by the upper decks with the wheelhouse, crew's quarters and kitchen.

The next step was installing a marine diesel to power her. Captain Nelson needed to square the stern to accommodate the new engine. The Fairbanks Morse Company made some of the best engines of the day, and a brand new two-cycle diesel Fairbanks went into the *JR Spear*, one of the few at that time on Lake Winnipeg. It was powerful but monstrous. When it was replaced 30 years later in the mid-60s, the *Spear's* carrying capacity increased by 250 fish boxes.

The *JR Spear* began plying the waters of Lake Winnipeg in the summer of 1933, with Captain Nelson at the wheel. She was 84 feet long, with a carrying capacity of around 100 tonnes. She could handle up to 1000 boxes, but that was a stretch. The distinctive thumps of the huge Fairbanks engine could be heard two or three hours before she arrived at the station. Many a night Dad walked to the other side of the island station at Berens River to listen for her. She handled the sea well, particularly a head sea. She rolled heavily in a side wind, but her grip on the water was never in question. The *JR Spear* would prove to be one of the great workhorses of Lake Winnipeg.

Securing the *Spear* was only one step in the next phase of Sig Fish operations. Building a station at the North End of the lake was next, and having the *Spear* to freight the catch south to Selkirk and Winnipeg made that possible. The first challenge was to find a location with easy access to the best fishing grounds. Strategically, one of the best spots was a group of three small islands known as Spider Islands in the heart of the big waters 20 miles south of the North End where the Nelson River broke out at Warren Landing to make its 800-mile rush to Hudson Bay. Norway House—upriver about 20 miles on Playgreen Lake—was the nearest major settlement. Along with Lower Fort Garry outside of Selkirk on the Red River, Norway House was one of the key pivots on which the Hudson's Bay Empire in Canada was built, with the mighty York boats plying their way across the rough expanse of Lake Winnipeg between the two forts.

Selecting an exact location wasn't easy. The islands were attractive, but aside from the Petersons of Gimli, who had already established a station on one of the islands, Booth Fisheries of Chicago had the rights to the others with the exception of one barren piece of rock almost too small to call an island. Notwithstanding Sig Fish's long-standing relationship with Booth, the Chicago company was not about to give the upstart young men access to any prime pieces of real estate where they would be in direct competition. Their relationship had never been based on inequality; it was a partnership of mutual respect. Booth was a giant, and Sig Fish was the mouse. But this applied more in the Chicago markets than the gruelling reality of the North Basin, where it took tough, strong-willed and independent men and women to survive. Booth understood that, and they understood the Sigurdsons. And the Sigurdsons understood Booth. So SV, Steve and SR proceeded with their plans undaunted by their reluctant partner. If necessary, they would build their station on the tiny island. And so they did.

In the winter of 1934, SV's younger brother Solli went north with his wife Betty, a gang of men and supplies to build the station at Spider Island. On that barren, windswept piece of rock and ice they built a modern (for those days) fishing station featuring an 800-ton icehouse. When the work was finished, only a few square feet of rock remained visible. Space was so limited that the outhouse had to extend out over the water.

Business was good, and there was money to expand the fleet the same year. Two whitefish boats were built for the emerging Sig Fish presence in the North End whitefishery: the *Shirley* and the *Bluenose*. They added the *Helen* and the

Eleanor the year after, named after Steve's daughters. The Sigurdson partners made a deal with Hjartur (Fatty) Hanneson and Barney Stefanson, top Lake Winnipeg fishermen from Selkirk, to join them and teach them those waters. They knew the grounds like no one else, and when you added the skills of SR, Valdi Johnson and Arni Goodman, Sigurdson Fisheries was in top shape.

In the summer, they made arrangements with the Big 6 Station operated by the Stefansons out of Selkirk to use their dock facilities. Then the final steps were taken. Three new forty-foot boats with gas engines (gasboats) appropriate for the North Basin were constructed.

With these accomplishments came tragedy. While building the Spider Island station, Solli became ill with a mastoid ear infection. Within a few days it developed into meningitis. He was taken to Norway House by dogsled, where arrangements were made to fly him to the hospital in Winnipeg, probably the first medical evacuation flight on the lake. Afi SV turned to Connie Johannesson, a member of the legendary Winnipeg Falcons, the all-Icelandic hockey team that won for Canada the Olympic gold medal for ice hockey in 1920, the first time it was awarded. Connie was operating what was becoming a famous flying school. He agreed to make the trip to Norway House to pick up SV. They landed on the river in front of the house in Riverton, and Solli was taken immediately to hospital.

He died shortly thereafter, leaving daughters Grace and Jorunn, and his wife Betty (Johnson), who had first come into the home to look after the two children, and who he later married. Yet once more, Valgerdur heard the bell toll. Afi SV was now the only surviving child. Another tragedy had hit them the year before. Dad was standing beside Afi at the dock in Berens River Station when Captain Hugh emerged from the pilothouse and spoke down to them from the deck:

"Siggi, the news is not good. The Big House burned to the ground. Your mother and everybody in the house are safe."

Afi dropped to his knees beside Dad, and weeping, cried out, "What more can she endure?"

Another major Sig Fish development followed the discovery of gold in northwestern Ontario. Their transportation efforts expanded into a partnership with Patricia Transportation, a company owned by the Richardsons of Winnipeg. Extracting gold requires supplies, from equipment to food, fuel to dynamite. Patricia Transportation had the heavy equipment suitable for hauling over winter roads to locations in northern Ontario, but their equipment was too heavy and ponderous to perform the ice haul over Lake Winnipeg. The Sigurdsons found themselves hauling mine supplies 120 miles across the lake to the roads Patricia Transportation used to access the mines. The Sigurdsons' leg of the journey was Riverton to Berens River, where Patricia had a holding area for supplies and equipment on the treaty grounds as a result of an arrangement made with Chief Berens.

Dynamite was one of the major parts of the haul; substantial volumes were shipped by boat before freeze up and then by tractor train over the winter. At times, the entire stretch of river in front of the Sigurdson houses and office was a continuous train of sleds loaded with dynamite. Barrels of fuel were moved, too, and supplies of all kinds, enough to provision an entire small company mining town.

In the 40s, from early January to the middle of March, the weekly trip involved nearly as much paperwork as supplies. Each item was documented on bills of lading six copies thick, two for the insurance company, one for the Patricia Transportation offices, one for the mine site, and two for Sig Fish records. This endeavour lasted at least ten years.

When the mine closed, the equipment was brought to Riverton and stored in the fish sheds and on the property. That brought Reginald Leach and his wife (a Mckay) from Berens River to Riverton. Reginald was responsible for overseeing the storage of the mine equipment and its eventual disposal. The Sigurdsons left the freighting business behind around this time. They saw limited prospects for the future after the closure of the mine.

Not so for the Sigfusson family who foresaw a much bigger potential ahead in the winter freighting business. Many of the communities inland off the lakeshore were isolated behind granite ridges and endless swamp and muskeg as you moved east toward Ontario. These were remote places with little contact. Soon, tractor trains over frozen winter roads were the work horses of the north, hauling in supplies to otherwise inaccessible locations. Riverton became their major centre of operations in the '50s, and over the next decades they made their way up the broad expanse of Lake Winnipeg, building a massive network of roads and trails to service all of northern Manitoba. Later, they moved their base north to the Channel area, in Little Dog Head, where they would cross the two-mile channel onto the east shore, just three miles north of Leaside.

CHAPTER NINE

Conceived in Catfish Creek

T he onset of the Second World War brought unexpected opportunities for Sigurdson Fisheries. Canada needed landing strips and airports, quickly. Governments had no time for red tape. Ministers turned to people with reputations for getting things done, men like Chris Fisher, a brilliant civil engineer of the day. The military gave him a commission and marching orders. Chris turned to men he could trust, like his good friend SV Sigurdson. Along with two partners, they secured a contract to help build the concrete runways, hanger aprons and gravel access roads at the Dauphin Airport. Oddur Olafsson of Riverton brought four Diamond T trucks to the project (Sig Fish also brought one), and other equipment and supplies were brought in from Oddur's Transport Operations over on the east shore and at the San Antonio Mines. Walters in Beausejour contributed the concrete and mixing plant. Suddenly the family was in the construction business, and Dad was abruptly spun from boats to tractors.

SV and Steve pulled him out of a Friday night dance and informed him he was leaving for Dauphin to run the construction operations. He was the first employee of what operated originally as Walters and Sigurdson, and later became Monarch Construction. He had just turned eighteen.

Within days, he found himself in the Dauphin Hotel, where he lived for a few weeks until the partners set up an office and living quarters. He was soon overseeing a fleet of thirty trucks hauling gravel from eight miles out of Dauphin to a crushing operation employing about thirty men, several of whom knew Dad from Riverton. If they minded having an inexperienced kid like Dad as their boss, they never let on. SV's old friend Chris Fisher always made himself available for quiet guidance and background support, which Dad tapped into often. He was there for close to a year.

In the fall of 1941, with the airport job complete, Dad returned to Riverton, went winter fishing in Fisher Bay, and continued to work in the family business. On July 29, 1942, he enlisted in the Royal Canadian Navy. The Navy was the only place he could imagine for himself, and his life on Lake Winnipeg had equipped him as well as possible for the horror ahead. He took up his station on the tin cans called corvettes that escorted the great convoys across the North Atlantic. The gravest threat was the U-boats, but there was no shortage of other dangers. Even the trek across icy decks to deliver hot cocoa to the midnight watch was risky.

I suspect Dad never expected to survive his time in the Navy, but he wasn't one to dwell on that, then or after. It was what it was. Perilous as it may sound, Dad was used to danger on the water. He often said the waters of Lake Winnipeg were even tougher than those of the North Atlantic. Fishing boats are much smaller than corvettes, and the breaking action of the lake's shallow waters can be remarkably strong.

He did share some stories. Living conditions on the boat were nothing like depicted in so many World War Two movies. They were dirty and crowded places. The men slept in hammocks four-deep attached to the walls of the ship. They kept their clothes on and life jackets within reach, as they never knew when the alarm would send them to their action stations. Within a moment, Dad was forced to go from sleep to dropping depth charges off the stern, setting them for the ordered depth, then pulling the lever to send them rolling down the slide into the deep. This was Dad's life for 18 months of four-hour watches, punctuating the water with the explosive rhythm of the charges.

The overall monotony eased briefly at eleven o'clock each morning when the two-ounce rum ration was distributed. The men weren't allowed to save the rum, but some furtively stockpiled it for when they went to shore. It told me a lot about Dad when I heard in one of his few "war stories" about his close encounter with tattoos, not a good mix with booze, especially for a man like Dad who was not one for self-aggrandizement. He explained to me that being at the long end of a line of "drunken sailors" in Saint John was the luckiest thing that happened to him, as he sobered up enough to get the hell out of the line before he reached the front. A twisted serpent emblazoned on his arm would have left him cringing for a lifetime, and wearing only long-sleeved shirts.

He was demobilized August 27, 1945. The first thing on his mind was a return to the fishing business. Other opportunities were open to him as a veteran, like financial support for university, but he knew what he wanted. A lot had changed in Riverton while he was away, but nothing was more striking than the appearance of a particular beautiful young woman. He soon identified her as Sylvia Brynjolfson. Her family had recently relocated from Hecla Island, where his own family had begun their life in Canada. His strategy was simple yet impeccable. Talking fish with her father Malli, an iconic Lake Winnipeg fishermen, would be the best way into her heart and then her life.

Dad was the first of his generation to marry. Their wedding in May 1946 was a grand affair, combining Riverton and Hecla's enthusiasm for their union with the jubilance of a brighter future signalled by the end of the war. They rode the train to Chicago for their honeymoon, and Dad convinced Mom to squeeze in a visit to one of the plants with which Sig Fish had long done business. One of the senior men at the Booth plant, Harold Erickson, an American who would soon find himself posted as the Booth manager in Manitoba, pointed to the purple stains covering his apron and announced, "That is the remnants of your dye!" He had worked there at least 15 years, since the dye was added to mark the embargoed tulibees for processing as animal food.

In the world Dad had returned to, as it had been for some time, a top strategic objective was to have your station at the most northerly point, as close to the "line" as possible, so your fishermen had the first opportunity at the fish pushed south by the big winds. The "line" for the productive fall fishery had moved gradually northward throughout the '30s, and there was no stopping it in the '40s. In anticipation of another move, Sigurdson Fisheries had started building a station in remote and difficult Catfish Creek in 1939. The "line" had not been officially moved, so many saw the move as "jumping the gun," but that didn't deter Afi, who had many of his dad's instincts alive within him.

On a rocky outcrop where Catfish Creek flowed onto a windswept shoreline on the east side of Lake Winnipeg (about two hours by boat south of Berens River), they constructed the station that would enable them to be first in line as the fish moved south on the wind tides. Catfish soon earned its reputation as one of the most productive and reliable locations in the fall fishery.

Catfish was a long way from anywhere, except in the fall, when it became command centre for some of the most productive fishing grounds on the east shore. The creek winds its way through rock outcroppings and deep swamps from the granite shield of the east to find a home on the open shoreline of the lake about 20 miles south of Berens River. The wind, especially from the north, whips the waves into a frenzy that sends them pounding onto the shoreline and up the creek. During the fall, the clouds lay low, their black inner lining a harbinger of the approaching winter.

The Catfish station sits on a low rock platform reaching into the waters where the creek meets the lake. A rugged dock struggles to exist between the icehouses and packing sheds, and the often swollen creek. The fall season inevitably began with the dock repairs that made it possible to land the tugs and load the rich cargoes of Catfish Creek pickerel for the trip south for processing in Winnipeg, and then on to destinations as far afield as Chicago and New York.

Mom and Dad spent the first fall of their married life in Catfish Creek. Mom helped with the books and Stefan kept track of everything else needed to keep the station running. The station was well established by then. Every night the men in the camp brought the cards out for endless sessions of bridge in the kitchen. Mom and Dad were aspiring bridge players, and SR was a master from years of games on the boats and in the camps. Mom honed her skills under the gentle guidance of SR and an old family friend, Geri Sigugeirson from Hecla. In anticipation of the quiet fall evenings, she and Dad rolled green tomatoes in newspaper and brought them north from home. They ripened over the fall, and the evening of cards was punctuated by cocoa and toasted tomato sandwiches at nine.

I was born in June 1947. Counting the months backward, I assume I can claim Catfish Creek as my place of conception, although I can't say whether the event was inspired by one of those delectable tomato sandwiches. My sister Elaine, born in 1950, and my brother Eric, in 1952, may be able to make similar claims.

Rugged Catfish Creek became Dad's home for many years from late August until the end of October. He usually made the 16-hour trip home to Hnausa on October 31, Halloween night, more often than not accompanied by the first winter storm and snowfall. As children arrived, Mom no longer made the fall trips to the Catfish camp.

Catfish Creek moved to the rhythm of any fishing station during the fall fishing season, starting with a bacon and eggs breakfast at six, usually with 60 or more in the cookhouse. The fishermen headed out as first light was breaking, or even earlier. The water was usually calmer at that early hour. They travelled out on twenty-foot yawls, some still wooden but mostly steel by then (now typically aluminum). Positioned in the narrow slot between the plank seat and the bow, the fishermen appeared bolted to the water as they bobbed and weaved through the lurching sea, moving along the nets pulling out fish with sure hands. Every day those hands were colder than the last, prey to the inevitable slide in temperature that would soon deliver the ice. They were finished by around noon and came in with their boxes of fish, which were not always full, but the odds were better at Catfish than most places. The shore then became the hub of activity, the shore hands busy chipping ice and preparing to weigh the fish, sort them by species and size, and box them in 60-pound weights. Everything on fish stations was counted, but nothing more rigorously than the scaly gold from the deep.

Catfish Creek was no easy place from which to operate. Nature knew the tug of no leash on its open shore. Dad tells of the time a huge storm tore a wall of water up from the northern expanse and heaved it onto the mouth of the creek in the middle of the night. The docks were destroyed instantly, and the many drums of gas located there were washed up the creek. The boats were ripped from their moorings, and with daylight were visible up and over the banks of the creek in the adjacent trees. Many of these were forty-foot gasboats used to haul three or four skiffs out to the grounds. The fishermen quickly realised the peril of the situation, for if the boats weren't pulled back into the creek before the high water receded, they'd be likely to be stuck there in swampy ground until winter frost. They retrieved the boats, and the challenge of rebuilding followed, starting with clearing the sand out of the generator shed and getting the power back up and running.

The perils of the location didn't end there. The creek mouth was difficult for the tugs to navigate, particularly in a blow from the northwest. There were prominent reefs on entry, and the tight turns required to move through the ranges was no easy feat even when the seas were reasonable. In the big norwesterlies it was downright dangerous. More than once the *JR Spear* hit bottom, with significant damage resulting. The only option for making the landing in a strong wind from the northwest was to run the bow straight onto the dock and secure a heavy rope with a heaving line and then use that line to pivot the boat so the bow faced the lake and the incoming sea. Sure hands and split-second timing were essential. Many times I stood on deck as we made our way in and watched Dad drop and stretch over the edge of the dock to catch a rope thrown short. He seldom missed.

It's not fair to paint too dismal a picture of Catfish. It came with certain risks, but it had a beauty all its own. The creek meandered up into the bush along marshy banks. The autumn trees were raging combinations of colours. Even in a monstrous storm, with deep grey clouds overhead and a pounding sea, Catfish had a rugged charm, and a strangely peaceful quality. To one man, it was home for many years.

Arni Goodman left an indelible mark on my mind. He was five-foot-six, perhaps a little more, a little less as he grew older. Aside from a brush of hair along the sides, his well-shaped head shone like a dome, allowing his crystal blue eyes to sparkle all the more. And he had a way with words. He fancied himself a womanizer, and over the years many came under the sway of his devilish charm. It served him well, except when he was drinking. Charm turned to fury as he fell under the power of an uncontrollably beguiling liquid mistress. Escaping that demon took him to Catfish.

A binge drinker, he'd end up in the Leland Hotel off Main Street when he was in Winnipeg. Just before the fishing season was about to start, my dad would get the call, and arrangements would be made to get Arni down to Riverton and aboard the *JR Spear* heading north. But Arni didn't need to go as far as Winnipeg to get into serious trouble. When the mistress beckoned, he would fight any weather in his yawl to cover the 20 miles north on the open lake to Berens River and Ma Kemp's Log Cabin Inn. Arni's reputation was large, and those who spoke of him on one of his "real tears" spared few details. He had a dark side, and had seen dark times. But Arni had almost escaped his reputation by the time he became a presence in my life (although, to be sure, I had some vivid glimpses into his past "glories"). Arni's only answer was to run from his ruthless mistress, and so he made his home at the remote Catfish Creek fish camp.

Arni was a man of many talents—a skilled fisherman, a trapper, a self-taught horticulturalist, not to mention a relentless reader. In the fall at Catfish Creek, he added damn fine bookkeeper to the list. With impeccable penmanship, he recorded every fish that came onto the station, plus whatever left on the southbound tugs. He tracked the supplies and their voyage to the kitchen or coolers or into the small store where the fishermen purchased daily provisions. Every transaction, large or small, was recorded by hand into ledgers and account books, and added to the click-clack of the hand-operated adding machine. Arni's accounting talents were not there by happenstance; he had worked in my great-grandfather Stefan's store at Hnausa as a boy and picked up skills he would carry with him throughout his life. When the season was over, usually October 31, life swept out of Catfish Creek as quickly as it had arrived. Little was left but fish awaiting the fast-approaching ice firmament, bears enjoying a final feast of frozen entrails in the dumping ground, and Arni.

As the last lines were thrown from the dock, Arni was sometimes left with company on the island. They were another breed of fishermen—the men who "froze out." It took three inches of ice for men and equipment to safely venture forth and set their nets for winter ice fishing. Lake Winnipeg didn't see that much ice until at least the third week in November, sometimes not until the beginning of December. Some of the year's best fishing was reputed to be at first ice, and several fishermen each year "froze out," waiting at camp so they wouldn't risk missing the bounty. Others headed south after the fall season ended, only to return after Christmas. The ones who froze out hoped to catch their limits by Christmas, or at least get close enough that they could finish up from home after the holiday.

Catfish Creek was a reputed first ice fishing ground, so December often saw a number of men waiting patiently in small log huts they would temporarily call home. Afi Malli was one of those men, usually with Uncle Grimsi beside him after the construction season had ended. The Baldwinson brothers, Baldi and Norman, would be in the next camp. Suppers were right up to scratch in the camp as the boys had earned their stars in pie-making from their dad, Herb, the cook on the *Spear* who had always made me jumpy until the risen pie was plunked down in front of me. (They became Grimsi's brothers-in-law when he married their sister, Collie.) I always thought of the men who froze out as the fishermen's fishermen. There was something mysterious, even heroic about them, but on the times they missed Christmas, the women and children alone at home no doubt saw things differently.

While the others were readying their nets, Arni got his trapping gear in order. He was a skilled man of the bush, moving with ease through the forests and muskeg along the creek, at peace with himself in a big and lonely land. A master trapper, he covered more than seven miles every day on snowshoes to tend his trapline. I was a lousy trapper and in awe of guys like Arni or others closer to my age like Brian Tomasson (Mundi's son), who could find a muskrat channel within one stab of the steel rod and make the perfect set. Maurice Oleson and his dog Peggy sometimes brought back fifty pelts a day, skinned where they were caught. I was lucky to get two. After school in the winter I snared for rabbits and set for squirrels. One day I stuck all the squirrels in my hood and toddled down the river only to arrive home itchy with fleas.

Arni also had many less rugged pursuits. His walls were packed with books, prominent among them his prized volumes on horticulture and botany. Plants became Arni's passion. Each summer he turned the grounds around his camp into a beautiful garden. He knew each plant by its ordinary name, and often the scientific name, too. He knew its characteristics and its typical stature. He anticipated the evolution of the garden over the growing season and located each plant carefully to weave a symphony of shape and colour. Few knew of this passion or saw the garden in its glory. It was past its prime by late August when fishermen started arriving for the fall season.

Arni took a turn for the worse in 1964. It wasn't booze, but rather a persistent cough that was causing him trouble. I was sent to the End of the Road to pick him up and drive him to a doctor in Winnipeg. It was an unnerving trip. Arni clearly wasn't well. He coughed the entire way, although that didn't deter him from chatting up my friend Carol Jorundson, who'd come along to keep me company. We were all shocked to hear the diagnosis of tuberculous. Miraculously, neither Carol nor I became infected. For Carol, TB struck particularly close to home, for her father Oscar spent over six years in the sanatorium in Ninette with the disease.

Arni left the sanatorium around 1967 with a fused knee, a gift from TB. Most didn't expect him to return to Catfish Creek, but he did, and he went right back to his trapline. He was no longer as agile on the seven-mile trek, but he had no less perseverance.

CHAPTER TEN

Each Season Had a Rhythm

N ot long after Dad returned home from the war, he walked into the Riverton Hotel and had a conversation that would transform Sig Fish. He had encountered Dori Bjornson, a man who could always be counted on to feed Dad's appetite for anything fish, all the more so after a few beers. Dori soon turned the conversation serious: "Stefan, the boys and I want to sell the outfit. We want it to stay in Riverton." Dad said nothing, but this was music to his ears, especially since Dori had singled him out as the person in the family with whom to share this information. The Bjornson brothers of Riverton were powerful and successful fishermen with eight whitefish boats. They had good locations at both Georges Island in the North End and Kenowa Bay on the west shore. Their principal business relationship was with hard-nosed and shrewd Mundi Jonasson, operating as Keystone Fish in Winnipeg. In Lake Winnipeg terms the Bjornsons were a sizeable operation, and merging it with the existing Sig Fish setup would almost double the size of the outfit. Dad told Afi SV of the conversation and they seized the opportunity. Within days they were in discussions to complete the transaction and make ownership adjustments in Sigurdson Fisheries to recognize the assets and business Dad and his younger brother Victor would bring to the table.

The three senior partners were not immune to the promise of a bigger and better future in the post-war years. They were itching to expand their business reach. The construction business had continued to grow and Afi was now spending much of his time developing it. They saw opportunities in Gimli and acquired much of the land on the south side of Centre Street. They built the Gimli Hotel in 1945, right next to Tergesen's Store, which had occupied the most prominent location in town since it opened at the corner of Central and Main. The Tergesen name was synonymous with Gimli. Hans Tergesen was Gimli's second mayor, after Johannes. Uncle Steve (my great uncle) ran the hotel in 1947 and 1948, but the partners didn't own it for long. Steve later explained the decision to sell: "If I stayed there much longer it wouldn't have taken me too damn long to become an alcoholic. Stay out of the damn hotel business!"

Around that time Sig Fish also acquired a partnership interest in the GM dealership on the property next to the hotel. They were never active players in the car business, but it was a valuable part of the operation. However far they stretched in their expanding operation, the fish business was always their anchor.

Each of the Sig Fish partners had his own space, his own role, and they came together seamlessly. They knew their jobs and when to do them. Everyone was responsible for a specific station. That was fundamental to their success. There was no room for big shots. Or, actually, they were all big shots. If I ever forgot that, it wasn't long before I was given a reminder. The Sig Fish partners stayed on the front lines of the operation; they were hands-on at ground level, every day. Standing back was not in their blood. There were tensions, to be sure, but challenges seemed to work for them, not against them. There was a lot of talk, and their decisions were all the better for it.

Each fishing season had a rhythm, and the approach of a new season brought a swell of activity. Spring saw constant comings and goings from the Sig Fish office. The conversation never stopped within the four corners of that small office. There was no need for a meeting in the "boardroom," and even if they felt the need, there was no boardroom in which to have it.

Outfitting for the season meant trips to Winnipeg, and I went along every chance I got. If Dad was in a suit and tie, it was a clear signal he was off to Winnipeg. We'd leave before seven to make it downtown just before nine. I loved this town. The wholesale district, not far from the corner of Portage and Main, was once the vibrant heart of the city. Winnipeg was proclaimed as Canada's Chicago for several decades. Both were in the middle of the country, both were major east-west rail links, and both were big distribution points for the West. Some areas of Winnipeg still play turn-of-the-century Chicago in movie shoots. The only thing it lacked was Al Capone. Enough Capone imitators emerged in Winnipeg during Prohibition, but they never matched Capone's notoriety. Winnipeg was no more than a town when Sigurdur first arrived, but it was approaching 20,000 people early in the 1900s. Unlike Chicago, Winnipeg was going through its heyday, which lasted for a few decades, while Chicago's never ended.

One of the storefronts in an imposing old brick building in the wholesale district belonged to Altman Sheps. Visits to Harvey Altman's castle were a highlight of my trips to the city. I don't recall meeting Sheps or hearing anything about him. I presume he was once connected with the store. As far as I ever knew, Altman Sheps was all about Harvey. In old Winnipeg, Harvey was the man for all seasons. He was Dad's great friend, and they always saw eye to eye. Dad counted on Harvey for everything from fishermen's equipment to dry goods for the store, and if Harvey didn't have something on any given day, he'd soon find it somewhere. Harvey's store resonated for Dad. Compared to most of the fancier Winnipeg places, it was a lot more like the Sig Fish stores on the lake.

The street in front of Altman Sheps curved in a broad sweep, a sign that the location was once one of the premier addresses in the area. It was a retail store in the front—although it looked nothing like you would expect of a store today—with what was essentially a warehouse behind. Along one wall was what must have been Harvey's office, where the books and records were kept. Unlike the Sig Fish office in Riverton, dominated by a hulking black safe, no such monstrosity was on view in Harvey's place. I expect Harvey relied more on his pocket than any steel box.

Harvey had a serious face but a warm smile, and there was a knowing kindness in the way he looked at you and spoke. He was no more than average in height and build. He always wore a dark suit, white shirt and tie. His presentation was nothing if not rumpled and ill-fitting, but those were the days for suits.

Harvey's suit matched his merchandise castle perfectly; neither was tight nor cramped. The store was narrow, but the ceiling enormously high. Only the garages in Riverton and our big garage behind the office had ceilings like that. And Harvey's second floor was fully functional. The odd time I went up there to help him look for something, I was astounded at all the stuff he had up there in case someone might need it.

Some of the sources of Harvey's wares left me unsettled. One season out at Berens I was planted in a bunk with Dad and another fisherman. As we were getting ready for bed one evening I noticed Dad had on a pair of black-and-white-striped boxer shorts, which struck me uncharacteristically bold. I've never been in jail, so I can't say for sure, but they looked an awful lot like prison garb from the movies. Dad turned around to get into bed, and now curious, my eye followed to look for numbers. To my astonishment there they were, stretching across his ass. "Dad, those are quite the shorts. Where did you get them?"

He was quick to answer, as he liked boxers (myself, I could never stand them): "From Harvey, a gift."

"Do you know that you have numbers blazoned across your bum? It's prison underwear!"

"What the hell difference does it make? Nobody except you has noticed, and no one cares. They're damn good shorts." And with that it was lights out. I suspect he knew about the numbers, but it wasn't a big deal to him. Perhaps he thought it was the fashion of the moment! Many a moment over the years I've had a smile cross my face thinking about that evening. I'm not sure where those shorts ended up, but I doubt they would have passed inspection by Mom.

Harvey was definitely not trading illicit prison wear. He was a man of great integrity. Harvey just knew where to buy stuff. Sometimes it was direct from the factory. Perhaps sometimes a receivership, or a train wreck, which was probably the source of the prison underwear. Harvey had plenty of money. I think almost everything he made he gave to others, especially the fledgling and oft-beleaguered State of Israel.

Usually Dad went to Winnipeg to see Harvey, but every winter, especially in my younger days, Harvey came down to the office in Riverton lugging several big suitcases of samples to go over with the boys in the office as they made their orders for the stores on the stations. Then he'd return to Winnipeg and make up the orders, package and mark them for the different stations, and send them on to Riverton Transfer to head down to Hnausa to be loaded on the *Spear*. The Sig Fish guys set the prices before everything left for the north, so fishermen would pay the same at every store.

Harvey always filled his orders on time. He knew the fishing business wasn't easy. Everything had to run like clockwork during the season, and Harvey wasn't about to have his corner of the operation jamming up the works. Harvey and Dad were good friends. He always had a special present for Mom, and when I visited the store he'd insist on sending me out with a pair of gloves or a scarf. Luckily, I was never offered any of his special underwear.

Around the corner from Altman Sheps and across Main Street was Ashdown's. Dad, and Afi before him, was in and out of Ashdown's regularly. Like at Eaton's, there always seemed to be Icelanders working there. That made doing business even more of a social event, as there was always gossip to pick up about the other fish companies and industry goings-on. Keeping up and in touch was just part of the day's business rounds.

Dad was also a supply and inventory man. He'd often head to pick something up in the West End at Marr Marine, where all the outboard parts were sourced. So many mornings when Dad was up north, the eight o'clock "sched" (short for "scheduled hourly calls") was a call to Marr Marine to holler out a parts order. In fact, Dad yelled parts orders over the phone for an hour every morning a few months a year for 30 years, either up north or in the store. It seemed like every part had as many numbers attached as could fit on it. It was annoying being in the Sig Fish store as Dad yelled out the numbers, and when he had to fight poor reception it really became irritating. Half the conversation then was, "Repeat, repeat." "Gasket 2-3-5-6-3-9. Do you read me? Gasket 2-3-5-6-3-9. Do you read me?" But Dad slipped into a mindless ordering rhythm, or was perhaps hypnotized into a trance. I avoided those calls as best I could, but halfway across the island I could still hear him bellowing.

But thoughts of Riverton were far from my mind on the streets of Winnipeg. No visit was complete without stopping to see Gordon Henders over at the Booth office. Gordon and Dad were close friends, so it was usually as much a social visit and industry update as anything. They'd been doing business together so long that any fine points needing discussion got put to bed quickly. Some would call the rest gossip, but I doubt they ever gave these important business exchanges such an awkward description.

Our last stop, especially in the hectic days before the summer and fall seasons, was the Leland Hotel, halfway between Harvey's and Ashdown's. One of the "boys" might need a pick-up, although he may not have even known his driver was in town. Some men like to go to Florida for drinks on the beach in the day, and then have a fancy dinner before retreating to an elegant room. Even battle troops on R and R are sent to high-class surroundings. But most of the men in Dad's troop had no such lofty ambitions. The Leland was Miami North for them—just as good, a lot closer, and you could drink a lot longer on the same dollars. Considering all the tough situations Dad walked into, and there were many, the most remarkable thing is that no man, to my knowledge, no matter how drunk or they were, ever laid a threatening hand on him.

Even with a few bottles of beer running through them, Dad's men always had a sparkle, a sardonic twist. I never heard this conversation, but I can't imagine it not having happened. "Why in the hell would I go all the way down to Florida?" a voice booms out from a chair in the Leland as the winds howl down the street from Portage and Main, in 40 below weather. "You can always count on Jack here, the manager, to help you out if you need it. The beer is no different here than in Florida … well come to think of it I've heard the Canadian beer is way better than that American stuff. The food is good in the coffee shop. The rooms are warm. It makes no sense to go all the way down south for a little break." There would be no piña coladas by the surf for those boys. "Outside?" they would have exclaimed if challenged. "I'm outside all the time. On my holidays I like to stay inside." It all worked out for Dad. If asked, he no doubt would have said, "That would be one hell of a situation if the boys started taking off to Florida and we had to run around down there to get this outfit in action every spring."

The Leland was once a classy Winnipeg hotel in the heart of the Exchange District. By the time I saw it, it was a dismal relic, like everything else around it. But it was better than most of the Main Street hotels down the way. Dad would have talked to the manager, Jack Dangerfield, earlier in the day to confirm his unsuspecting passenger's whereabouts, and Jack would quickly point Dad in the right direction as he walked in the front door.

"Stefan! Lucky break for me running into you here," the wayward fisherman would bellow when Dad spotted him in the Safari Room. "Stefan, I need a few dollars to get to Riverton in the morning. Is the boat still leaving tomorrow?"

Dad wouldn't pause. "I'm leaving now for Riverton. Forget about the taxi. Get your bags. Let's go."

"Okay Stefan," the man would say, disconsolately.

Dad would call over to Jack, "We'll get you settled up in a few days, Jack."

"Good, Stefan."

And that was it. We were back in the car, off to Riverton, a few words from the back seat and soon a guy sound asleep. If time wasn't pressing (but likely not if we had a weary passenger), Dad would turn into Gimli for some fish talk over coffee with his old friend Oli Josephson, the manager of the BC Packers operation in Gimli. Then he'd walk across to Olson's Fish Market and say hello to Ted and Paul, and then perhaps make a quick stop for a gossip with Ted Kristjanson or one of the Petersons as he was heading back to the highway. The rounds completed, we were off and home within the half hour. Another season had begun.

The fish business didn't consume every moment. There was also work at home. Every minute he could spare Dad spent digging and pruning and expanding the damn garden. It sounds harmless, but there was a dark side. Raspberries. Sure, I liked to eat them. Growing them was another story. Dad enjoyed both. Perhaps it was because the rhythm of the berries was like the rhythm of the fish. Energy surged into the bushes about the same time the ice started melting from the lake. When Dad returned in late summer, the fish had been harvested, and his lovingly tended berries were ready to be picked.

The garden was huge, a seigniorial farm in my mind, growing constantly longer and wider from the house to the river. Dad added vegetables to his raspberry repertoire, then a maple tree for shade. It's amazing he didn't build a small summer home to sit in back there!

The big push to get the garden in shape occurred in the days just before Dad left. He'd have me in there digging away. Or, more often than not, some unsuspecting fisherman (Beggi Gibeault from Berens River was often a candidate) that he'd picked up at the Leland and driven down to Riverton. Dad never made his reasons for these entrapments clear, but I suspect he believed the warmth of the earth in your hands helped a man sober up and get ready to pack fish. I'm certain that most of my erstwhile garden buddies shared my dim view of the enterprise, but we all sensed Dad's passion for the mission and thought better of debate. We just shovelled and pulled weeds relentlessly, knowing it couldn't last forever.

Gardening was not my strength. One year, for reasons that now bewilder me, but were presumably some teenage outburst of rebellion, I joined the most unlikely of clubs, the new 4-H Garden Club. Upon return, I announced to my mother that I was now the club's president. Perhaps I believed a presidential position of authority would render me too busy for mundane tasks like weeding. Whatever may have motivated this most bizarre of developments, it didn't work, and waterer and weeder I remained. The resignation of the founding president within days of the club's founding appears to have dealt it a fatal blow, as that was the last I heard of it.

Berries covered the bushes by late July, many visible but even more hiding under the leaves. When Dad returned from the camp, he would take one look at the patch, and the next moment he'd be attired in his berry-picking garb and out the door with a beer in hand. Fishing season was over, and berry season had begun. The summer sun would have pushed the bushes up about three feet in his absence.

There he sat, hour upon hour, bowl after bowl. The more berries Dad picked, the more those remaining flourished. There was something deeply peaceful about Dad in the berry patch. Berries on a branch were child's play compared to fish in the sea. Watching him made me feel guilty about the malicious thoughts that surged through me as I grappled with those damn weeds.

I think Dad's love of the berry patch resulted from some deep genetic stirring, like the one that seemed to be alive in Amma Kristrun, his mother. When Dad wasn't on the lake, he often made the short walk from the office to the house to have morning coffee with her. He found her in the yard most days, busy in the flowerbeds or the garden. Her quiet, unassuming manner perfectly matched her garden puttering. When Dad arrived she led the way into the house and put the kettle on if she hadn't already done so. Soon there was toast on the table, with crab-apple jelly or peach jam. Those were her specialties, the crab apples picked from the three big trees she and Afi had planted those many years ago, and peaches from a big box she bought each fall.

They'd sit at the table chatting quietly and looking out on the yard. Theirs was a gentle relationship, as deep as it was close. Conversation came easily to them. They had much in common in the way they looked at the world. They struggled quietly with their own problems, while giving strength to others. Amma puttered around her flowers and Dad beavered away with his raspberries, both in their own special places, and understanding each other more through their love for gardening. As I grew older, I often went to visit Amma, and while we didn't share a passion for gardening, we had deep and meaningful conversations about many things. Amma was not one for small talk or gossip. A lady with a gentle touch and an easy giggle, she was deeply religious in a very quiet way,

Amma came by her faith as a birthright, and the boy next door as her husband. Her father Bjarni Marteinsson had arrived in Canada in 1883, later to establish himself on a farm one mile north of the Hnausa dock, neighbour to Stefan and Valgedur. Bjarni was a highly intelligent man who had studied in Iceland under Reverend Jon Bjarnason while eking out a living as a farmer. His talents flourished when he became the first secretary treasurer of the new municipality of Bifrost, as well as the local school board. But was as chairman of the local Lutheran Church, and teaching youngsters preparing for confirmation where his greatest devotion lay. His roots in the Lutheran Church were generations deep with many distinguished pastors among their ranks, exhaustively chronicled by Amma Kristrun's sisters, Kay Palmer and Anna Marteinsson. Anna was a remarkable scholar, the Parliamentary Librarian in Ottawa for many years, and later a respected professor of library science at the University of Ottawa. I often visited her during one summer I worked in Ottawa as a student intern at the Dominion Bureau of Statistics typically meeting Anna in her labcoat in the stacks of the university library before we were off to dinner.

Meanwhile Amma, this tiny lady, was busy bringing up the eight children she had brought into the world. You could tell as soon as you saw her that she was conscious of being short. Amma always wore high heels, not just heels that were high, but long, sharp, pointed heels. She wore them in the house and she wore them to walk down the street downtown. It was an anomalous sight in a rural village that only had gravel roads until the '60s. But her shoes somehow seemed to be such a part of who she was that you stopped noticing them. Except, of course, when you saw her shovelling in the garden. It was difficult on those occasions to see anything but those long, sharp pegs and marvel at how she stayed upright in the soft earth. But she never quivered and she never wavered. She walked on the lawn as smoothly as on her kitchen floors.

Dad had his own garden clothing to cause wonder and amazement. His berry garb wasn't fancy, but the hats were another thing altogether. When the mosquitoes were in their full fury, the headwear reached its glory. He preferred a straw hat with a yellow bandana mounted along the back, which swept alongside his face and down past the back of his neck. Whether the mosquitoes were prevented by the bandana from approaching the juicy flesh they lusted after, or whether they were simply scared away by the atrocious hat remains an open question.

With the freezer full of raspberries, the action shifted to the jam and jelly operation. Headquarters moved indoors, with Mom in the captain's chair, and

Dad as first mate. When the cupboards were filled with jam, soon Dad would be pruning and readying the bushes for the winter ahead.

Spring was time to ready the boats for the summer season. Most of the gasboats (which had come to be called "whitefish boats," as they were used only for the whitefishery operations in the North End) had been pulled up in preparation onto the shallow banks of the river on a narrow stretch of land the company owned north of town. Each stood at attention, wooden crutches on either side holding them vertical. There were up to 20 boats at times. Whether wood or steel, they had to be scraped and painted. The wooden boats needed to be corked. Without this assiduous work, year in, year out, the boats would quickly deteriorate. Every year there were fewer of the wooden old-timers on the water. The gas motors, most of which started as car engines from the 1930s, had been overhauled innumerable times over the years, and each new year brought a fresh round of repairs. Steve, and later Victor, usually took charge of that, and would be back and forth, picking things up, giving directions, placing orders, keeping the crew going.

The leads that had been pounded onto the nets for the previous season had been removed so they could be melted down and recast and then reattached for the next season. They used a big vat in the garage behind SR's house to melt the leads down, a roaring wood furnace pumping heat from below. Boiling lead spurted unpredictably from the cauldron, making ladling it into the moulds a tricky operation. After a few minutes of setting, they pulled the moulds open and the freshly-minted leads tumbled onto the counter. Next, they cleaned and shellacked the corks, at least until a few years later when plastic corks were introduced. SR ran these operations, and like Steve he'd be in and out of the office many times throughout the day.

Most of all, they needed to ready the *Spear* and the *Kathy* for the season ahead. This meant scraping and painting and repairs of one kind or another, and usually an overhaul of the engine. Both boats would need to run day and night for the next two-and-a-half months, so it was critical they could be counted on. Victor headed up that mission, often with Steve barking over his shoulder.

Victor was a capable man, smart and tough. He was a sea captain by profession, trained when Lake Winnipeg was known as major water and you required a "ticket" entitling you to run a vessel of 800 tonnes, while most of the boats on Lake Winnipeg were only 100 tonnes. Victor required eight years of sea time to secure the right to take those exams, which on Lake Winnipeg took 16 years, because there was open water for only six months a year. He moved with an authoritative and commanding presence on the deck of any vessel, and could walk into the dirtiest of situations and tough it out. He would have been one hell of a man on the front lines of any combat mission. He was only a boy when he started working as a man. He was 16 when he started on the boats, and he was no stranger to life on the ice. He spent years alongside SR operating the tractor trains to the north. It was Victor who took the crews north to fill the icehouses with ice each year. He didn't mollycoddle himself, or others, in anything or in any way.

As soon as the equipment was readied, the logistics of running up to five separate stations at different locations began. Nothing was left in these remote locations from one year to the next. Every pot, pan and dish from the kitchens was packed into trunks and hauled out. Supply orders needed to be created for each station in the spring and sent to supply houses in Winnipeg. The station stores needed to be stocked with everything from fishermen's gear to dry goods, groceries and candy bars. Each station, in addition to its fishing operation, operated stores to supply the fishermen, and the stores were a major source of supplies in the communities. The other stores had to pay freighting costs, but the Sigurdsons provisioned their stores with goods brought North in empty holds soon to be filled with fish on the trip south.

Dad was the nerve centre of the whole operation. He spent the day meeting men, co-ordinating purchasing, putting transport arrangements in place, and generally putting forward the face of the operation politically and administratively. There were deals to be made, with the fishermen and with Booth. Each fisherman was his own man, but if everyone wasn't set up with everything they needed the operation couldn't get on the water at full force, so anyone's problem was Dad's problem. Sometimes it was lining up a man for work or digging a man out of trouble. Perhaps it was a problem at home, like a fisherman's family short on food. On occasion they'd need help getting the father out of jail, or more often off of a drunk. Anything that could distract from the focus on fishing had to be dealt with as efficiently and effectively as possible. Dad was a diplomat, a general, and a logistics officer. There was nothing he didn't do, from loading fish boxes to commanding the troops.

There were people and parts, and most critical of all ... the fish. They were on Dad's mind every step of the way, from pulling the product out of the water to keeping it fresh until it could be passed over the scales and purchased then sold again, to ensuring a fresh final delivery. They bought and sold on their own account and at their own risk. Always on the partners' minds was the allowance for evaporation. The fish were weighed in at 62-and-a-half pounds per box, and they paid the fishermen for 60 pounds. They were on the hook for the fish as soon as it crossed the scale. If they delivered the fish at less than 60 pounds in a box, they lost money.

Keeping the fish fresh was a constant concern, on the water and off. As the boxes came out from the icehouses ready for transport, every cover was lifted and another shovel of ice tossed in. If they needed to hold the fish at the station due to bad weather, they were at risk for all they had bought. Dad spent half the day sometimes making sure the men took ice out onto the lake. The last thing he wanted was for the product to be beaten up by the sun. The first sign of deterioration is a softening of the flesh, and when bones were visible, sticking out through the flesh. The men would slide those fish straight off the dressing table into the gut barrel. Dad was in constant communication with the boats, stations and suppliers. Just monitoring how much fish was coming in so they'd know how much room they would need in the tugs was a major undertaking. And half the time Dad oversaw all this from a boat in rough weather with frequent breakdowns and two-way radio interruptions.

In the summer, unlike the winter, while individual fishermen operated independently, they were highly dependent on the "packer" companies, called such because they bought and packed the fish to be sold to the larger companies for export into the US markets. The packer companies typically owned the boats and equipment, especially the big whitefish boats, and rented them to the fishermen. They would provision and supply on credit everything needed for the operation, from gas to food. Accounts were settled at the end of each season.

This dependency grew alongside the gradual decline of the fishery, with the fishermen caught in the grip of diminishing fish receipts and increasing operation costs. The packer companies supplying exporters were in turn tangled in the vagaries of Chicago and New York markets, grinding away to maintain their margins, bearing the brunt of the risk on the downside, but not enjoying the benefits of the big swings in prices on the upside. The exporters had their own challenges, as they were vulnerable to the influence of a few buyers who controlled the markets. This collage of interests gurgled over the next few decades, morphing from an uneasy soup to a witch's brew of ever-fewer fish, puzzling prices and an uncertain future.

The toughest time for Dad was settling accounts with men who had nothing left on the table after the season. He had to take back literally everything they owned, and perhaps not even issue a meagre cheque in return. Days when that happened were not easy for Dad.

Dad was versatile enough to take care of it all. He had to be able to connect to prominent businessmen (he wore his suit then), and he needed to connect to the people who ultimately drove his business, the men from whom he bought his fish (no suit then). He brokered a conversation between many different people, all of whom needed each other. He wasn't so much a middleman as a man in the middle, immersed in many different realities. He moved in a comfortable way with many different people.

Every day Dad faced this enormous web of pressures, including the complex interactions among the powerful personalities of the Sig Fish partners. Nothing happened at Sig Fish until everyone was aboard, with one mind and one voice, but before that place was reached there was, inevitably, a lot of talk. Plus he had his own family to look out for!

Somehow it all hung together, and I think I know one of the most important reasons why ... he treated everyone with respect. He needed to, because in a business as complex as he was running, he couldn't afford to create problems. But it was deeper than that. No man or woman was ever different in his eyes—he was a genuinely "colour blind" man. He just didn't see differences in value in other human beings. He was never in your face—he always left space for other people and other perspectives. To be sure, he had a strong and determined will, but he always left room for others to help shape his actions. He was not judgmental, but rather, profoundly accepting of people's strengths and foibles. He was unswervingly loyal, and constantly vigilant not to betray who he was by overlooking someone in a way they could see as hurtful. He was a gentle man, a good man, but not a man who asked for or expected that endorsement.

Some men purposefully figure out how to be leaders. They work hard to gain influence, spend their energy gathering the trappings of power. They don't worry about stepping on people who get in their way—"that's just business." But there's another type of leader, a natural leader, who commands respect by giving respect. Everyone is important to these leaders and they believe they get what they give. They accept people for who they are, seeing right past weaknesses to strengths. They have power, but are seemingly indifferent to wielding it. And they don't focus on doing one huge thing, at any cost, but on doing a million small things at no cost, because they're good things to do.

Dad was a natural leader. Actually, many of the men in my family were. The risk of someone thinking it arrogant to say so is far outweighed by the injustice of not saying it. The kindest people should get their due. Anyone would understand if they could look into my dad's eyes, be touched by their warm and open confidence. He didn't need to be anything. He just needed to be. Dad was never in the business of transforming people. He accepted them for who they were. His was a tough business, operated in tough places, run by tough men. There was a lot of heavy drinking. In all Dad's years on the lake, walking into the middle of difficult situations and drunken fishermen, no man ever took a hand to him, or even tried. Nor did he lose a dollar, for what was owed one year was always repaid some later year. The men and women with Sig Fish were there season after season, for a lifetime.

CHAPTER ELEVEN
A World of Unimaginable Characters

Let there be no doubt. If you were on a tug on the North Basin, in the heavy seas of a ripping norwester, with a motor in trouble, you'd want Dori Benjaminson with you. Dori spent most of his time in the repair shop beside the small store on Sigurdson Island at Berens River, working to get the outboard motors going again. He'd go in every day to give Dad the list of parts for the next day's call. Or, just as often, he'd march into the office scowling and grumbling about the young native guys taking the covers off the outboard motors, which exposed the motors to water in a blow and triggered mechanical failures. They couldn't hot-rod up a car, so they wanted to soup up their outboards. Dori spotted them like a hawk as they roared past the island on their way to the fishing grounds.

Dad knew how vital good mechanics were on Lake Winnipeg, for if the motors weren't running, there would be no fish. It was that simple. Dori was a genius with motors. He could lay on his back in a hold full of greasy water and coax a marine diesel motor back to life with ingenuity and baling wire, no matter how hard it was blowing or how tough the going. Four years as a tank mechanic on the Allied front lines taught him all he needed to know about working under pressure on any kind of engine.

Dori was short, wiry and tough, and tough looking. Strangely, he looked bigger than he was. Dori was grumpy at the best of times. He was Dad's man, there was no doubt about that, as Steve reminded Dad whenever Dori was on a "tear" (shorthand for a long drunk). There were plenty of those; Dori was never one to restrict his partying to social events. When the spirit moved him, or the fire inside was eating him up, Dori could start a lonely party quickly, and once he started he was relentless, until he burned down like a wick on a candle. He lived with demons that tormented him in ways hard to fathom, but the fact that he was a good man was never in question. Dori had come back from the Second World War "shell-shocked," as people called it back then. Now, we know it as "post-traumatic stress syndrome." Whenever someone started calling

Dori out, Dad would defend him with an angry edge: "Where in the hell can you find a man who can do what that man can do no matter how impossible the situation?" And that would end that.

Dad and Dori spent most of their lives together. Dad could get mighty angry with Dori, but abandoning him was never an option. Dad was lucky enough to return from the North Atlantic intact in body and mind. Dori hadn't been so lucky. Mom, without ever talking about it, understood completely. As I grew older, I understood the silent but special bond between these two very different men, each unwaveringly loyal to the other.

Dori didn't do much drinking at the station over the months he was there. There was work to be done. He did his real binging down south. Nevertheless, he slipped on occasion, and made his way to the Log Cabin Inn, where the river meets the mouth. The motors in the shop would go lonely for a day or two while Dori built up his own head of steam. Eventually, he'd come rolling to a stop back in his bunk (hopefully), or else Dad would go and find him.

On one occasion, Dori was on the move with an amorous friend he had met upriver. When he arrived at the station he was on a ripsnorter, and the fact that the generator was out and the electrical equipment down was insignificant to him at that point. Dad had to plead with Dori to get his act together and fix the generator so they could get the ice machines going before the fish spoiled. Dori slowed down long enough to get out his tools and go to work. Even dead drunk and crazy, there was no piece of mechanical equipment Dori Benjaminson couldn't get going.

Dori usually took a winter holiday, but not to the sunny south. He preferred the Safari Room of the Leland Hotel and a "luxury suite" on the second floor. Finding Dori and sobering him up was part of the ritual of getting ready for each season. Usually, Dori went north on the tug as it left for the season, except for the odd year when he was angry with Dad for something and took off instead with Tom Rasminsky to repair bush planes up north. One way or the other, Dori was always back for the next season, or the next year.

Back in Riverton, Dori often showed up at the back door of the house for a visit. Whether Dad was home or not was of little concern to Dori; Mom was no less tolerant of his carryings-on. There was fear in Dori's voice one night when he came to the door.

"I'm having a heart attack, Sylvia," I heard him say as I stood behind Mom.

"What makes you say that, Dori?" Mom replied. "Is it because you walked over here in the cold?" She was right to be sceptical, because Dori was three sheets to the wind.

"This arm ... and my hand ... they're ice cold. Feel them."

Mom recalls my helpful three-year-old interjection: "Why don't you put a mitt on if your hand is cold?"

Mom tried to reason with Dori, but reason had no place with him that night. He announced that he was heading to the river. This would be the end of him, he told us solemnly. "You'll never see me again in this life," he said. And with that he trudged off in the blackness of the cold fall night towards the river.

Mom had seen Dori in all types of crazy situations, but this had become alarming. Dad was away, so she phoned over to Afi SV's. She was hoping that for a change he wasn't off at a job site. Fortunately, she reached him, and moments later he was at the back door. Mom pointed him in the right direction. He plunged into the pitch-black marsh along the river, probably expecting to find Dori with a beer in his hand somewhere in the field sitting on the beer case. When Dori was on a drunk, he usually carried two "24's" as each cardboard box of 24 bottles was commonly known. One day I asked him innocently, "Dori, why do you have two cases of beer? Isn't one enough?"

Dori fired back, "Can't you figure that one out on your own?"

"They must be heavy to carry. Why not drink one, and then go get another?"

"Do you know nothing?" Dori replied without hesitation. "You need one to sit on and the other to drink from." I guess he had a point.

It wasn't unreasonable to expect to find Dori drinking in the field. But not this time. SV found him lying in the water beside the river. He pulled Dori from the marsh and marched him out of there. Dori spent the night on a bed in Afi's basement. He had reached a height of agony that needed no further words, only sleep. To be sure, there would be disgust at his antics, but no irreversible critical judgments. That wasn't Afi's nature, nor was it Mom or Dad's. Dori was Dori.

Dori was still in Riverton one December. He usually would have made his way into Winnipeg after the season or headed out on some other job, but not this year. He was sleeping in the basement at our place every night. He'd come up to spin his tales while Mom worked in the kitchen in the evening. She sometimes laughingly recalls how she was writing cards one such night and signing them "from Stefan, Sylvia and family," and almost found herself adding "and Dori."

When Dori got rolling, a couple of the Berens River dames kept a close eye on him. One was Ma Kemp. There will never be another like Ma. She came to Berens River from England in the 1930s, and began building her dream, the Log Cabin Inn. Her sister came, too, heading farther north to Norway House where she built and ran the Playgreen Inn. The Log Cabin Inn was a giant log structure, or so it seemed to my young eyes. The main room towered up 30 feet to the roof, fur and skin memorabilia of the fur trade adorning the walls.

What struck you first about Ma was that hair, white as driven snow and bursting from her head in every direction. She was short and sturdy, but there was no way her enormous personality could be bottled up inside that small package. She magnetized everyone who entered her orbit, and curious and lively little characters like me were drawn into her spell and held there at her will.

"God in Heaven, darling," she'd begin, as she captured the hapless folks who came in weekly on the *Keenora* on their Lake Winnipeg trip-of-a-lifetime. Invariably, the stop in Berens River involved a walk along a narrow trail from the Hudson's Bay Company dock to the Log Cabin Inn to meet Ma and taste her famous "rose petal jam." Not one tourist, I am certain, ever escaped her clutches without having bought a jar to take back home. Many of them had come to know her from prior trips or had heard of the Inn and were there to stay for a few days as a guest in a room or one of the log cabins.

The heart of Ma's castle in the north was her kitchen. In the centre was the huge wooden table that seated the guests for their daily meals. Everything happened in Ma's kitchen. She presided as the lord and master, the entertainer and the chef, the raconteur and the preacher, all in one five-foot-nothing bundle of energy. The heat of the old wood stove beside which she stood day in, day out, passed through her into the centre of the conversations she shared happily with all she encountered.

Ma kept a watchful eye for Dori's funny business when he was on the move in the community. That was infrequent, but happened enough over the years that she had a solid grasp of who he was and how she would handle him if he showed up. No doubt part of her expertise arose from belligerent exchanges in the past when she had refused to sell him a case of beer. Word of his wanderings in the community usually preceded him, and Ma would be in a state of alert ready with her sermon as soon as his face appeared on the property.

Dori's other guardian angel was Dollie. He did not see her that way. She knew him in much closer quarters than Ma, sharing the same small Sigurdson Island and three meals and two coffees a day with him. If you needed a label, Dollie would have been called the station's cook, but she was much more than supper. She had no problem with men like Dori. Who they were and how they lived was just a fact of life. They elicited frustration, to be sure, sometimes disgust, but she had her own life to live, so she accepted them. Dori reciprocated with his own collage of emotions. He made his feelings crystal clear when he realized that Dad was having his breakfast at 7:30, not 7:00, and that Dollie was serving him his preferred one egg on toast. Soon, Dori began arriving in the kitchen every morning at 7:30 expecting precisely the same treatment. So the morning conversation came to include Dollie, Dad and Dori. One had the sense that Dollie wasn't as enthusiastic about this as Dori.

Dollie was the only other person with Dad's radar for "who's up and what's up." Your first thought when you met Dollie was not necessarily that she was a somebody; that understanding came later, after you got to know her. It washed over you in time, like a rising sun. If Dad was the ostensible king of Sigurdson Island, the little hunk of granite at the mouth of the Berens River, let there be no doubt that Dollie Berens was the queen. First of all, she kept the food coming. That was hard work, and all the camp cooks knew it. Maria Sigurgeirson (nee Baldwinson), Grimsi's sister-in-law, wrote in *Train Stories from the Icelandic River* that, "I was a pastry cook one year at Black River for Leif Hallgrimson. I had to bake for 70 men, so I had to bake 70 pies and stack them on a pie rack—and all the donuts. I used to keep them in washtubs because there was nothing else big enough to hold them!" A pie a boat will keep you busy, and Dollie at least equalled that in her kitchen.

Dollie's charisma wasn't limited to her ability to entice with food. She was simply a part of the land. When she put her arms on the windowsill and peered out from the back of the huge cookhouse up towards the mouth of the river, she was looking at her world. She knew it like no other. Her home was a mile down the river, on the height of land looking down at the bay in the river before it began its eight-mile rush to Sturgeon Falls. Across the bay, on the other shore and up toward the lake, was the Métis community. Just downriver before it broke into the mouth was the Log Cabin Inn. The rest of the community was upriver, houses on both sides.

Dollie and Dad were workmates, but beyond that they were good friends. They understood each other. Every morning they chatted over the breakfast she set in front of him after he finished the first "sched" on the radiotelephone. Most of the men came at seven, but Dad had to walk over to the store, which doubled as his office, and start the day checking in with the other stations and the boats. In the old days when the camp was feeding 70 men heading onto the lake, breakfast was at five. These days, the kitchen was mostly for the land-based shore crew, since most of the fishermen were from the community and went home each night. Dad would tell Dollie the gossip from the stations in the morning, and they'd discuss the other meals for the day. After that they each oversaw their own kingdoms.

I always found it ironic that more meat than fish was consumed in the fish stations. After Dad and Dollie decided what should be on for dinner, he'd go down to the shed and dig into the meat locker to bring up what was needed. The beef came in quarter sides wrapped in cheesecloth. In a fish station you had to be able to do everything, so Dad was a satisfactory butcher, or at least good enough to render the quarter into a variety of cuts. SR took the butchering job on with enthusiasm when he was around. In later years, Roy Shonberg, who, like another of his German countrymen, Fitz Metzker, arrived sometime after the war, took on the task with the same relish as SR. Roy was with Dad for many years, adding to his life as a fishermen responsibility for the station's caretaking.

Dad had more of a penchant for eating fish in the camp than many other station operators. His favourite was fish livers. On days when whitefish were turning up in the nets, he often sent me down to stand by the fishermen as they dressed the fish. My job was to pull the livers out of the guts and drop them into my pail until we had five pounds or so. They were an incredibly rich liver, far better than chicken livers, and a real delicacy when fried fresh. Some of the women from the settlement would show up when dressing was underway with spoons sharpened at the edges and scoop out the pickerel cheeks, often sending up enough for dinner in the kitchen that evening.

Dollie was square. She wasn't tall, she wasn't fat. She was square. She had a round face, a warm smile and a soft voice, except when she was angry. And Dollie could get angry. Anyone from the community who acted out faced her wrath. Whenever there was trouble on the island, Dollie jumped into action. She wasn't happy when somebody set foot on the island drunk, and believe me, she knew everyone who came onto those rocks. She knew they were there, she knew their wife, their kids, their mother and their father, and their parents before them. She knew their strengths, and every weakness, especially if they were drinking men. It was one thing to be drunk on the island, but something else altogether to try to come into her kitchen, as some were bold enough to do. I couldn't understand what she was saying in those cases, but the response of the interlopers told me what they were hearing, and when the broom came out it was definitely time for the troublemakers to head out. Dollie was absolutely fearless.

 . Dollie's husband, Jacob Gibeault, was always right beside her, adding his stature and sombre tones to the moment. Jacob was a fisherman, a quiet man, a respectful man. He was tall, stately and dignified. Somehow you always had the sense that Dollie ran the show. He respected her deeply, and he was proud that Dollie was his wife. Both of them were proud of the grandkids Dollie always had in tow. How many she helped raise over the years I can't imagine, but they were as much a part of her as she was of them.

Dad knew how things worked in Berens River, like he did in Riverton. When you'd lived and worked in a place as long as Dad, you came to understand who was who and what to do and not to do. And for any questions Dad might have about who linked how to whom, Dollie was always a reliable source, or, more accurately, a fountain of information. Dad knew many generations of people at Berens River, and around Lake Winnipeg, for that matter. He knew who their families were, and he knew their character. It was through his relationship—and his father's and grandfather's—with people like Dollie that he acquired this knowledge. With Dollie on double duty, in charge of the kitchen and on the lookout from her post beside the back window with a view onto the dock and the bay beyond, and Dad at the helm at his desk and in the shed, things in that small corner of the globe ran in step and on time.

Fishermen are like anyone else doing a job; not everyone has the same ability or motivation. Some guys found it tough to get going at four in the morning when first light was breaking and the wind had died down. By the time they got going at eight the winds had picked up and they couldn't get out to their nets. Most fishermen were steady and solid, but the odd guy, not surprisingly, just didn't have the knack.

Then there were guys who you knew might try to pull a fast one and slide some bad catch through at the bottom of a tray, fish the next guy would have thrown into the gut barrel. Some guys always forgot to pick up ice on the way out, or were just in too much of a hurry because they wanted to get back to do something else that day. But Dad and the weighmen were alive to all of this in the action-filled packing sheds. Everyone running the stations developed a nose for fishy business, excuse the pun. They knew their fishermen. Just like everyone else, I had to learn the hard way to keep my guard up.

Tom Bittern, from Berens River, had worked with Dad since he was a kid. He was a little older than me, but not much, and we'd played around the station and nailed boxes together. Tom was a first-rate guy, a top-notch shore hand who went on to become the weighman and the shed boss, the man in control of the packing operation. When Tom left to run another station up north, he gave me a crash course as a weighman. Then the torch was passed and he was gone. I was left alone, and those first days were stressful. The fishermen hovered as I dithered over each lot. Were there a few sauger at the bottom? Was that flesh a little soft? That fish small? Thankfully, there wasn't a man who didn't know me, and I them, and we all knew that everyone has to start somewhere. There were a lot of jokes and much laughter flying around. When the laughter came from around a dressing table from five guys in their oilers with blades flashing as the fish spilled out in every direction, speaking Saulteaux and watching me dither around, I knew who was providing the entertainment. Even so, things were coming along okay. Until the incident.

"Dad," I reported, "there was a guy in already, with a hell of a lift. Over 600 pounds." Fishing hadn't been heavy for a few days, and Dad's curiosity was piqued.

"Who was that?" he asked, looking up from the books he was working on at the back desk. I told him. "Who?" And I gave him the name again. "When did he come in?" I told him around 9:30. "There's no damn way he's been out to the lake and finished lifting and back here with that amount of fish by this time in the morning." My heart sank. "I don't think he's brought in a pound for about four days," Dad said. "Give me those weigh bills from the last couple of days. I don't remember a single entry from him." A quick check confirmed his suspicions. "You better get back down to the shed and see if you can get the boys to locate those boxes and check every last one of them. There's no way that fish is in good shape." So off I went.

Sure enough, in all the bullshitting he'd engaged me in when I was weighing, I had missed the telltale signs on the flesh of the pickerel. At least half of it was unacceptable. He had made one fatal error; he was still hanging around the station. In moments, Dad and he were in a heated conversation.

"You better get the hell out on the water more regularly and not try to pass that kind of shit over the scales," was the gist of it. That episode concentrated the mind of this young weighman from that day to the end of the season. That was my first and last season on the scales. Tom was back in the saddle the next fall.

In 1966, after spending three summers on the tractors excavating the massive new Red River floodway, I decided to go north on the lake. I had been out the fall before for a couple of weeks before university started, but this year I decided to spend the whole summer on the lake and hope for a few more weeks' work on the floodway before school started when I got back. Sig Fish Management 101 with Professor Steve, right there on the dock at Black Bear, is indelibly stained in my mind. That's how the season began for me.

It was a grumpy day on the lake. The clouds were a foreboding grey, dark and puffy along the waterline, overstuffed, as if they were gulping up the lake as they lumbered along. Mist was hovering, and the wind was picking up. It was late May, and the ice had just left the lake. I had passed the final box to the next set of hands in the chain, and the boat was loaded and ready to pull out. Steve put his arm around my shoulders and walked me down the rugged plank dock. He wasn't a man who took a long time to come to a point.

"You're going north to Berens to get that station started for the season," he said. "You're the boss. Do you know what it takes to be the boss?" My mind was rushing for an answer, as it always did when he started peppering me with questions. Before I could blurt anything out to escape this face-to-face at the end of the dock, he was back at me. This wasn't my first learning experience from Steve, so I knew when expectant silence was preferable to talking.

"Just listen now. Are you listening? I'm only going to tell you this once." I heard him all right, but I knew he wasn't expecting an answer. "There's just one thing you need to know about being a boss. Your job is to work harder than anyone else on that station. As long as you keep working, everyone else will keep working, and the harder you work, the harder everybody else will work. Have you got it?"

I knew the time had come to say something: "I got it." And to make sure this would soon be over, I looked him in the eye again and said firmly, "Steve, I got it."

"Jump on that boat, then, and get going. I'll let the lines go."

I had passed Management 101 at Black Bear.

He was quite a man, that Captain Steve. He was about six feet, slim and angular, with a penetrating set of crystal blue eyes. He was tough. He was disciplined. He was demanding. He had a penchant for detail. He counted every penny and, not surprisingly, ended up with a lot of pennies. When I was twelve, we pulled up to the garage in Riverton after a long trip together. I took a Coke bottle and heaved it mindlessly into the river. Steve grabbed hold of me: "If that's the way you deal with every two cents that goes through your hands, you'll never have a pot to piss in." He could always be counted on, and what he said he would do, he did. He could be overwhelming and overbearing, but just as often, his soft side was exposed. He knew how to round the hard edges of his crusty shell.

Steve had a nickname for almost everyone, like "Johnny Holiday," or "Two-Day Bob, two days late for the job." He kidded and cajoled. And he was a master of the rhetorical question. For all those reasons, he wasn't intimidating, but he could sure get your attention, and, on occasion, get you pretty rattled. He took command naturally and with confidence. Even when he was exasperating, he enjoyed respect and I learned from him. You knew where you stood with Steve; his messages were clear and straightforward. And although they were not always delivered in a manner conducive to relaxed absorption, later reflection revealed that they were saturated with the wisdom of common sense.

After Steve had released the bowline and the boat reversed out into the harbour following my brief management seminar, Steve came running down the dock. He always seemed to be running. His baggy pants flowed over the top of his rubber boots, his blue nylon parka had the hood pulled over his head with the beak of his cap sticking out, and he hollered at me to get ready to pull the stern line aboard. I watched him head back up the dock as the boat made its way out of the picture-perfect horseshoe bay that was Black Bear Harbour. Steve might not have been dressed in the usual costume of a captain of industry, but in that place, that day, he left no doubt he was the bear in that lair.

There had once been five fishing stations operating around Black Bear Harbour, a major real estate play for any part of Lake Winnipeg. One by one, the stations closed with declining production, and after the lake reopened in 1972 there was only the Sigurdson station left. Steve had run down that dock for over thirty seasons toward the red icehouse on the shore, and up the hill to the place he called home for four months each year. What set Black Bear apart from almost any other station was that everything that happened there other than the handling of the fish took place in one two-story log building. The kitchen was on the main floor, with the store and office behind, and on the second floor was a bunkhouse that slept around 50 in double-decker bunks. Some might, in a kindly way, call it cozy. To be sure it was compact, and it was surely heat efficient, but however you chose to describe it, it was Captain Steve's world.

Let's not gild the lily too much. Steve could be difficult, and unreasonable, and very cheap. He could be hard on people. In the final years of the station's operation Steve became increasingly self-sufficient, to the extent that he determined he could save a few more bucks on costs if he served as the cook as well. That's when he pulled out the garlic sausage and bologna, and God help the man who found himself unhappy with the grub. Obstinacy aside, however, Dad through long years had learned, as did Eric and I, that even Steve could revisit decisions when you stood your ground firmly.

Life for Steve started in a very difficult place. Grade Three was the extent of his early formal education. As a young man he went to Winnipeg in 1928 to study at Success Business College, and a decade later he spent a few months studying in Toronto in preparation for writing his captain's papers. He was captain on the *Spear* for many years, and that time moulded him, and became the window into the man he would become. Nothing was more important to Steve than his family—to whom he was absolutely devoted—and his commitment to education. He was determined that his children would never battle the insecurity he faced as a boy, or have to fight so hard for an opportunity to live an easier life. He extended those same feelings to me and my brother and my dad. Steve wasn't one to open up about such things, but I know those hopes were embedded as deeply within him as the lake that had trained and sustained him. That is who he was.

The endless hours Steve had spent gripping a boat helm had clawed one of his hands; his fingers would never extend fully again. He started to run the stations in later years, and Black Bear was his home base. You felt like he was in command as soon as he walked aboard any boat, whether he was or not. Not only did he convey an aura of authority, but he had the showmanship to go along with it. He'd take hold of that big wheel in the pilothouse and start barking commands to those on the deck and dock below, churning the wheel around with gusto, confidently manoeuvring the tug, always perfectly positioned to make safe passage out of whatever harbour he was in, no matter how tough the weather. Those tugs were his home for many a year, but working from land became more his wont as time passed. Although Black Bear station came to be his ship on land, he was never far from taking control of any tug when the need arose.

Life at sea held a special challenge for Steve. He didn't feel well in a head sea, complaining specifically of headaches. I often had a far more gruesome experience in storms as a kid. Given that my dad could be turned upside down like a saltshaker without feeling anything out of the ordinary, I felt I had a soulmate in Steve when it came to my problems. That ended in no uncertain terms on one trip north.

My friend Rudi Leach and I were going north to Berens River. Rudi's mother was a Mckay from Berens River, and he was being sent up to visit relatives for the summer. I was heading to the Berens station to spend the summer with Dad. It was blowing hard from the west, at least 40 knots. The tug had a deep hold in the water but a narrow beam. She was rolling so ferociously that I thought she was going to lie down on her side and drown. As the storm worsened, Rudi and I made our way to the back bunk on the upper deck. An agony that only the rolling sea can bring was upon us. We groaned as each swell surged from below and lifted us like a feather in a twisting motion, up and down, up and down.

Our tortured perseverance was soon shattered. Steve pushed open the door and wanted to know how the hell the two of us were making out in the storm. Not well, Steve. Sick as dogs, as if he couldn't tell from the state of the room. He sensed desperation in our voices and determined quickly to find a remedy. Confident that a crisp wind would get us back on our feet, he tied us to the back lifeboat looking out at the frantic sea. The fresh air failed utterly to be our salvation, and no more horrendous fate could await a couple of twelve-year-olds than we met in the hours before arriving in Berens River.

The storm's fury was finally subsiding as we approached the ranges on the way into Berens, and we were released from our roped captivity. I'll never forget the feeling of standing on the dock, firmness under our feet. The relentless motion, however, stayed alive in my mind for some time. There's nothing worse than seasickness. The hours of incessant retching lead you to the irresistible conclusion that the lining of your stomach is struggling to make its way to freedom.

For two days I walked about like a ghost, feeling as if I was still rolling and heaving. I felt the aftermath in other ways, too. As a little guy squeezed into the corner seat of the bench in the kitchen on the *Spear*, I usually felt like a big guy when the cook banged the plate of bacon and eggs onto the flowered oilcloth in front of me, just like for all the other men crowded around the table. I was older now, but bacon and eggs were still the morning ritual on the tug. This time, memories of those seasick hours were punctuated by that breakfast in ways that were uniquely and perplexingly enduring. For years, the very sight of bacon and eggs reawakened a dreadful taste in my mouth. Mercifully, this malady of the mind slowly retreated, and within about five years I was back at breakfasts of bacon and eggs.

My younger brother Eric experienced his own version of Management 101 from Uncle Steve. Dad was sitting at his desk, the chaos of pre-season preparations swirling around him, when Steve stormed into the office.

"The kid thinks he's a boss, so we better make him a goddamned boss!"

"What is the problem, Steve?" Dad was quick to call out upon hearing the shouting.

"That damn kid of yours," Steve barked. "He's out there telling me how to load that fridge on the truck. I told him there was only room for one boss on any job, and I'm the goddamn boss on this one."

"Is the fridge on the truck, or do you need me to come back to help?"

"The fridge is on the truck. We're ready to go. But this kid thinks he knows enough to run a job, so we better get him going. Let's send him north to run a station," Steve hollered back.

Steve's demand that Eric take his place alongside the rest of the bosses wasn't all that surprising. His capabilities were already clear. At 18, he was sent north to run Georges Island, one of the largest and most important stations on Lake Winnipeg. He had twenty senior whitefish boats, each with a crew of four, and it was his job to ensure that the station operated like clockwork in handling their fish and servicing their needs. He had a crew of around ten under his control. He kept all the books of account, issued the daily fish receipts, and checked every bill of lading against goods received. And, he was expected to be the statesman who kept the place going and deal with any issues that might arise. His link with the rest of the family was by two-way radio.

The only management lesson Eric received was the same one I did: work harder than everyone else, and everyone will keep working as hard as you. But there was never a shortage of practical lessons. Eric learned from one of the best up at Georges Island, fisherman Joe Bjornson, one of the famous Bjornson brothers that Dad bought out. Joe hadn't caught much for several weeks running, insisting on fishing close in near "Little Georges," a much smaller sister island a couple of miles away. Others were running miles out, burning gas and time. Joe breezed along calmly with small daily lifts. Eric, a man-kid, was running the station and was worried that Joe wouldn't fill his limit. Eric was stressed, because he was in charge of encouraging the men to hit their maximums. Every pound that one of the men failed to collect was a pound the Sigurdsons couldn't buy and then sell to the bigger companies.

But since the fishermen were all independent, Eric had no real leverage over them. He and all the others needed to be great persuaders. They couldn't come down hard like bosses; they needed to soft-pedal, use diplomacy. They didn't command the fishermen, but rather worked with them. Eric was particularly suspicious of Joe because he knew Joe's proclivities. Joe was days late coming in from the north one season, after an "unexpected" delay at the Log Cabin Inn in Berens River. My dad had been waiting for him for days. When Joe finally rolled in, with a clearly amorous, yet highly unqualified new firstmate, all he had to say for himself was, "Are all the other boys in yet, Stefan?"

Just as Eric was nearing his wits' end, he saw a gasboat approaching the dock one day, its gunwales only inches above the surface, as if it were sinking. It was Joe. His lift was so enormous that the boat was literally swimming with fish! The holds were filled, and the decks were filled. Standing in the midst of it all, laughter shaking his round belly, was Joe. As he tied up at the dock, he announced in his low, raspy voice, "Eric, you see I told you the fish would be coming to Little Georges. It always comes a little later. You just have to wait for it!" Those waters had been home to Joe and his brothers for decades, and they knew them like the backs of their own hands. Clearly Joe had penetrated some of the mystery of the lake. Having the wisdom and patience to wait for the fish was his strength. He knew they'd be there, but he didn't know exactly when. Eric allowed Joe (he had no choice) to use his wisdom, and it paid off!

Eric then watched a second gasboat pulling into the harbour, equally loaded with fish. Lloyd Jonasson stood on deck, his face twinkling with that winsome grin, fish halfway to his knees against his yellow oilers, and his curly black hair standing on end. As he pulled in beside the dock, all you could hear was that Lloyd Jonasson voice, so deep it was as if it came from inside a mountain: "Fishing was pretty good today."

SR was understated compared to his larger-than-life younger brother Steve. He had charisma that worked its own brand of magic on a young mind. You could see and feel the warmth inside him. He wore his emotions openly, a grimace when grumpy or tears when moved. Inside that strong man rested a tender soul. He'd been self-sufficient since he was a boy, losing his young mother to illness and his elderly father Sigurdur not long after. He was sent to the States to live with an aunt for a couple of years, while Steve and their sister Runa stayed with Stefan and Valgerdur in the Big House. The separation was difficult to endure, and SR came home as soon as he could.

SR had known hard work ever since he was a boy, and his legendary prowess as a fisherman powered the Sig Fish partnership in the twenties and thirties. They say you know a person by the little things they do. I never understood that more clearly than when SR showed up on the Monarch job site soon after I started on the tractors when I was 16. He hunted me down to check up on me. When he found me aboard my tiny crawler tractor, pulling a giant sheep-foot roller, he could see my pain in the two Band-Aids on my nose and the sweat pouring down my face. The temperature was in the 90s and the redheaded, freckled kid was burning alive on twelve-hour shifts before the era of sun cream. That was all SR needed to see. He directed me and the tractor to the shop and told them he wasn't leaving until a steel roof was welded to the frame of that tractor. Every time I saw him from that day on, the first thing I pictured was the roof over the tractor.

Sigurdson University was also open every fall offering its course in fish heads. Uncle Steve's transportation artery of choice was increasingly "the North Road," the gravel road built by Monarch draglines in the early '50s after the winter road had been pushed through to save the fish in the 1949 season. Steve's sense of commercial opportunities expanded accordingly. Now with road accessibility to the mink ranches in the Interlake, he found a way to turn even fish heads into a buck. At two cents a pound, they made fine mink feed. That's where I came in.

I was to meet Steve two or three times a week at the "End of the North Road," where it runs head-long into Lake Winnipeg at the mouth of Fisher Bay, with Matheson Island two miles across and Black Bear Island just behind it. There I would receive my cargo, a load of fish heads for the area's mink farmers. I was allocated an old brown van, far past its prime, and as I completed my 90-minute trip, he was inevitably waiting for me at the dock. He'd be wearing his blue nylon parka and rubber boots, standing beside the "gut boat," the old gasboat he used to haul the offal from the dressing operations. He wasn't inclined to small talk when there was work to be done. I can't recall him ever saying hello before he started throwing plastic bags of fish heads at me. Inevitably, as I scrambled to keep up with the barrage of bags, one would break open, thanks to the razor-sharp bones around the pickerel's cheeks. Fish heads would then be flying in every direction on the floor of the truck, and I'd be slipping on their slime as the next bags came flying my way. Then it was over, as fast as it had begun. The truck was loaded.

Encounters with Steve could be instructive in many ways. Occasionally he'd drive in with me to get other business done. As soon as he got behind the wheel and the old beast lurched into gear, the questions began: "So what the hell are you going to make of yourself?" As I stumbled with my reply, he'd admonish me, "Just make sure you stay out of this goddamn fishing."

Steve and SR were used to giving orders and organizing men. They'd seen it all in their years on the lake, but there was one man who drilled into their nerve endings like no other: Arni Goodman. SR could become moody, a quiet grumpiness that contrasted dramatically with his brother Steve, who was in-your-face and volatile. They'd known Arni all their lives, in his better days and in his darkest days, but they had a deeper and longer memory of his bad times. Arni's infamy had been secured in 1934. It was a heavy sea, and Valdi Sopher was at the wheel of the *Whoopee*, a forty-foot gasboat, struggling to see through the water-drenched windshield to the tug ahead, the *Spear*, and follow in her wake. Only the occasional outline of its stern was visible through the waves crashing onto the deck in front of him. The *Whoopee* had been in tow since they'd turned north at Barrel Rock, the last of the ranges on the way out of Berens River. She'd been tucked in more tightly behind the *Spear* as the storm built, and was now in the tug's immediate wake. Suddenly, on the *Spear*'s upper deck, Valdi thought he saw a man emerge through the spray. It was a man! He was climbing onto the railing of the *Spear*. Valdi realised it was Arni, and the instant he saw Arni jump he ran out onto the deck. When Arni hit the deck of the *Whoopee*, Valdi grabbed him to keep him from bouncing overboard. He dragged Arni across the deck into the cabin.

"No goddamn man is going to be behind the wheel of this boat other than Arni Goodman," Arni spluttered. He was stone-cold drunk, had been since they pulled out of Berens. Not even his miraculous jump had sobered him up. And it was miraculous. You just don't jump between boats, especially in a storm. The fact that Arni made it, while drunk to boot, could have caused a skeptic to embrace the divine.

Steve had thrown him in a bunk on the *Spear* to sleep off the booze, putting Valdi in charge of the *Whoopee*. Valdi was an "all-purpose guy," who spent years with the Sigurdsons. There wasn't much he couldn't do, from fixing motors to running the stores to keeping books. But I doubt he ever bargained on rescuing this flying wonder in the night. Arni had awoken, seen someone else in charge, and infuriated at the presence of another man behind the wheel of his boat, made the mighty leap. With it, he leapt forever into the folklore of the lake.

Arni was going home, back to Catfish. He had been discharged from the sanatorium, and just as I had driven him south a few years before, I was now tasked to drive him north, We arrived at the "End of the Road" where Steve and SR were waiting for us to make the trip north to Berens River aboard a small fish freighter, the MS *Kathy*.

Arni was an engaging conversationalist. His particular brand of wisdom and the stories of his agonies made our drive pass quickly. The MS *Kathy* was waiting for us when we arrived—Steve was always on time. It was an awkward boat for Arni to climb onto, thanks to the stiff leg he developed from his bout of TB, but we managed to manoeuvre him aboard into the wheelhouse and throw his bags into the front hold.

Steve took us out from the dock. There was a brisk breeze, but it wasn't a heavy sea. Arni lay down in a bunk in the small living quarters behind the wheelhouse. Standing on a rolling boat with that stiff leg wasn't easy for him. An hour out of Berens, he called out to ask if I would bring him one of his bags from the hold; he had pills he needed to take. I delivered the bag and went back to the wheelhouse. Arni wanted to join us there, so we helped him up. Soon he was into one of his rambling conversations, but SR wasn't in a talkative mood and Steve had little patience with Arni at the best of times. He always told me that Arni, like Dori, was my "Dad's man." Arni was aware of Steve's sentiments, and had considerable sympathy for them. He knew Dad was his ally in the family, and, through Dad, he presumed, so was I. So Arni focused his patter at me.

I listened more intensely as I noticed he was starting to slur his words. We were now within minutes of landing, and Arni was not only slurring but was becoming increasingly indecipherable. SR grimaced at him disgustedly, and then at me. I knew what he was thinking: Arni was hammered. Steve put it to me straight: "What the hell did you do? He must have had booze in that bag you gave him. He's dead drunk. You deal with him when we land." SR had gone from grumpy to full-on angry. Arni babbled on, increasingly oblivious, and a sense of dread settled over me.

I jumped onto the dock as we approached, and SR threw a line my way. No one was at the camp—we were there to open the station for the summer. Our first task was to unload Arni, which was now even more complicated, because to his tricky leg had been added what appeared to be a major drunk. High water complicated matters further, because it meant a drop from the boat down to the dock. We just about had Arni on land when he slipped out of Steve's and my grasp and lurched into the arms of SR (who had his own bad knee), almost knocking him to the ground. To say that words were used that cannot be restated here needs no mention other than to suggest that you allow your imagination no bounds. The upshot was soon declared. I was in charge of Arni, and I better do whatever it took to get him into a bunk and out of the goddamn way.

Arni was now wobbling lopsidedly, and I was becoming more alarmed. I was baffled at how he got hammered so quickly, no matter what he'd got his nose into on that boat. I grabbed him from behind with my arms locked under his and began to push him awkwardly up the ramp, tilting from side to side as we inched upward to the small store at the top. SR had opened the door to reveal the double-decker bunk at the rear. My mission was to get Arni onto that bunk, unfortunately just a bare spring with no mattress. First, I had to get him through the door. SR came to help, and I could see that he was alarmed now, too. I wiggled Arni across to the bunk. That achievement brought momentary relief, until I noticed he'd lost control of his bladder and his pants were soaking wet. I took hold of him face to face, and with an intensity that finally seemed to penetrate his fog, demanded to know what the hell he drank on that boat. Through glazed eyes and a frozen tongue, he blurted out, "It must be those pills I took. I must have taken the wrong ones together."

"What kind of pills? Where are they?" I ran to grab his bag and find the bottle. It contained every colour and description of pill imaginable, all mixed together. "Which ones did you take?"

"I must have taken the heart pills and...." He mumbled another type of pill, but I was no longer listening. We had to get him to the hospital. I needed to get Arni moving under his own steam, and quickly, so I told him to start moving his arms back and forth. My words must have awakened some primeval survival instinct in Arni, because he began flailing his arms with a fury difficult to imagine. (It must be noted that Arni's survival instinct had been called into action many times in his life, but never in quite the same way as that day.) He struck the tin stovepipe on the heater, sending the sections flying across the store. SR reappeared in the doorway, watching the scene with a look alternating between deep pain and complete horror. I yelled out that Arni had taken the wrong pills and that we had to get him back onto the boat and over to the hospital at the Roman Catholic Mission complex across the bay.

Moving him back to the boat was easier, because it was downhill, but the challenge had taken on a new dimension, as Arni continued to flail his arms wildly. Steve's comments were anything but pretty when he heard we needed to go to the hospital, but all I could think of was getting Arni into the hands of the nurses at the mission. The narrow doorway into the wheelhouse was no longer a viable portal for boarding the boat, as Arni's flailing arms had taken on the propulsive power of missiles. Steve nudged the bow into the dock, and we boarded him directly. There Arni and I stood, me with my arms locked under his underarms and a solid grip across his chest, and Arni with his torturously contorted face, his arms still swinging madly as we churned across the bay.

It was twenty minutes before we pulled into the dock and got Arni off the boat. From the path up to the mission I spotted the fulsome personage of Mother Superior peer through her office window and then disappear from view. Mother Superior knew Arni well. He had "rested up" there after many a Berens River "tear." By the time I dragged Arni up to the back door, she was there with a surprising greeting even for a hospital. She was clutching what looked like a foot-long hypodermic needle. Before Arni had placed a foot onto the porch he had his first injection, and then two more in quick succession as we tottered into the hospital.

"That will settle him down in a hurry," said Mother Superior. "I don't want him causing trouble like the last time. We have a full hospital of sick people here. I could see that she was firmly seized by assumptions she had made as she witnessed us disembarking and coming up the path. Finally, I was able to get a word in and explain about the pills.

The chaos was soon to be history, as the flailing stopped, the eyes shut, and Arni was rolled down the hall on a stretcher. He didn't awake for two days, and I was sincerely concerned that he might be on his way out. I was there shortly after he finally came around. He was trying to piece together what had happened, and with the ironical innocence that Arni had long mastered, he asked, "Why are my arms so goddamn sore?"

CHAPTER TWELVE

Remember the *JR Spear*

The *Suzanee* went down in 1967. She was about the same length as the *Spear*, but squat and flat-bottomed. When she rode down a wave in a big head sea, it gave you the same feeling in your stomach as on the elevator in the Eaton's store in Winnipeg as it lurched downward. The *Suzanee* was headed north, loaded with supplies. A yawl was lodged across her main deck. It was longer than could be accommodated within the confines of the boat, and so it protruded through the open hatch on the main deck. The *Spear* met her going south and attempted to radio with news of heavy seas ahead, but she didn't hear the transmission. One hour later she was on her side, and then down to the bottom. The captain had made the fatal error of attempting to turn the boat in the night, and the *Suzanee* was thrown onto her side by a powerful wave, and was no doubt drawn further into a circle of death by the yawl extending out into the water.

Clifford Everett, the mate, was the only man to survive. Seven of his shipmates died. The next season he was mate on the *Spear*. I was impressed that he had the courage to go back on a boat so soon after a terrible trauma. I spoke to him about it in the wheelhouse of the *Spear* one day, riveted to his every word. Clifford told me it was the captain's watch, but he was roused by a heavy sea. He got out of his bunk and pulled his pants on, then pushed open the door of the cabin and made his way up to the wheelhouse. It was blowing like hell. He had just made it inside and pulled the door shut, when the boat lay over on her side. The next thing he remembered was being in the water with the captain, Allan Sveinnson, beside him, hanging onto the detached roof of the wheelhouse. He clung to this makeshift raft for the next eighteen hours before finally washing up on shore at Hecla Island. Allan died in the night, beside him.

I'll never forget my first encounter with the lake's full force. It was around four in the afternoon. Storm clouds were moving in rapidly, and a looming darkness was descending upon our small island at Berens. Dad was on the two-way trying to raise word from the *Spear*, which was on her way north. Several whitefish boats were on course into the station, and they were uppermost on

Dad's mind. There were also men on skiffs. The storm was foreboding in every respect, the sky filled with lightning, and the thunderclaps relentless. But most eerie were the rising wind and descending blackness. I was around twelve, and I was frightened. Dad ordered everyone into the largest building on the island, the cookhouse. I remember waiting with him as the boats started making their way around the close beacon and the final turn into the lee of the island and the safety of the dock. Cecil Goodman, Arni's son (who fought on the same boozy battlegrounds as his dad most of his life), was on the last skiff, and as he pulled into the dock and tossed Dad the line, all fury broke loose, with lashing rain and fearsome winds. The three of us ran to the cookhouse, and were no sooner inside than the dead darkness of a starless night descended and the storm howled, shaking the foundations and showing no sign of relenting for an hour.

That was tame compared to a trip north on the *Spear* with Dad a couple of years later. We were heading from Berens River far north to the station at Spiders, for no particular reason other than it was Dad's practice to visit the other stations from time to time. When we arrived at the three tiny islands, the smallest of which housed the station, a late afternoon wind was blowing hard from the south, so hard that we couldn't pull the tug up to the docks at the station to load the cargo of fish boxes. So we anchored in the lee of the largest island and a smaller freighter carried the boxes over from the station and offloaded them into the hull of the *Spear*. This precarious operation was complete before nightfall, and we were ready to begin the trip south. If anything, it was blowing harder than when we arrived, but that was nothing new in this remote end of Lake Winnipeg.

The wind grew stronger as we made our way south. Dad estimated that it would be hitting 70 knots by the lighthouse at Georges Island, which was our destination four hours, or 40 miles, to the south. The tug was heavily loaded and was having an uncharacteristically difficult time weathering the head sea. This trip was different than any other she had made in over 30 years. The heavy old Fairbanks Morse engine she'd had since Ed Nelson had rebuilt her in Selkirk in 1933 had been taken out the previous winter, and a new GMC Marine diesel installed. It was much smaller and lighter, but more powerful, and the tug could now carry more than 200 additional boxes of fish. They had poured concrete into the hull as ballast to compensate for the redistribution of weight.

What became clear over the course of the night was that the ballast had overweighted her front end. The bow was plunging deep into the water with each wave. The front end of the boat was slowly breaking apart, and the propeller at the stern was lifting clear out of the water and running free with an eerie whir. It was going to be a difficult night.

Dad installed me in a bunk on the upper deck with strict instructions not to leave the room. He had never given me directions that firm and final on the lake before. I lay on the top bunk and looked out the window at the expanse of sea. The swells were enormous, higher than the boat itself. I strained to figure out how I would survive if the boat were to break up in the night. The morose sound of the prop running free haunted me all night. And with the propeller engaged only minimally, the best we could do was to maintain our position throughout the night.

Dad was down below with Mundi Tomasson. The two of them, with the help of the two deckhands, were doing their best to bolster the bow, which was showing increasing signs of stress. They braced and hammered furiously. Twice, Dad came up to my room to tell me everything was all right. It was still heavy going, he said, but with daybreak the winds should ease; there were signs of the barometer starting to rise. I was still frightened, but I had absolute confidence that as long as Dad was on the boat we would never go to the bottom.

Mundi usually looked glum. He seldom laughed. He was a serious man in a serious job. But having a serious man about wasn't a bad thing, and others knew that. He was a careful man, hesitant to take risks. He was a thinking man. Mundi Tomasson had spent his life on Lake Winnipeg, and he understood the lake as well as anyone. He never took it for granted. And on the open water you depended on him every minute to keep those engines turning, and get them going again when they stopped. When you saw Mundi looking glummer than usual, you knew there was big trouble. Dad and he had spent many years together; each trusted and relied upon the other. Up in my bunk, I never had the slightest suspicion that a storm could get the best of them.

That night, as on many others, the lake finally spent her fury. With daybreak came a let-up in the winds. Georges should have been only four hours to the south, but after six hours we were still two hours away. As we moved south we increasingly came into the lee of the island, and our speed continued to increase. Finally we were outside Georges.

Lake Winnipeg is not only one of the world's largest inland lakes, but it has an extraordinarily long and intricate shoreline. The men who live around and make their living from the lake know every point and every island. They understand the lake's merciless rampages, when their boats are an uncertain sanctuary at best. It is a complex body of water, where the real skill required is more that of a pilot than a navigator, for the entrances to its harbours are tricky channels that twist their way around menacing reefs both on the open water of the lake and in the rivers, conditions ever changing with the shifting water levels.

While there were many a "real lake man," none exemplified the description better than Dave Sayers. "He knew where every rock was from one end of the lake to the other," as Dad put it. Dave spent a life on the lake, including years with Steve as the mate on the *Spear* in the '40s. Steve in his usual way had given him the nickname "Captain Soccer" for reasons no doubt connected in some way to his passion for soccer. The task at hand was to take the hapless *Phyllis Williams*, the Abitibi Pulp and Paper Company steamer, from its location beside the mill on the Winnipeg River near Pine Falls to dry dock in Selkirk for a major overhaul. Dave was one of the few men who knew the river well enough to undertake this rescue mission, so the job went to Sigurdson Fisheries and the *JR Spear*. Dave and Steve, with Dad aboard to experience the trip, made their way up the river, delicately weaving their way around invisible rocks, guided only by the radar screen of Dave's knowledge of every turn in the river and every landmark along its shores. They strapped the much larger steamer to the *Spear's* side and began the dangerous task of manoeuvring the lopsided and unwieldy coupling of vessels through the precarious journey to the open lake, across the South End, and up the Red River to Selkirk for repairs.

Afi spent the first fifty years of his life on the lake, so he knew it as well as any man. However, to make way for his sons in the company, his focus started to shift from water to mud in the late '40s. Monarch Construction was coming into full swing, and Afi's life increasingly focused on building the company. He was already a man of 50 when he started the serious work of building the company, and soon he was leading a growing army of men and equipment building roads across the province. With dragline roads and drainage in the north and big tractors and highways in the south, Afi was becoming a major player in the growing Manitoba Road Builders Association. In 1955, he won the contract to build the first cloverleaf overpass in Winnipeg—at Highway 75 as it pushed southward to the US border—and the perimeter highway circling the city. Monarch Construction had entered the big leagues. That only whetted Afi's appetite.

By 1962, Monarch was big enough to bid for and win the first contract on the Winnipeg floodway. The first mud moved on the job was thanks to a massive bulldozer with Afi at the controls. Premier Duff Roblin and his young son, along with Dad, Eric and I, watched as he pulled the levers. Only a few of us knew that Afi had spent the last three days practising for what was a momentous day in his career. He was 67 years old. Fifty-nine years before, as an eight-year-old boy in the Big House in Hnausa, he would have been revelling in the excitement as his mom and dad entertained in grand style the young and

204 VIKINGS ON A PRAIRIE OCEAN

energetic Premier Roblin's grandfather, who led the province at the turn of the century. That was not a memory Afi shared, but I have no doubt that his mom and dad were alive in his mind on the bulldozer that day. There is equally little doubt that had my great-grandfather Stefan—always alive to an opportunity for "putting on the style"—been alive, a celebration no less grand would have capped that momentous day on the future floodway.

The next seven years of Afi's life he travelled up and down that floodway day in and day out as Monarch construction completed four more contracts. Amma was beside him throughout it all, making a home in a mobile trailer at one job site after another, or sitting patiently in the waiting room of the Marlborough Hotel for him to pick her up. I was in university those years, and I knew that if I wanted to see them for a visit, I could find her in the waiting room of that once grand landmark, then only so slightly losing its lustre after many decades of grandeur. Most weekends, they would be back in Riverton. Sometimes Amma stayed at home for a week, but usually she was right back in the car beside him the next.

Afi had brought a younger generation of the family into the fold—his sons Ralph and Gordon, and SR's son Johnny. Tragedy struck early. Ralph died in a head-on collision coming home from building a highway near Dauphin. It almost killed Afi. I can still hear him crying in the church. He was out of commission for months with grief.

A few years later, just a high school kid in Grade Eleven, I joined the Monarch men, along with many other young guys in town taking their first summer job. It paid "big money" compared to any other summer jobs. The two weeks preceding my entry into that world was fast-paced. I turned 16 on June 14, and hurried down to the local garage-keeper Gudjon Johnson to get my driver's license. Gudjon was standing by the wide-open doors of his garage on Main Street.

"Gudjon," I said as I approached, "I came to get my license. I am 16 today."

"I've seen you driving down the street," he replied. "You seem to be a pretty good driver." I'd been driving intermittently around town for months. To my surprise, Gudjon revealed himself to be more observant than expected. The only things I assumed he looked at were the undersides of cars, and wrenches and bolts.

He sauntered into the garage to get his "driver license book," and propping it on one of the garage doors, wrote out my license with his big greasy hands, carbon paper recording the official record for the licensing authority in Winnipeg. He gave me my license and off I went. That was my first and last driver's test.

In ten days, Dad sent me on my first driving job. A Model B tractor, the same model that witnessed my infamous burned-mitts trip years before, had to be taken north to Catfish Creek to perform daily hauls of fish guts into the bush. They had become a bear attraction for miles around. I drove the tractor the first 15 miles to the ferry landing, where I took the next ferry to the island and then started the final ten miles to Gull Harbour. I was travelling on a narrow gravel road built by draglines. Gravel and dust were flying up from the tracks, and suddenly a speeding truck drowned me in an avalanche of gravel. One tractor track went off the side of the road, dropping two feet to a berm running alongside, with the deep ditch below. I grabbed for the hand throttle, but lurching about made it impossible to grasp. Suddenly, the tractor rose up, pivoting on the idler arm that extended the track out. I was unable to leap from the tractor as it toppled sideways. It did a complete flip and landed right-side-up on the bottom of the ditch with the motor still running and a terrified me in the seat. Escaping serious injury or death that day was nothing short of a miracle.

I walked into Hecla, where my cousins Helgi and Beggi Jones came to my rescue. Once they were satisfied I wasn't hurt, they drove back with me and pulled the tractor out. The muffler was bent, but luckily they were able to straighten it. I was very uneasy about climbing back on the tractor. Helgi urged me on.

"You better get back on that tractor and drive it the rest of the way," he coaxed. "It's the only way you'll put this behind you. It will be harder to do so later. It's like falling off a horse."

I reluctantly settled into the seat and ever so carefully drove the tractor another ten miles to where the *Spear* was waiting. Uncle Victor was the captain. I told him what had happened. He looked at me, and the tractor. "Are you all right?" I told him I was. As he jumped on the tractor, he turned to me and said, "Don't worry about it. That's bugger all to a big outfit!" He flew down the dock onto the loading ramp, ducked his head at the last moment as he flew through the hatch, and screeched to a halt on the lower deck. The next minute he was on the top deck yelling to the deckhands as he ran into the pilothouse—"Let the spring line go!"—and the next minute likewise with the bowline, and off he steamed.

Over the next week, I completed my Grade Eleven exams. Afi SV called a couple days later. "Glenn, I have a job on a tractor for you. You can start right away. Your first shift will be this Sunday night at seven. You'll be starting on a small tractor pulling a packer. Do you want the job?" I was still feeling the effects of my mishap, but I remembered Helgi's advice and took the job.

That Sunday night I found myself on the Winnipeg floodway job site number one, on St. Anne's road, where the southernmost part of the floodway was to intersect with the Red River. I think Afi wanted me with him. I thought he was just offering me a job, but now I realise it was something deeper. He wanted me for company, to have me as part of his life in ways none of his younger grandchildren could be at that point, because of their age or because they were a long way away. He wanted me to be part of his world.

Dad must have known this, too, judging from his encouragement: "It will be a good experience for you, Glenn." Whenever I was off shift, Afi seemed to appear at an opportune moment, and soon I'd be sitting on the front seat beside him. There wasn't much we didn't talk about, from the roulette game of winning the next "big bid" to keep the cash flowing and pay down the massive equipment debt, to what made people "tick." He taught me that business, and I came to understand him in ways that most boys could never know a grandfather.

My first shift started Sunday night at 7:00 p.m. Freddie Johnson, the foreman, sat beside me on a tiny HD5 Caterpillar and gave me a ten-minute lesson on its operation. The little tractor was dwarfed by a monstrous "sheep-foot packer" attached to it. My job was to pull the packer back and forth, compacting the dike along the ditch as enormous, lumbering earth-moving machines arose from the river being dug below. It was terrifying as they lumbered up in front of and behind me, onto the embankment where they dropped their 24-cubic-foot loads. The tractors circled around at 9:00 p.m. for coffee break, and I made my way over. Back to work, darkness soon descended, and with it my sense of where I was on this ocean of mud in the confusion of headlights punching holes that twisted, turned and tilted in the blackness of the night as the monstrous machines lurched around me. I could still see the bobbing lights of the massive machines, but they were off in the distance now. As midnight and dinner approached, I realized I was lost. The hours that followed were pure terror, as I wandered aimlessly across this massive and alien expanse of mud.

The dark blue hue of dawn was just washing over the horizon. The rumble of machinery and the whine of engines were everywhere in the crisp air. When I saw a truck approaching, I quickly popped the tractor out of gear and scrambled over its tracks. By the time I hit the ground, the foreman was in my face: "Where in the hell have you been all night? I've been looking all over hell's half acre for you. Don't you know where you are?"

After the hours of torment I'd just come through, the only response I could offer was a stunned silence. Freddie soon broke it: "where in the hell have you been? I have been looking for you all night. You're on the Simkin job site, a mile from the Monarch site. Get on that damn tractor, put it in gear, and follow me." So, like a sorry puppy following its mother after a bite on the behind, I clattered along on my tiny Caterpillar behind foreman Freddie's old blue GM one-ton truck. Days of merciless ribbing followed.

I survived the rest of the week. The nightshift ended Saturday at 7:00 a.m., and the next week I'd be on dayshift, starting Monday at 7:00 a.m. I was on my way to becoming an operator. Life in camp was plain and simple, rough and tough. Except for when the job site was shut down due to weather conditions, the roar of equipment was silent only 26 hours each week—from 5:00 p.m. Saturday until 7:00 p.m. Sunday. The shifts lasted 12 hours, starting and ending at 7:00. Time was measured to the beat of the kitchen, serving up to 150 men every day. Dinner came at noon and midnight; supper at 6:00 p.m.; breakfast at 6:00 a.m.; and coffee at 9:30 a.m., 3:15 p.m., 9:15 p.m. and 3:15 a.m.

The food was always good and always too much—bacon and eggs in the morning, pork or roast at dinner, donuts filled with gooey jam, and always coffee. The kitchen trailer was no banquet hall, though. The quarters were tight, and the men ate quickly and talked little. When they did speak, it was more like a screaming match than a conversation. This was long before good ear protection became available, and the unmuffled exhaust pipes of the vehicles, smoking and snarling just feet away from the operators, left most of them deaf, or nearly so, for several hours after a shift. It eventually caused lifetime hearing impairment, as my wife so often informs me today.

The bunkhouse trailers were a cozy eight-by-24 feet and slept eight men on four double bunks. There was no running water and no toilet facilities. The men played a lot of poker, and almost as much cribbage and bridge. There was usually a case of beer somewhere on a bunkhouse floor and never any shortage of Five Star whiskey. When it rained too hard and too long the job had to be shut down and the men, mostly from Riverton and the area, went home.

Teaching me to drive was another of Afi's missions, a baffling prospect to all who knew him. Afi's driving record on highways was impeccable. He logged up to 50,000 miles every year—he lived in his car. The same cannot be said of his record in the city or on the floodway. In the city the incidents resulted in what I like to think of as "character bruises." I've had quite a few myself. On the embankments and dikes of the floodway he prowled by car and foot at all hours of the day and night, he kept every operator on "high alert" with concern they might run over him with the monstrous machines they were driving with limited downward visibility.

Afi's favourite haunt sprang up wherever the tractors circled around like buffalo for coffee breaks. He'd pull up beside the big Cats and join the guys for 15 minutes wanting to know how everything was going. That was a risky place to park. A broad blind spot in the Cats made it impossible for the operators to look down and see anything beside their machine. Reliable sources report that four cars were squashed like pancakes as one swing out on the big D9s grabbing a few inches of metal would stretch it out in seconds and flatten it like a pancake. Exaggeration perhaps, but rumours always start somewhere, so I wouldn't discount anywhere from one to four cars. I can still hear Frankie Vigfusson grumbly at the best of times, hitting his top notes of utter disgust in talking about Afi's wandering about in the dead of night, or Maurice Thompson on the truck to camp for dinner: "Did you see him on the goddamn embankment earlier? I damn near ran over the car, and there he was waving me over to stop." He wanted to know how things were going down in the pit. Jesus Christ, we are going to run over the old man one of these nights."

I'd been on the job only a couple of weeks when Afi and I were in the midst of a driving lesson around the city. I zipped around a corner headlong down a one-way street, cars rushing at us, and Afi calmly said, "Turn into that lane on the left, fast." I did as instructed. "Watch for the traffic and back into the street, and get going the right direction. You have to watch out for one-way streets in the city. This isn't Riverton." We zoomed along.

Then came the second incident. I felt the seat was too far back. Without a thought, I reached down to disengage the seat and move it up, and as I did so I stepped on the brake. I torpedoed into the steering wheel and Afi's face almost imprinted the windshield. The seat slammed back and locked. I was shell-shocked. Afi looked dazed. He pulled himself together and in an only minimally shaken voice said, "Never, never do that again. Now let's get going. We're late." I didn't talk much about these "driving lessons" to the likes of Frankie or Morris, who still cheerfully reminded me whenever the moment was ripe about my first night on the job.

Over the next few years, after Grade Twelve, and in the university years that followed, I spent most of the summer working on the floodway. Whenever I had a few weeks, usually at the end of the summer when fall season was beginning and school was still three weeks away, I would go north with Dad on the lake, and in 1966 spent the full summer on the lake.

Now I was back on the tractors. The work was long and hard, but the money was good. I had long left my little tractor in the dust, and had just climbed onto my D9 Cat, the biggest Caterpillar made at the time. Moments before, we'd all been standing on the back of the foreman's truck bouncing across the embankment and down the dike to where the equipment was parked between shifts. I saw "the Old Man's" car coming toward me. "Old Man" was the affectionate name the 120 Monarch Construction men had given Afi. He was on those job sites in his car at all hours of the day and night, so there was nothing unusual about seeing him first thing this morning. But as soon as he got out of his car, he waved me over. I knew something was wrong, as I jumped off the tracks to the ground.

"Afi, what's wrong?"

"The *Spear* has gone down. We need to go Riverton. Shut the tractor down. We'll leave right now."

"How do you know?"

"There was a news report on the radio."

"Is everyone safe, Afi?"

"I don't know," he responded.

"Where did she go down?"

"I'm not sure, but apparently north of Berens River last night."

"Have you spoken to Dad?"

"The signals are out. I haven't been able to reach anyone."

"Why go to Riverton?"

"I want to see if I can raise your dad," he explained. "The two-way in the office should work, because it's farther north."

Like Afi, I feared the worst. We drove past the camps and the cookhouse, heading down the dirt road to the highway. Afi had driven the highway north to Riverton hundreds of times, but I am sure never with the sense of foreboding he felt that day.

I know that he, like me, was agonized unbearably with the uncertainty of the fate of those on board. And boats become in their own way like people. We give them a name, and a sex. Boats are with us for a very long time. We get to know their quirks. We work to their strengths and protect them from their weaknesses. We depend upon them for survival. They become part of us. The *JR Spear* had been with Afi since 1933, its thumping engines the heartbeat of the family business. For me, too, it was a part of life.

Not a lot was said as we drove along. One of us would say something, and then we'd wander back into our own quiet thoughts. I remember to this day some of the things that were rolling around my mind. Dad flashed into my mind. I could see him in his characteristic walk-run across the granite rock at Berens River, heading to get a vantage point on the lake, not to try to see the *Spear* on the horizon, but rather to listen for the distant thump of the two-cycle Fairbanks Morse engine, the heart and soul of his beloved tug which had been part of him since he was a boy.

"Afi, they're talking about the *Spear*," I said, jabbing my finger toward the radio. "Turn it up."

"The *JR Spear*, owned by Sigurdson Fisheries of Riverton, has apparently gone down north of Berens River with over 20 people aboard. The whereabouts of the fish freighter and the status of those aboard are unknown at this stage. We shall update information as it becomes known."

Afi, like I, was numbed to hear the number of people aboard.

"Why would there be so many people?" he asked.

"Afi, I don't know, but this must be the first trip north and they will be going north to get the stations up and running I expect. It's only May 27."

"That's right," he said softly. "She'll be loaded down with people and equipment to open the station at Spiders."

"When I spoke to Dad last weekend, he said there was still a lot of ice moving in the North End. She could have run into heavy ice. The weather was a lot better in Winnipeg. It's changing the farther north we go."

"Who is running the boat this summer?"

"Erland Settee is the captain, I believe."

"If this is the first trip north, Victor will be aboard as well."

"Probably, but I don't know."

Afi stopped the truck in front of the office in Riverton, and we rushed inside. Everyone connected with the operation had gone north, so there was no one around. Soon Afi was fumbling with the knobs on the two-way and shouting into the speaker:

"This is Riverton calling Berens River. Do you read me? This is Riverton calling Berens River. Do you read me?"

The signals were still out. We were going to have no more information than we had in Winnipeg. I don't think he remembered how to operate it, and it was one of the older phones so neither was I.

"Glenn, jump in the car. We're going north."

"Where are we going, Afi?"

"The signals may be better farther north."

"Nobody has a two-way on the road."

"There may be a tug tied up at the end of the road; they may be in touch and have some information."

The "North Road" was an extension of the family. Monarch Construction had built it with draglines operated by Uncle Grimsi and Leslie Olafson. Today I have that same sense of deep connection as I cross those 60 miles of gravel every summer to the cottage, all the more so because the road is in essentially the same rugged inconsistent condition almost 50 years later. It reached north from Riverton to enable direct access from the Channel area in the middle of the lake to the North Basin, the same North Basin that had drawn Afi's father into the major leagues as a young fisherman.

I thought about Dad, and the agony he must be living through. What Afi and I didn't know at the time was that in addition to the usual crew of ten, there were twelve passengers heading north to man the stations for the June 1 start of the summer season on the North End. Nor did we know that the *Kathy* was travelling beside the *Spear*, or that the winds had apparently reached 70 knots at the Georges light that night. All of these factors would have been in play in Dad's mind, but none greater than the realization that the entire Peterson family was on board. They had been friends and neighbours on the tiny Spider Islands for decades. In such a remote place neighbours have a special meaning, and our families had counted on one another often. The Petersons didn't have their own tug, so their entire operation was on the *Spear*.

Dad had often spoken of the haunting call he had received one morning in 1957, and I knew that same thought would be alive in his mind. That day, he had turned on the short-wave and heard the eerie words, "This is the last call of the *JR Spear*. This is the last call of the *JR Spear*." Where was she? That's all there was, just those eerie words. And each time, "Berens to the *Spear*, do you read me?" No answer was forthcoming. The boat was floundering on its side, and the receiving switch must have been turned off in the panic. She was only transmitting. Mercifully, the *Spear* survived that night. She washed aground on the one lonely sand beach along the rocky shoreline of Humbug Bay, just north of where the *Suzanee* went to the bottom 10 years later. Everybody made it safely to shore.

Seven years later she hit ground again, this time going into Catfish Creek, 20 miles south of Berens River on the east side of the lake. Navigating the tight turns on the buoys going in on the ranges to Catfish was no small feat. In a big blow, there was no forgiveness. After she struck, she was able to carry on and reach harbour. My uncle Steve managed to plug the hull with mattresses and planking to get her seaworthy the next day, and he got her to the Selkirk dry docks under her own power.

I could hear in my mind's eye Dad calling desperately. "Berens River to the *JR Spear*. Do you read me? Berens River to the *JR Spear*! Do you read me? Berens River to Georges. Do you read me?"

Finally we reached the end of the road. The boats Afi thought might be tied up to wait out the storm were not to be seen.

"What now, Afi?"

I expected him to say that we'd need to go back to Riverton.

"Let's call over to the island to see if we can get them to send a skiff to take us across."

"Why would we do that, Afi?"

"Bill Bennett must have a two-way. Given how far north we are, the signals may be stronger."

He wasted no time, when he spotted telephone in the little box at the end of the dock which connected to the island. Almost immediately we could see a skiff making its way across from the island, rearing up one minute and out of sight behind a wave the next. Every so often, the boat cut through the top of the frothing snowcap, the spray arcing alongside. Slowly, the man sitting by the engine came into sight, his green rubber oilers covered in a slippery sheen from the spray. The only wind that the mile crossing from the island to the mainland was not protected from was the blow from the northeast, and that was exactly what was powering the lake that day. The trip back was going to be rough and wet. Thankfully, we didn't need to go out into the main channel. There the lake would be a white froth.

It was a dull and grey day, the sky ragged and dirty. Even so, the fresh air and mist blowing from the lake felt good after three hours on a dusty gravel road. There was no one in sight along the shale-covered shoreline. The fish station on the adjacent property was dead quiet; fishing season was still a few days away. There were a number of cars and trucks parked behind us, waiting patiently for their owners to return. That might be in a few hours or some weeks. Most of the drivers would be over on the island. The rest had left their vehicles when they went north to the fishing stations to prepare for the season. This was the End of the Road, and from here the only way beyond was by boat or air.

We could see the skiff coming into sight, as it crashed through the waves sending an arching spray to either side. We were at the end of the dock as it pulled into the lee side of the harbour, and the man clad in a green rubber outfit called out over the roar of the engine "Do you have oilers with you?" It had been a long time since the old man had had a pair of fisherman's oilers on, much less had them in his car.

"It's going to be a wet one. Let's get the two of you wrapped up in this tarp," the man hollered over the snarling engine. My grandfather was strong, and in good health, but he was 73, and it had been some years since he'd regularly crawled in and out of boats. He was now used to a flat and dusty workplace, not the wet and rolling scene of the previous generations. I made sure he got onto the boat first. Soon we sat crunched together on the plank seat, our backs to the front. The captain shoved a torn and dirty old oiler into Afi's hands as we roared away from the dock.

The ride was rough, as expected. But the fury of the storm had passed. Now it was just a steady blow and a dreary day, the kind of day when fishermen sat on the dock talking and waiting for the sea to die down. Our makeshift protection did little to protect us from the spray, but soon the docks and houses along the two miles of shoreline on the south side of the island came into clearer view. The captain throttled the motor up as we moved within the protective embrace of the land ahead, and we sped into the small government harbour and pulled up along the wharf.

Minutes later, soaking wet, we were at Bill Bennett's doorstep, soaking wet,

"It's good to see you, Siggi! It's been a long time since you've been on the island. I wish the circumstance were better for your visit."

"It sure is Bill. Have you heard anything from up north?" Afi wasted no time. Afi had heard terrible news many times in his life, and it was natural for him to fear the worst. Afi feared the lake as much as he loved it.

Afi and I sat with Bill and his wife to wait. Bill, with his distinctive island accent, was such an engaging man that even in that very difficult time he made the situation seem easier.

"Not yet Siggi. The damn signals have been out for almost two days now. It's been blowing steady and hard from the northeast. You can hardly make anything out over the two-way. I think I heard Steve talking to Stefan a while ago, but I couldn't make it out."

"Where's Steve?" Afi asked me.

"Afi, I'm not sure."

"Let's try again," Bill offered."I think Steve is in Georges."

Afi struggled to follow the conversation, but I could see his mind was elsewhere.

Bill finally heard Dad's call through the static. Bill got on the two-way, and within minutes we were in radio contact with Berens River, forty miles north.

"Matheson Island to Berens Island. Do you read me?"

"Roger, roger, reading you loud and clear." Suddenly Dad's voice boomed into the room.

"Stefan, Siggi and Glenn are here with me. Any news on the tug yet?"

"The *Kathy* had been travelling with her, and has just got into Georges. Everybody is aboard her, and safe."

"What about the tug?"

"She's on the bottom. She broke apart in the night on the Poplar Reefs. There's nothing left of her. But everybody got off."

Relief flooded Afi's face. With this news we were soon on our way back to Winnipeg. He was a different man on the return trip. Everyone had survived— the 22 people aboard had miraculously been transferred from the sinking vessel to the *Kathy*.

Talk came more readily as we returned south. Afi often seem preoccupied and he had every reason to be. He had found himself on a treadmill of having to winning more bids to support more equipment needing more financing. The competititve bidding process was nerve racking. As a result of a last minute decision to lower the price on the last tender, he was way below the next bidder—"$400,00 left on the table"—very big money on a contract of just over one million. And the job was proving unexpectedly difficult, requiring the big cats to run day and night in frigid conditions through the winter.

As we made our way down the highway, he suddenly asked, "What do you see ahead of you?"

I thought the question curious to say the least. I answered, "The road, Afi."

"What else?"

Now I was becoming bewildered. "The lines in the middle."

"What else?" he persisted.

Now I was getting frustrated. "The shoulder and the ditches?"

"What else?

I barked out, "The fields with grain!"

"You missed the most important thing," he said.

"What is that?"

"The poles. The hydro poles." I looked carefully at the poles, little more than a blur as we zipped by.

"If you have to take the ditch, that's one thing. It's avoiding the poles that's everything."

That lesson has stuck with me. There's an elemental truth there that has applied in so many ways, and in hindsight I realize that it applied that day, too. The poles had been avoided, but only by the narrowest of margins. It was the courageous seamanship of the captain, Jones Everett from Berens River (later to captain the *Goldfield*), and the crew of the *Kathy*, that had saved the lives of everyone aboard. They had threaded their way through the perilous reefs on which the *Spear* had become impaled, positioned themselves in the lee, and miraculously evacuated everyone to safety. Had the *Spear* been alone that night, as she usually would have been but for this being the first trip north, everyone almost surely would have been lost.

Afi's head was always "busy." He wasn't the kind of person who felt uneasy with dead airtime, nor was my dad for that matter. Afi always had a bag of peppermints in the car. Often it was after offering me a peppermint that he said something. He thought deeply—I know that from our surprising conversations. It may even have been on that trip when he suddenly asked me: "What do you think are the most powerful human emotions?" I remember answering "Love and hate." He pushed on. I added "Pride." He agreed. "What else?" I struggled. He answered for me: "Jealousy."

That conversation has taken on different meanings for me over the years. At the time, I took it as a personal reflection on Afi's own encounters with jealousy over the years, but I understand our discussion differently these many years later. What he was telling me was the importance of being my own person and not being pulled down by what other people said or thought. This is not to suggest that he was in any way detached from others, or indifferent to their circumstances. It was quite the contrary. He could stand in the shoes of others. He cared for people in every sense of the word. He had a big heart. He was, I think, much like his father in those respects. All the men who worked with him were unfailingly loyal to him. He was an emotional man, not afraid to cry. Often when speaking publicly his voice would break, he would struggle through a pause, and his voice would come out higher on the other side.

While Afi and I made our way back, there was already a plane in the air bringing the Peterson family back to Riverton where they would soon be having coffee with Mom before returning home to Gimli.

How had she gone so far off course? The night was rugged, to be sure, and the winds were gale force. The area was perilous, as the reefs there project well out into the lake, and the standard course was to keep three miles outside them. All of these could have been contributing factors, but it is perhaps Clifford Stevens, who captained the *Spear* when I was making my trips as a boy, who unlocks the mystery. In his article, "A Rugged East Shore,"[58] he explained how he was suspicious of his compass one night a decade before the *Spear* sank, as he was taking her southbound from Spider Islands. He sensed that the *Spear* was pulling to the right, and his instinct was confirmed a few hours later when a course correction needed to be made, prompted by his mate advising him that he couldn't see the light at Big Georges when expected. The reason was discovered the next morning. A magnet in the engine of the lighting plant on the main deck below the wheelhouse was affecting the compass. Captain Stevens reckons this could be the key to unlocking the riddle of the sinking of the *JR Spear*. She was heavily loaded with supplies and equipment, including lighting plants. These were always stored on the starboard side of the boats, and would have pulled her off course to the east. The *Kathy* would have simply tracked the running lights on the tug ahead. And the weather was far too heavy that night to have ever expected to spot the light at Big Georges.

The *JR Spear* went to the bottom, but parts of her soon rose from the depths. The divers were able to retrieve her new marine diesel engine. Years later, in 1977, Dad received a letter explaining that the lifeboat had been found intact on the shore of Reindeer Island. But it was through Solli's lyrics in "Remember the *JR Spear*," from the "Lake Winnipeg Fishermen" album he wrote and performed, that her soul was reborn. He tells the passion of her story on the back of the album:

> The *JR Spear* was much like any other boat on Lake Winnipeg except it was more of a family boat than any other. But like people boats take on personalities and the sinking becomes all the harder to take. It would be impossible to name all the people associated with her. The few mentioned are outstanding. There are thousands of people I don't even know who will remember the *Spear*, fishermen, the tourist passengers, Berens River Indians, lighthouse keepers, fishermen's wives and families, but especially the "boys who ran her" will "remember the *JR Spear*."

Solli had been one of those boys, a deckhand wheelsman throwing fish boxes into the hold and hanging onto the *Spear's* great wheel. He felt her loss as he would the loss of a member of the family, which she was. Singing was definitely not a talent bestowed upon me, but my relationship with Solli ran deep. He babysat me when I was little, and in my formative years he was like an older brother. We spent many hours together, including driving non-stop from Winnipeg to the Miramichi River in New Brunswick and back to attend one of the original Maritime folk festivals of that era, with the endless tales of drama in the woods or on the sea sung by folks no less character than the gang from Lake Winnipeg.

Nothing galvanized the crowds at the Riverton Hootenannies like Solli's renditions from the album. His first song was "Black Bear," which he wrote to capture the essence of the fish station where his Dad (Steve) had spent so much of his life. The last two lines say it all: "When it comes one more season, they won't need a reason / To pack up their duds to fish at Black Bear." But the pièce de résistance was always the story of the *Spear*, which Solli would bridge into with the equally compelling story of the sinking of the *Suzanee*. This refrain from the *Spear* song captures its heart: "A mighty water Lake Winnipeg to some a lifelong friend / But do not take her for granted, or this shall be your end."

The cover of the album speaks to the story. There, kneeling on the deck of his whitefish boat, is Afi Malli, his long-time companion Roy Mason beside him, in a photo attributed to my brother Eric. In his opening note, Brian Oleson describes the songs as capturing "the joys and tragedies" of the people of the lake. Fittingly, the album was recorded in 1970, during Manitoba's centennial year, a province whose history has been greatly shaped by the people of Lake Winnipeg.

The album is deeply nostalgic, and there's a great joy in reliving those times through songs coming so deeply from within the heart of a man. Solli was Sigurdur's grandson, the son of Steve, who was born to Sigurdur in his 70s. Sigurdur's frisky genetic coda so late in life turned the family's generational rhythm from a quiet melody into jazz, and I have little doubt that had he been alive at 133 years of age, as he would have been in 1970, he would have stood proudly in the Hootenanny audience watching his grandson perform.

CHAPTER THIRTEEN

"How Do You Make Change Work for You?"

The winds of change blew hard as I grew from a boy to a man. The comings and goings of Lake Winnipeg fish have always been mysterious. "Cycles" was a word you heard often. (As early as 1887, Stefan wrote about fish cycles in *Heimskringla*.) By the '50s and '60s, filling a whitefish limit of 20,000 pounds in the North Basin would take up to two months, using around six miles of nets, and to preserve freshness in the warm summer waters they had to be set and lifted each day, gruelling work from 4:00 a.m. into the evening. Theories about cycles abounded and stimulated endless talk on the dock.

The fact was that there was a simple answer: too many boats chasing too few fish, and immature fish, worth too little money, with too many companies supporting the fishery and competing to buy its catch to sell in the US markets. The lake couldn't withstand such a harvest. To be sure, pockets of fish emerged. Some fishermen were more adroit than others at finding them, by savvy or by luck, and that only fuelled the endless hope that next year would be different. All too often the fishermen were pawns, working at the margin of self-sufficiency and forced to return their boats, nets and equipment to the company each year because the returns had been insufficient to meet their expenses. The next year they'd begin over, cap in hand back to the company to finance for yet another season the gear it would take to get back on the lake and a cash advance to leave with their wives and kids. It was a brutal system. Everybody knew it, companies and fishermen alike. No one liked it.

By 1957, times were sufficiently tough that Sigurdson Fisheries, upon the announcement that Great Slave Lake was being opened for commercial fishing, saw an opportunity. Exploratory trips followed. All signs pointed to Dad heading up the operation and moving the family to Hay River. Mom strenuously resisted. The decision was taken to send eight whitefish boats north. They decided to "test the waters" with Victor going north to do double duty as a captain on a Mackenzie River tug while keeping an eye on the operation.

Afi Malli made the decision to go, and his boat the *Elaine* (named after my sister, built in 1950, the last wooden boat built on Lake Winnipeg) went with him. After a couple of years, the pull of Lake Winnipeg was too great. He returned home without the *Elaine*. Many others did likewise, but a substantial number of Lake Winnipeg fishermen moved north or made the long bus trip back and forth each summer. The Sig Fish partners were too deeply rooted in Lake Winnipeg, as were their many other business offshoots, so they decided not to pursue these operations. In the early '70s I was in Yellowknife and learned that the *Elaine* and most of the other boats the Sigurdsons had sent north were now in service on Lake Athabasca.

Fishing continued to be very difficult on Lake Winnipeg. The temptation to put small-mesh nets in the water to ensure production sufficient to cover operating expenses and eke out a meagre living was becoming irresistible. Finding fish was not enough; dodging fish inspectors was the new challenge to survival. And, a few years later, W.D. (Bill) Valgardson would dip into these waters with a famous short story "God is not a Fish Inspector."

Then came high water in the early '60s, which threatened the stations. The Catfish Creek icehouse was in the greatest peril, and if the icehouse was out of commission, so would fishing be that fall. Dad called Harrison Boulanger in Berens River and asked him to help assemble a crew of ten men to sandbag the station. Harrison was one of those remarkable fishermen who disproved that fishing was all about luck, for he was always the top boat day in day out, year after year. Dad respected him. They were close friends, and Dad missed him deeply when he died prematurely. But that was years later, long after Dad and I left for Catfish and met up with Harrison and the gang. We worked from daylight to dusk for two weeks, inundated by black flies drawn to the hot black plastic with which we wrapped the buildings before piling sandbags along the walls. Upon arrival, Dad advised that my duties had also expanded to camp cook. I was 15.

The government concluded that using more selective gear than gillnets might be part of the answer to the low stocks. They encouraged the use of trap nets. Only the big operators were able to buy these expensive nets and refit boats to handle them. The leads to the boxlike traps were extended out onto the shallow shorelines where the pickerel swam, redirecting spawning fish into the traps. The nets worked brilliantly—enormous harvests of pickerel were achieved. But they worked too brilliantly. Even those at the receiving end of the bounty, like Sig Fish, who had three trap net boats, were alarmed at the possibility they would "fish the lake out." They and the specially outfitted boats were soon taken out of commission and "parked."

Other changes were occurring. The Indian people were mobilizing politically and becoming more vocal players within the province and the country. In the early '60s, the Manitoba Indian Brotherhood was formed. From those roots arose many great Aboriginal leaders, several of whom I am privileged to count among my long and good friends. Mom and Dad were invited to one of the founding Brotherhood events as guests. Native communities along the lake were pressuring for expansion of their stake in the fishery as a foundation for their economies. There was growing recognition within government of the importance of integrating the people of the isolated settlements of the north into the economy, and those on Lake Winnipeg much more directly and fully into the fishing industry. This was part of the community development movement that began in Manitoba in the mid-1950s, and would be given expression with the rise of co-operatives in the 1960s.

Governments responded to these larger forces taking shape, with implications for the companies and regulators of Lake Winnipeg. Berens River had been restricted to the summer season. No fall fishing was allowed north of Catfish Creek. For some years Sig Fish had been pushing to have the fishing line moved northward for the summer and fall seasons. Berens River had operated as a summer station for some years, but having stations in action at both of the most northerly locations in the fall would be an important strategic advantage. This would also eliminate the challenging and dangerous trip for men anxious to go back and forth to the settlement to see their families during the heavy fall blows.

Sig Fish had deep connections with the Berens River community. Dad, like his father and grandfather, knew everyone—their parents, their grandparents, their kids and grandkids. He worked closely with Chief Willie Swain to secure the regulatory change. In the early '60s, the Berens station was opened for both seasons, to be fished exclusively by community members. Similar community-based fisheries, open exclusively for area residents, were established at other locations. Several fishermen in Berens River established a co-op, which began operating out of Cubby Jacobson's old station on the mainland across from Sigurdson Island.

The challenges plaguing the industry in those years hit on other fronts as well. Markets were controlled by a limited number of buyers in Chicago and New York. They controlled the price, and the demand/supply equation was tipped all the more heavily in their favour by the perishable nature of the product. If not sold fresh, every day the fish spent in cold storage reduced the quality and increased the cost of carrying the inventory. After six months the fish was worth essentially nothing. There was talk in the early '60s of a "syndicate" buying everyone out. Who the so-called "syndicate" members were remained a mystery as best as I can recall. There were a variety of reports and recommendations made, and other freshwater lakes were subject to similar forces.

In 1969, after years of lobbying and a Royal Commission under George McIvor, Ottawa acted with legislation to create the Freshwater Fish Marketing Corporation with responsibility for controlling the marketing of all freshwater fish in the interior of Canada. The Sigurdsons found themselves in a different position than most of the other companies as these developments took shape. Their culture and allegiance had always remained closely tied to the lake and the fishermen, relying on their long alliance with Booth Fisheries for marketing. They were lake men first; marketing was a distant second. Most of the other companies on the lake made their money selling fish, not producing it, so the advent of a governmental marketing corporation eliminated their core business. Not so for Sigurdson Fisheries. They were the one major company on the lake prepared to continue as production agents for the corporation.

The provincial authorities stepped in with limited compensation for stations and equipment made "redundant." No compensation would be made for the loss of the good will. Many of the fish companies were not unhappy with the prospect of exiting the fishery, but not without compensation for the loss of their business

For Sig Fish, the loss of the *Spear* had represented another challenge, but an unexpected solution was around the corner. BC Packers left the lake like all the other companies, and their freighter, the *Goldfield*, was for sale. Sig Fish acted quickly. The summer season of 1969 was grim, but there was one positive and surprising mid-summer development. For reasons that remain unknowable, the North End suddenly surged with small whites. Sensing a glimmer of hope ahead, but worried that these small fish could also fall victim to fishing zealousness, Dad recognized that tough decisions needed to be made. He visited Winnipeg in late July to urge regulators to shut the season down to give the young fish a chance to grow. Soon after, the season was called to an end.

Then came danger from the most unlikely of sources. I remember Dad's call shortly after I began law school.

"Glenn, you won't believe what the hell has happened now." I could hear anger and alarm in his voice.

"What's going on, Dad?"

"They shut down Lake Winnipeg! Those damn scientists in Ottawa have gone completely crazy."

"What are you talking about?"

"They say there is mercury in the fish, coming from Dryden, Ontario. Nobody can make head or tails over this. I've been called into some meeting at the Freshwater Institute tomorrow, and should find out more then. How in the hell is that stuff in thermometers going to make its way hundreds of miles from Dryden, down the Winnipeg River to the South End of the Lake and 300 more miles to the North End of Lake Winnipeg?"

The results of widespread testing of the entire water basin were soon released. In the North Basin of Lake Winnipeg, more than 800 miles away from Dryden, excessive levels of mercury were detected in the fish populations. The scientists were firm; the threat was real. Lake Winnipeg was closed.

If and when it would reopen, no one knew.

The prospect of the end of fishing on Lake Winnipeg was too much to absorb. My heart fluttered. For Dad, it was his life. He heard the alarm bells ringing in Ottawa as a death bell tolling for Sigurdson Fisheries Ltd., and the four generations of our family in the fish business on Lake Winnipeg. Everything that Afi Malli had ever said about the insidious threat of chemicals took on new meaning. The fact that mercury was an element, not a chemical, was child's play to his thundering rhetoric; he was now assured that the "chemical war" he had long feared had finally begun. But this was a war unlike any other, for you could neither touch nor feel nor smell the enemy, and the battle would be decided in labs and office towers in Ottawa. This was a blow that struck to the heart of our identity.

It would be three years before the lake fully reopened. "Make work" projects were put in place as a condition for qualifying for the minimal compensation. Afi's project was feeding carp at the mouth of the Icelandic River. Each morning he filled his skiff with sacks of barley to drop into the marshes at the river's mouth for these valueless scavengers that destroyed the spawn of other fish. His indignation at government stupidity reached new elevations.

But the long arm of the bureaucracy would lash back and try to take its pound of flesh from the old man. This was the year of Amma and Afi's fiftieth wedding anniversary, and the gift from the family was a trip to Iceland. Tickets were acquired for a June departure before the opening of the season was announced. The first fishing allowed to resume was the summer whitefishery on the North End. The rest of the lake stayed closed. Government regulators were stringent in the requirement that anyone intending to continue fishing after the closure and all the other changes on the lake would have to be on the lake in person, and not by proxy. Afi was told he would lose his license permanently if he weren't personally on the lake. He had no intention of letting that happen. He asked Roy Mason to operate the boat that summer. Roy and he had been together for more than twenty years. Roy would be fishing alongside Oswald and Wally Hudson and their father Bill, each with their own whitefish boats. They, like Roy, were from Fisher River, and had been his travelling partners for many seasons.

High-handed tactics persisted with the old man. Word reached his old friend, and my former teacher, Wally Johanson, now a cabinet minister in the Schreyer government whose spirited years of boarding with Amma and Afi to feed on vigorous debates over statistics and world affairs was still inside him. Through whatever combination of entreaties and threats Wally employed, the situation was resolved and Afi and Amma were off to Iceland and the men from Fisher River he had spent many years with, Roy Mason and Lloyd Sinclair, went to Warren Landing. Roy and the other men from Fisher River were so excited to tell Afi about the outcome of the season that they were waiting for him at the Winnipeg Airport when he returned. After all those years on Lake Winnipeg, Afi Malli missed the season to end all seasons.

Dad went north to run the station at Warren Landing, as Berens remained closed. Mom went north with Dad, just as she had the very first season in Catfish after their marriage, and as she had done so often in her life. She would say today that she wasn't busy at the time, so that was a good place for her to be. I suspect that a deeper reason was to be with Dad, as what lay ahead for the industry was far from clear. The most important question was, "Would there be any fish?" The deeper question was whether circumstances would prove to be a new beginning or a sudden end for Sigurdson Fisheries.

God smiled. God really smiled. Dad's instincts in the summer of 1969 proved prescient. To everyone's utter disbelief, the lake was absolutely full of whitefish. At one point fishing had to be halted because the freighters and the Marketing Board in Winnipeg couldn't keep up with moving and processing the bounty. Mom punctuates this with the story of Philip Orvis, several days late in arriving at the station. Every limit was filled and the operation was ready to close down and head south. Philip was not a popular man, but that would quickly change. He filled his limit in three days. His final lift may have been the largest ever seen on Lake Winnipeg. Mom was on the dock and greeted him when he arrived. Fish were everywhere, flowing over boxes all over the decks, and the boat was nearly sunk. Philip stood on the deck in fish up to his ankles, and as everyone watched with awe, Philip explained as if in a daze: "I always dreamed about going to the nets, and they would be floating with fish, and today it happened, the nets floated with gleaming whitefish like a blanket on the water."

The next year, 1972, the entire lake was reopened for fishing. As agents for Freshwater, Sigurdson Fisheries needed a new facility that could also act as a receiving depot for fish. The classic, original Sig Fish office was demolished and replaced by a long, flat modern building covered in blue tin. The symbol of an era evaporated within a day. The rationalization of the fishery that had been so long in coming had been thrust upon the industry in the form of mercury. Everything had transformed over those years. There were fewer stations on the lake. Eighty whitefish boats had shrunk to 44, and the big *Goldfield* was essentially alone. She would no longer make the long trip to Selkirk. Her terminus point would be the End of the Road, where trucks would take over and travel the 18 hours into Selkirk and the Booth sheds. From there they went to Transcona to a modern plant of a federal corporation operated by a professional management team under the direction of a federally appointed board of directors, with two fishermen representatives. And the fish stocks had returned. Afi Malli's six miles of nets was now down to less than half a mile, and he filled his limit in less than three weeks in the North End that first year after the reopening. The whitefish youngsters had matured and were all over the lake. Pickerel and sauger were also plentiful.

Critical regulatory changes were also made at this time. Licenses were turned into quotas. As opposed to a revocable privilege issued by the Crown, fishermen would now "own" the right to produce a designated "quota," and could buy and sell these quotas, along with their boats, motors and equipment, as an asset. When a headline read, "NDP allows fishermen to sell quotas," it was a first in North America, introduced by the provincial NDP government of Premier Ed Schreyer in 1974. To enter the fishery in the future, fishermen would need to acquire a quota from an existing quota holder, and while the possibility of this changing in the future was not foreclosed, at the time only one person could hold one quota per season. Within a few years that requirement was eliminated and fishermen became free to buy and sell their "quotas."

Alongside this development was another significant institutional innovation. The ability of the Manitoba Agricultural Credit Corporation (MACC) to provide loans was extended to fishermen. Two very able men with a long history as managers in the industry, Siggi Sigurdson and Oli Josephson, lifetime friends of Dad's, were given the responsibility to manage these activities. An important financial tool was fundamental to the lending operations: repayment was to be on the basis of a ten percent check-off arrangement under which the fishermen would repay the loan and the accumulating interest on the basis of their actual production, not on a fixed repayment schedule. Siggi and Oli brought to this task a deep understanding of the industry and knowledge of fishing and fishermen. In their quiet and unassuming manner, they could help with the development of business plans and give sound advice. Dad often said that the single most important factor in ushering in a new era for the Lake Winnipeg fishery was this development and the ability and experience both men brought to the assignment.

Many good years followed for the fishermen of Lake Winnipeg, and Sigurdson Fisheries as the agents of the corporation. Fish was once more abundant, and individual fishermen were able to rely on a consistent return. There were fewer fishermen. The equipment was improved. Prices achieved by the Marketing Board were significantly higher. After receiving a base payment at the conclusion of the season, what became known as "final payments" were made by the Corporation when its final profitability was known, and profits were distributed on a proportionate basis back to the individual fishermen.

Sig Fish, for its part, worked very closely with the Freshwater Fish Marketing Corporation and the MACC. While Sig Fish was referred to as an "agent," the relationship was in fact more complicated, as they bought and sold fish on their own account, at a fixed margin, with full responsibility for all costs of production and transportation. Hence, Sig Fish was at risk for the fish from the moment it went over the company's scales at the stations across Lake Winnipeg until it reached the Freshwater Fish Marketing Corporation (FFMC) in Transcona within Greater Winnipeg. The margin remained constant over the succeeding years, but the costs continued to rise. Communities in several locations wanted to establish more local control by setting up their own operations, often in the form of co-operatives. The production volumes Sig Fish was handling were slowly shrinking, which put further pressure on the viability of the business.

In 1987, the decision was made to sell the operations of Sig Fish to the Freshwater Fish Marketing Corporation (FFMC). Clyde—Victor's oldest son and a partner since 1972, the fourth generation in the business—said, "You've got to think about that history a little bit, but unfortunately history does not pay the bills." Steve and SR had retired some years earlier. My brother Eric, a partner in the business for some years, had left to begin a prominent career in business a decade earlier after completing his MBA. Dad had retired in 1985. An era had ended. Many members of the family, however, continue to have a strong presence on the lake. SR's son Johnny and Victor's son Clyde stayed with the FFMC for several years. Clyde eventually moved on to other employment, but Johnny stayed as the Lake Winnipeg manager until his retirement. Three of SR's grandsons are successful fishermen and Johnny has returned to the lake as a fishermen. Kevin, another of Victor's sons, now owns one of the oldest names on the lake, Leckie Nets and Fishing Supplies, and remains actively engaged both in the business of selling nets across Canada and the production of fish.

It would be impossible to imagine how I could have ever received a greater training for the work that would later shape and define my career than living through the events I have chronicled here. Throughout my career, I have inevitably found myself in the middle of complex dynamics around fisheries management. Invariably, it is fish and their habitats that first bear the brunt of environmental pollution of mines, pulp mills or industrial operations. But the lessons are far more far reaching, for they trigger complex change processes that have profound implications for people, leaving a wake of uncertainty, conflict, realignments and adaptation. Inevitably, people have to come to the realization, as my wise friend Peter Sakich, longstanding Chair of the Commercial Salmon Advisory Board on the West Coast puts it about a fishery that has been facing the headwinds of stock uncertainty and restructuring for two decades "Change is here. You can't change that. What we need to ask each other is 'how can you make change work for you'?"

PART FOUR

SHAPED BY A PRAIRIE OCEAN

CHAPTER FOURTEEN
Beavers to Kilowatts

Engineers had recognized since the 1930s that the waters and rivers of northern Manitoba represented a potential treasure chest of hydro electric power. In the 1960s, their dream would come true. Kilowatts would replace beavers, as Manitoba Hydro became the commanding presence of what was once the exclusive mercantile domain of the Hudson's Bay Company. In the 1960s the province struck a deal with the federal government to construct a transmission line that would carry the power south to service the growing domestic demand with ambitions set on export dollars to be earned in the voracious US markets beyond over the longer term.

Many great rivers of the centre of the continent drain into Lake Winnipeg—from the east, the Winnipeg River carrying a vast flow from northwestern Ontario; from the south deep into the Dakotas, the Red and Assiniboine Rivers; from the west, as far as Edmonton and Calgary, the Saskatchewan as well as a host of other rivers, lesser known but no less significant, such as the Little Black, Bloodvein, Sturgeon, Leif, Poplar, Big Black, Dauphin (connecting Lake Manitoba and Lake Winnipeg), Fisher, and the Icelandic I still call home. Only one river, a goliath, the Nelson, carries this vast liquid cargo to the sea, racing and tumbling over 800 miles, dropping 800 feet to the shores of Hudson Bay. It is much more than a river. It's a complex amalgam of waterways; treacherous channels; long, looping stretches; and lakes. Here is where the dams to generate the power would be built.

A century and a half earlier, the merchants and moneymen of London knew Norway House as the centre of a great mercantile empire, a strategically located trading post on the fur trade route stretching from York Factory on Hudson Bay across Lake Winnipeg and on to Lower Fort Garry on the Red River. Located on Playgreen Lake, part of the Nelson River system that sits like a hat on top of Lake Winnipeg, it was a place unknown to most Manitobans in 1974 when one of the community elders (I remember his name as Harry) and I had the following conversation:

"Glenn, what will happen if we can't stop the project?"

"That's a good question, Harry. The project is already so far advanced that the chances of stopping it now are not good."

"What will happen then?"

"We'll have to go to court and prove damages."

"Damages. Everything is damaged here. Just tell those people in Winnipeg to come here and take a look around."

"Well, maybe at some point we'll need to do that, but we will also need experts to help us explain to the courts in what specific ways this project has affected you."

"Tell them about the land. The best land is finished. The land along the shoreline. That's the land us people up here rely on to travel, to hunt and to trap. I want my land back. Tell those guys that."

"We can't get the shoreline back. Courts can't give land for land. Courts can only turn land into money. Lawyers and judges call that damages."

"They got guys in Winnipeg who know how valuable this land up here is to us people. I never saw those guys up here."

"No, but there are experts called appraisers who are specialists in knowing what land is worth, and we'll need to teach them about the North."

"We can teach those guys that? What about the moss in my nets? They don't fish a damn anymore. Who is going to get rid of the moss?"

"Well the courts can't do that, but they can give money for damages. We'll need some experts in fishing nets to tell how much fewer fish you've caught because of the moss."

"There's guys who know about our nets and moss up here? What kind of guys are those?"

"I'm not sure what they're called. There are experts for everything. I'm sure there must be net experts who can tell us how much fish you would have caught without moss in them. Then we'll probably also need guys called economists to tell us how much money you have lost."

"Those guys have never been around here. I can't see them knowing anything about us people up here, and how we live. Glenn, this is hopeless. We cannot go down there to Winnipeg. Those guys don't know nothing about us people up here. You got to get these people who are doing all this stuff to us up here to talk to us. We have to talk this thing out. That's the only way. We got to tell these people what's going on and find a way to make sure we don't get pushed out of here. This is the only place I know. I'm worried these dams are going to break one day and flood us all out, and if not me, my grandchildren."

Harry is the name I remember him by, but my memory as to his name may have dimmed. Perhaps it was some other common name like William or Kenneth

John all quite common British names. Quite possibly in generations past the blood of a young man from the Hebrides, or an Englishman from York or an Irishman from Galloway had combined with a Cree mother, and his name was now like a tombstone reminding us of his once presence in these lands with these people. Likely had been recruited as a 20-year-old, barely a man but soon to become one, good with numbers and ambitious to run a trading post, with a dream of making his fortune and returning home to enjoy it. Many years later, with thousands of entries in the log book that the Adventures Trading into Hudson Bay required him to fill out daily on the speed and direction of the wind and the number of Indians who had entered the post that day, he came to realize that the land and its people had swallowed him whole. There was no returning home; he was home.

Now my wise friend Harry's world was being turned inside out and he was struggling to understand what was about to come. In writing and teaching I often found myself often returning to this conversation. I have come to realize it was a pivotal moment in shaping my life and work, as it was for Harry each of us in our own way.

Harry had walked this young lawyer into the the University of Real Life with a quiet compelling eloquence that afternoon in Norway House. It would begin to inform what I had taken from many classrooms, not just with the experiences of the lake, but from the many rivers that flow into it, and the one river, the mighty Nelson that carries its waters north to the Hudson Bay, and the people who live along them. Lake Winnipeg was to be lassoed as a "storage basin" for water in the summer and to be deployed for hydro generation in the winter months when southern markets were hungriest for power, in effect a southern extension of the Nelson. Through Harry, and many others like him, I came to know the Cree and be taught by them about the great rivers and lands north of Lake Winnipeg, their way of living, their history on those lands from time immemorial, and the waters they travelled and fished. The Cree became my valued teachers. This was a land of which I knew little, but home to a people with whom I felt at home, a gift from growing up on the lake.

I heard Harry in ways many others would not have. To be sure, I heard him through the ears of a lawyer. To "protect and advance the interests of my clients," my professional charge, I was coming to understand that I would need many more tools than law school had given me. I had a lot to learn. However, the anxiety and bewilderment within Harry's words hit me in a deeper and more sensitive place than it might have for others, for they could have easily been the words of my Afi Malli. Harry on Playgreen Lake, and Afi on the shallow waters of Mossy bay at the far North End of Lake Winnipeg, were separated by only a narrow band of land two miles across. Their worlds, close yet far, were about to become much closer with the construction of a two-mile channel to move the waters more quickly northward to the dams. While Afi and Harry were quietly living out the vision of their lives, another very different vision was taking shape.

Linking their worlds was only one part of Manitoba Hydro's vision. Because it was cheaper to move water to dams than dams to water they set their targets on another mighty river to complete their assembly of huge hydrological playpen. The Churchill River —almost as formidable as the Nelson— tears across the prairies from the foothills, crossing into the Canadian Shield to begin its final plunge to the sea. Midway across Manitoba, the river widens out to form South Indian Lake. At Misi Falls, where the river leaves the lake in its final rush to the ocean, they would construct a mighty dam. Here, the land mass runs in a direction opposite to what nature intended, falling downward from north to south as opposed to the other direction towards sea level on Hudson Bay. The Churchill would be stopped almost dead in its tracks, and diverted southward with the construction of a thirty-mile diversion channel. The Diversion Channel would redirect the water into the Burntwood River and redirect its flow to bring the waters of the Churchill to the dams on the Nelson. A geological accident, and reversing a river would now become a hydro asset.

Enormous controversy surrounded this project, dominated the public consciousness for several years, and distracted attention away from the impacts that would be experienced by the communities along the Nelson. Communities like Norway House, Cross Lake, Split Lake, Nelson House and York Landing. It was not until 1973, when construction was well under way, that these communities, and their fiduciary protector the federal Department of Indian Affairs, became politically alive to the serious potential implications of this development, surprising in hindsight because there were extensive studies underway in those years.

Manitoba Hydro's northern ambitions had first become known to me a decade earlier, with the construction of dams on the Saskatchewan River. These developments had flooded a vast territory and created the third largest body of water in Manitoba, Cedar Lake. The waters had poured over a massive landscape, flooded out two communities, and forced their relocation to a new community known as Easterville. My cousin Solli Sigurdson had been retained to prepare a report on the communitites before they were buried on the bottom of a huge storage basin to be known as Cedar Lake. Solli was around those summers. Often he would respond to a Sig Fish request to deliver something or pick up some fish at the "End of the Road" and I would go with him. Inevitably our conversation would include Solli's struggle to interpret what was happening to these communitites and their likely futures with this monumental disclocation to their lands and lifestyles brought about by this project.It was the lens of our common experience on the lake that grounded our discussions.

My sensibilities had been enlivened in other ways close to home. The Interlake had been designated one of three "poverty areas" targeted by the federal government.This label irked most everyone, especially the Icelanders like my mother and her dad, my afi. We were besieged by social sceintists and consultants studying and planning us—"social engineering" was coming into full swing, and we were the laboratory. But revamping the Interlake was a small pond; there were bigger plans to sort out the prairies. Rail lines were being dismantled. The push to "farm rationalization" was in full force and schools were being consolidated. In Riverton Mom and the ladies were fighting to keep our school and drawing some of us senior students into developing the briefs of war.

Drainage systems to turn wetlands into fields were being planned. These developments clearly left a deep impression. I was startled to discover a long forgotten prize-winning essay reprinted in the *Aurora Borealis*, the 1963 Riverton high school yearbook, this sentence: "...the trend in the world is to large-scale social and economic planning. Through this system people are beginning to rely on the government to solve their problems." The notion of experts telling other people who they were and how to go about living and organizing their lives had already deeply imprinted my young mind.

My journey down the "tracks from Sandy Bar" began in 1964, when I left Riverton for the University of Manitoba. I gravitated to economics. The honours program was almost entirely seminar based with no more than ten students writing and defending at least two lengthy papers each term. It was lead by remarkable teachers and mentors who combined wisdom and rigour. These were the heady emerging days of mathematical economics and econometrics, where the messy world of political and social realities was being washed away with assumptions and equations. Teachers like Clarence Barber and Ruben Simkin were not about to be suctioned whole body into this new paradigm; we were challenged with penetrating questions and thoughtful reflection. I still saw potential for myself in economics. I secured a summer internship with the Dominion Bureau of Statistics, a numbing experience trudging daily into a big office structure called DBS with 3,000 clerical people manually producing the gross national product and other statistics of Canada. A scholarship to McGill the following year proved too seductive to turn down, notwithstanding Clarence's views that there were other programs elsewhere that might suit me better, but then, they were not in Montreal!

But how relevant was what I was learning to the real world? Was I suited to what appeared to be an academic career ahead of me? Montreal was an exciting place, but was this the path I wanted? I asked myself those questions every day as I walked up the hill toward Mount Royal. The answer became clear toward the end of my first term. This was not the career I wanted. I was growing increasingly skeptical of the practicality of what I was studying. I needed to get much closer to the reality of life, to the operational nitty-gritty of how things really worked. I wanted to work with real people and real problems, closer to the gearboxes of life—the machinery through which people did stuff and made things happen. I wouldn't be satisfied just watching and writing about it.

Perhaps, law would take me there. I resigned my fellowship and returned home. My biggest concern wasn't my parents, who gave me the gift of independence at a very early age. The words of my mom amidst our tears after my car was finally loaded to leave for University for the first time have stayed alive in my mind all these years. "Glenn. You are on your own now. Your dad and I cannot be around every day to checkup on what you are doing. Our hope is that what you have learned to this point and are taking with you will be with you every day in helping you make good choices." They questioned and worried, sometimes challenged, but never second-guessed. They understood it was my life, that the only right choices were my choices, and that I had the right to be wrong.

Some of my strong-willed and successful mentors within my extended family were more direct. One such conversation began like this: "You gave up that scholarship. What are you going to do now?"

The words caught in my throat: "I'm hoping to go to law school. I'm applying now."

"What the hell do you want to do that for? Lawyers are just intellectual mechanics."

Larry Kristjanson, a Commissioner of the Canadian Wheat Board, gave me that advice when I visited him and Helen, my cousin, at their cottage in Hnausa one summer afternoon. The only lawyer he had any use for was Henry Monk who was the Wheat Board's lawyer, and had drafted its original legislation. Larry and his five brothers, all with PhDs, several in economics from the University of Wisconsin and already with major careers, were legendary sons of Gimli, with a national profile in Canada's *Time* magazine *Maclean's*. But I wasn't about to be knocked off my perch.

"Larry, if that's what it takes to work in the world and understand it that's what I have to do." And with that I began a vigorous defense of a profession of which I knew little to nothing. But that wasn't something that would have deterred me in those days.

I returned to Winnipeg and sought the guidance and security of my mentors, now friends, Ruben and Clarence. I knew they would help me find a way, and I had a vision to share with them which had been taking shape in my mind. My real interest was economic development, specifically in Canada's northern communities and among their Native populations. If intrusive yet distant meddling could happen in Riverton, I already knew something of what was starting to take place in the North as the new playpen for experts of every kind and description paddling in on theories, not canoes. This was where my passion lay, and that was where I would go. I knew I could count on them to help me find a way to break trail from conventional wisdom, maybe even combine law and economics together when doing so.

They did, introducing me to Dr. Paul Deprez, a young up-and-coming economic demographer from Belgium who had just joined the department. Canada, to say nothing of its indigenous people, was entirely unknown to him. I knew nothing of demography. We introduced each other to our different worlds, and as unlikely a duo as it might seem, we were the perfect blend of energy, and intellect, to work together. We became close friends and collaborators, and had fun on the way. I could always count on Paul for a zany punch from the day I saw him bandaging with great flourish an injured passenger in response to a pilots request on a bush plane in Northern Saskatchewan "is there a Doctor on board?"

Ruben Simkin would continue as my great supporter and mentor. Many Saturday mornings he would have me over to his house at 56 Matheson Avenue in the North End for a visit to review what I was doing and writing, and give me his humble brand of deep wisdom. He was a very wise and human man. Pancreatic cancer would take him suddenly, at a point in which he was preoccupied with "the limits of growth," a prescient pathway in which I have no doubt he would have become recognized as leading thinker.

The focus of Paul and my work at the Centre for Settlement Studies at the University of Manitoba was the role and realtionships of native people and their communities with single-enterprise towns, and relationships in the Canadian North. For the next year and part-time throughout the following three years of law school, and even the year following graduation from Toronto's Osgoode Hall Law School, this was my work, my preoccupation, my passion, and persisted as a theme throughout my career.

I travelled across northern Canada, to places like Fairfort Manitoba where an entirely native crew from the community was assembling the first transmission lines from the northern hydro stations, to a mine in La Ronge, Saskatchewan; to Moose Lake Loggers in Northern Manitoba cutting pulp for the new mill at the Pas, and into the Northwest Territories and the Yukon. I went just about anywhere there were enterprises with significant involvement of the native labour force. What were the opportunities? What were the barriers? What was myth? What was reality? Were people in northern communities being pushed south by poverty or lured by potential? Paul Deprez and I authored our first major publication together in 1969: *The Economic Status of the Canadian Indian: A Re-examination.* Other work and publications followed which took me to the newly opened Cominco (now Teck) lead zinc open pit mine at Pine Point on the south shore of Great Slave Lake in the Northwest Territories, and down the "road"—in those days a roller coaster ride over bumps and ruts—to Fort Resolution and a large logging co-operative that operated there.

The 100-page publication received widespread distribution. When I look through it all those years later I am surprised how deeply many of my values and views were already lodged by the time I was 22. The first chapter is entitled "Cultural Integrity or Economic Development: A Meaningful Dichotomy?" in which we framed hypothetical polarities as a basis in which to set the discussion and our findings on the role of Indian people in economic development—framing at one end a "romantic" imprint, and at the other "an imperialistic," both of which echoed into policy responses. One particular sentence stands out for me these years later:

> The unilateral state of dependency between the Indians and the various groups of government officials must be changed and replaced with a more dynamic sense of Indian involvement in economic and social activities, at the local, provincial, and national levels. Incited to action that all is not well, there is a tendency at various levels of policy making and policy implementation to forget a fundamental principle of human development, namely that no society can impose development upon its members.[i]

But more disturbingly it is a reminder of how long the road has been, and how short the distance we have travelled.

A provincial election was called in the summer of 1969. Edward Schreyer, the youngest ever federal MP at the time, was persuaded to return home to Manitoba to run for the leadership of the provincial New Democratic Party. The environmental movement was first appearing over the horizon. There was a growing controversy over a huge dam being constructed in Northern

Manitoba where the Churchill River continues beyond South Indian Lake to Hudson Bay, and media coverage was moving this issue to centre stage in the election campaign. Schreyer seized the new tempo of the times and energised his campaign on a platform that would have Manitoba Hydro alter its plans from a so-called "high-level" to a "low-level" diversion to minimize impact on this small northern community.

In no small part on the back of this controversy, Schreyer took power from the Walter Weir Conservatives and became the first NDP premier to lead Manitoba. Ironically, from that day forward it seems that young Schreyer's political fate moved in lockstep with the fortunes of Manitoba Hydro. In ways I could never have anticipated, my career would soon veer headlong into both.

On election night I happened to be in Moose Lake, Manitoba, undertaking a case study on Moose Lake Loggers, a local logging operation becoming a success story of local native entrepreneurship. Jock Gibb was a local trader who also ran a store and a guest house, and operated a "muskrat ranch" for his father-in-law Tom Lamb, a charismatic bush pilot and businessman who, with his sons, built up one of the first big bush plane operations in the North. The other house guests were two elderly Jewish gentlemen, salesmen lugging their huge black suitcases of samples, like Dad's buddy Harvey, making their annual sales trip to northern stores. We sat listening intently, sometimes through static drowning the signal. We sat together in the living room listening to the returns on the radio. Sitting ever more stiffly on wooden chairs in the dining room, their furrows deepening across their very bald heads and their eyes bulging with tears, they forecast the rise of the communism and fascism that had driven them from their homes in Europe. Over the course of that emotional night their life stories emerged, including their rescue and two-year refuge in Iceland after the merchant vessel on which they obtained passage was torpedoed.

One afternoon a young Scandinavian-looking man burst into my office at the Centre for Settlement Studies at the University of Manitoba. He grasped a cigarette between his fingers and punched out in very distinct Scandinavian accent:

"Are you Glenn Sigurdson?"

"Yes."

"I am Yngve Georg Litman from Stockholm. I like what you write. I want to talk to you."

I liked him the moment I met him. He had a burning intensity and drove straight to the point. He explained that he was a Swedish graduate student studying social anthropology. He had come to Canada to more fully understand the social and institutional connections between marginalized groups and highly developed societies around them. For his PhD thesis research, he said, "I am going to go and live on a reserve." Now he had my full attention.

I asked why this topic was of interest to a Swedish academic. He explained that Sweden had a growing immigrant population of Turks and Gypsies, and that racial tensions were building. He wanted to understand how Indians on the reserves in Canada related to the communities and society around them.

I asked where he was planning to live. He said he'd been down at the Manitoba Indian Brotherhood (MIB) and had met the then Grand Chief, David Courchene, who had introduced him to a young guy called Phil Fontaine from his home community, known as Fort Alexander. That night I met Phil, his wife Janet, and Yngve's partner Eva. So began a set of lifelong friendships, Yngve, Phil and I collaborated on projects often, punctuated with conversations late into the night. Phil was starting his march down a political track and was back and forth between Fort Alexander and the MIB.

Soon I would be combining my continuing work at the Centre with studying law at Osgood Hall in Toronto. This was the first year of Osgoode's affiliation with York University, and relocated from downtown Toronto (and the jurisdiction of the law society of Upper Canada) to the York Campus. I would spend the next three years there, taught by a strong faculty. The teaching style was Socratic—questions upon questions, framed by an endless series of new facts each drawing out different implications. I came to understand that law was not about memorizing laws and cases, rules and prescriptions. It was about knowing how to ask questions and find information. It was a process of reasoning. Osggode left me with many legacies, but none greater than an extraordinary network of good friends across Canada, which has lasted a lifetime. My real learning was yet to come. That would take place in the demanding early years as a lawyer where I had to learn to transform ideas into tools, and papers into persuasion.

In the summer of 1971, I went home for a few months. Graduation was months ahead but I was already resolved that a big-firm career in Toronto was not for me. I consulted with my cousin Leifur Hallgrimson, QC, then deputy attorney general of Manitoba, always a gentle and caring guide to me, as to his thoughts on an articling position. Leifur knew the place for me —Richardson and Company—where his good friends Scott Wright and Charlie Huband had a very successful practice along with their partners Reeh Taylor, William Norrie and Garth Erickson. One discussion was enough. No more interviews elsewhere. Leifur's judgment was never sounder. The mentoring, the relationships, friendships, became bedrock to my career. Scott, who signed my papers, oozes enthusiasm in all things, and both likes to give, and gives, good advice.

"Don't worry about making money. Worry about being the best lawyer you can, and the money will follow," was among the first of these jewels.

By the time I began a career as a lawyer in Winnipeg, my friend Phil Fontaine was making his first run as Chief. Yngve and I celebrated his victory with him in Fort Alexander, now Sakeeng ("the place where the waters meet") the night he was elected, flanked by his many brothers gushing proud of their young brother "buddy" for whom they saw big things ahead. That night Phil was starting down the road that would see him become the National Chief of Canada, serving for over nine years, and a man of stature across Canada, and internationally. No doubt his older brothers, his greatest boosters, would say that they could see it all ahead then! Soon I became Fort Alexander's lawyer, with one foot still in articles, but under the watchful eye of Garth and Scott as I started to work with what I now realize would have been my very first client!

Not long after, Phil's wife Janet's father, Dr. Ahab Spence, was elected head of the Manitoba Indian Brotherhood (MIB). Ahab was a remarkable man. Ahab as I recall was the first Cree Anglican minister, the developer of Cree syllabics, the first Director of Education within the Department of Indian Affairs and Northern Development, a teacher, and now a politician. Ahab was a tall, distinguished, wise and gentle man. He was good to me. He became my friend. Soon, I found myself working for the MIB, requested to help with rewriting the organization's constitution. I concluded within a month that this would likely be my last assignment for the MIB, for the endless debates and unending wordsmithing that erupted would surely bring about its demise. Somehow, it all came together, the MIB survived, and I endured, "smarter and savvier."

The next phase of my life would take me to the rivers entering and leaving Lake Winnipeg. One of my early assignments at Fort Alexander was to investigate any possible connection between the Manitoba Hydro dams, (the Seven Sisters as they were known) on the Winnipeg River and the dramatic erosion taking place on its shores crumbling acres of reserve land into the river.

The implications of the mammoth hydro project taking shape in the North were emerging on the political radar screen, with the spotlight focusing on two communities in particular. Nelson House, along the diversion route, would face rising water levels and the prospect of a significant loss of land. Cross Lake, downstream from the main control dam for Lake Winnipeg at Jenpeg, would have to cope with the consequences of abnormally low water levels. That there would be consequences for all the other communities along this system was certain, but in what way was far from clear. To the east the battles that the Cree of James Bay were having with Quebec Hydro became major national news. The moccasin telegraph was beating out the messages across the country. In

June 1973 in the basement conference room of the Balmoral Hotel, the representatives of the northern Manitoba communities met for the first time. Billy Diamond, the leader of the James Bay Cree, and James O'Reilley, their prominent and flamboyant counsel from Montreal, were invited to share their stories and strategies.

With my growing connections to the aboriginal community, I had become increasingly aware and drawn into discussions about these emerging developments in the North, and given the very strong firm around me, it was not surprising that Charlie Huband, Garth Erickson, and I were asked to be part of the meeting, as the need for some kind of organizational and legal strategy to respond was becoming clear. Energized, the communities resolved to start working together as the James Bay Cree had done. We were instructed to advise Premier Schreyer that we would seek an injunction to halt further development of the project. I still recall Charlie's closing the letter with the hope that further proceedings would be conducted in the spirit of the underlying reality, that the parties would have to continue living and working together. Much organizational activity flowed, and soon I was drafting the letters of incorporation for the Northern Flood Committee Inc (the NFC).

Meanwhile, the folks on Lake Winnipeg were even more oblivious to what this might mean for them and the lake. Afi's and my Norway House friend Harry's futures were about to become interlocked, but nobody had bothered to tell them. They were fishing on grounds less than 20 miles apart as the crow flies, and the moss from Mossy Bay could now move into Playgreen Lake and Harry's nets. Harry's world felt the impact directly, and quickly. Afi did not know the questions he should have been asking: What were the possible consequences of changing the flow patterns on the lake? What were the potential biological consequences of connecting these water bodies, thereby making the encroachment of smaller "Grade B" Northern Whites from Playgreen swimming south and combining with the legendary fat Selkirk Whites of the North? In Afi's world these impacts would work stealthily and slowly. Fortunately for Hydro, he would die long before the answers would start to emerge.

CHAPTER FIFTEEN
"We Speak with One Voice"

Litigation carried significant risks for both sides in the Hydro dispute. Courts declare things, stop things, and give and take things away, but they cannot solve problems like moss in nets or falling into a crack in the ice on a trap line, some of the many possible implications of the developments. Charlie Huband suggested we propose an arbitration instrument to Dr. Stuart Martin, QC, special counsel to the premier, that would have a much broader remediation authority than achievable in court. Martin, who also had a labour relations background, was surprisingly receptive.

His response had a deeper underpinning. Presumably on the basis of advice he was receiving, Martin stated, in his usual confident (some might say smug) manner, that the system would be operated within historic highs and lows. The fact that the state of nature was being reversed—low water when it should be high, and high when it should be low—was an ecological detail seemingly perceived by Martin and Hydro as of little consequence. This confidence proved to be Hydro's undoing. Martin laid it out simply: "If you can prove damages, we should and will pay." He embraced Charlie's suggestion to develop an arbitration instrument. I had a significant interest in labour law, having studied under Harry Arthurs, one of Canada's foremost academics and labour arbitrators, and was already actively engaged on labour relations files within the firm. It fell on me to develop the initial draft of the arbitration instrument.

Another set of developments was unfolding as this possibility was being explored. Charlie Huband became leader of the Liberal Party of Manitoba, and it would be inconsistent with his new role to continue his involvement in such a high-profile, politicized case. Garth was a commercial lawyer. Scott was now a Court of Queens Bench judge. It was too early in my legal career to take on such responsibility independently. Our clients already had an eye out for Darcy McCaffery as lead counsel, so together the decision was made to approach him. Darcy had turned a unique combination of brilliance and flamboyance into a towering reputation as a trial lawyer.

Never one to fear the unorthodox, but prudent in his own way as he grew his young firm, Darcy turned the dark old basement of a building at 290 Gary Street into his personal residence. There, over a long afternoon of whiskey and cigars, Darcy and I bonded, and from that day until the day he died we were brothers. His offices were next door to Richardson and Company, and soon I was walking between the two offices many times a day. I would take him into the North, and he would turn me into a real lawyer.

He was a great mentor, always opening and never closing doors. He often told the young men and women who walked with him, "My job is to make you famous!" Voted one of Manitoba's ten greatest lawyers in an informal professional polling a few years ago, a great trial advocate to be sure, Darcy's true genius was the art of the possible and the pragmatic, and his impeccable sense of positioning and timing to achieve that. He was no ordinary man. His mother, who was more like a sister to him, was only 16 when he was born. His father was a cowboy rambler who took off to Alberta not to be seen again. He and his brother and sister and their mother went on together to build remarkable lives and successful careers. Darcy had a well-earned reputation as a lover and a fighter. He had no difficulty taking that set of talents into any setting, whether a bar or community hall, a board room or a court room. Over the years ahead we were inseparable on the Hydro case, and ultimately our friendship was the basis for the formation of a new firm created out of the merger of Richardson and Company and the McCaffery firm to become Taylor McCaffery in 1979.

Before he moved precipitously in situation, Darcy "sniffed" the ground carefully. "Glenn, we need to go to the North for a week to meet the folks." So, in the summer of 1975, we travelled from community to community absorbing and assessing to be sure, but doing so in a blur of talking and drinking, all of which he elegantly labelled his "bonding mission." Darcy was fully "bonded" upon our return, and soon he would be sporting the "We Speak with One Voice" T-shirts he had helped inspire on our journey.

Darcy's relationship with the Cree people would become a profoundly important part of his life and legacy. Darcy, as was I, was entranced with the eloquence of the Cree speakers, men and wome alike, who spoke freely, simply, and powerfully building on each others stories and metaphors at meetings lasting most of the day with speakers lined up one after the other. His pen filled scribblers. What made the Cree language accessible was the genius of Allan Ross. Allan was part of the Robertson family, the name of the last great "factor" (manager of a post) for the Hudson's Bay Company. He had been brought up by his Cree grandmother who taught him the language with such mastery that he was regarded throughout the North as one of its greatest speakers,

and certainly the finest translator. It was as if he was in a trance when he translated, listening so intensely sometimes for what seemed like ten minutes or more,
making the odd note in an old scribbler, and then interceding to explain what
had been said. Later Allan would complete his law degree, but would never
actively practise, becoming in later years Chief at Norway House.

What should the response be to the arbitration proposal that appeared
to have traction? We met with the Cree leadership from across the communities in a lodge south of Thompson for two days, where we discussed the proposal's pros and cons inside and out. The Cree were resolute. They would not
hand control over their destiny to a man in a suit, an arbitrator with final decision authority, with even broader powers than a judge. If there was to be
adjudication, they would only accept its conduct by a man in black robes in
whose presence the honour of the Crown and the commitments given at the
time of the treaties would be at stake. The clear instruction was to reject the
proposal. They would accept nothing but getting face-to-face with these people and institutions.

The dispute between the Cree and Hydro was now a regular headline. The
acrimony was intense. The rhetoric rising every day, with Canada tangled up in
its own feet with a fist full of dollars invested in a transmission line in the '60s,
and a sackfull of fiduciary obligations to the Indians coming home to roost in
the '70s. Skirmishes were already coming into public view between the province and the feds, and Prime Minister Trudeau and his ministers' relationship
with Premier Schreyer were becoming increasingly less warm and fuzzy. It was
a tangled mess; our goal was to make it even more tangled, knowing full well
that to have a serious conversation our clients needed to be taken seriously.

The possibility of war makes peace possible. A fight is easy to start; finding a way to make peace is much tougher. We knew we would need a form of
intervention to help bring about any meaningful face-to-face discussions. "If
not an arbitrator, what about a mediator, someone who could help advance the
discussions as a middleman working with and among the parties, but without
the power to decide?" we asked. The Cree leadership agreed.

It was in the spring of 1975 that I first met Leon Mitchell, days after he
was agreed upon as mediator for the issues involving the Northern Cree and
Manitoba Hydro. I'd read through the terms of reference developed with respect to his mandate. One of the terms stipulated that the mediation was to
be completed in 30 days. This was completely unrealistic, and I made my view
known to Leon, energetically, as I was inclined to do in those days. Through
bushy eyebrows, and with the hint of a smile on his wise face, Leon said, "I
will keep working until somebody tells me to stop." His sagacity was revealed.

What surprises me in hindsight is that I understood his implicit message. He knew that debating the length of the mediation at the outset, amidst the acrimony among the parties, would have doomed the process before it began. So when the 30-day clause found its way into the draft, Leon saw what others failed to see. The likelihood of someone pulling the plug as long as Leon said there was progress being made was remote. And in any event, no one would halt the proceedings without Leon's voice being heard, as the power to write a final report on his efforts remained in the text. I had my first lesson from the master. He became my mentor, my colleague and my great friend.

As Leon was wont to do on occasion, with the legacy of years of old-style labour relations bargaining inside him, he pulled a mickey of scotch from his drawer, offered me a drink, and lit up a cigar. Leon and I bonded that afternoon, and my career was already moving on a new trajectory, although I didn't know it then. Leon understood how people worked, and the things they did with and against each other. His greatest strength was empathy, and on that foundation a deep respect for others and their circumstances. No doubt much of his understanding of people was born from his own life story. As a young Jewish boy growing up in Winkler, Manitoba, Leon began his working life as a fruit peddler in the 1930s. In the early '40s he was struck down with a neurological disease that left him paralyzed for 18 months. Slowly the paralysis withdrew and he regained most of his mobility. He made his way to Winnipeg, and soon became active as a union organizer. Leon is credited with setting the foundation of the first civic employees union. Leon next set his sights on law. By 1955 he opened his own offices, and by 1969 had developed an immense practice and an enviable reputation as Manitoba's foremost labour lawyer. Never overtly political, he was admired as a champion of social justice in every way. Edward Schreyer offered him an appointment as chair of the Manitoba Municipal Board in 1969, and after his many long and intense years of practice he was ready for a change. A few years later he was appointed to the Federal Public Service Staff Relations Board as vice president in charge of interest arbitrations. During his Ottawa years he dealt with the thorniest issues in public sector bargaining, and specifically the acrimony associated with the harnesses on wage increases imposed by the anti-inflation guidelines of the mid-70s as inflation burst out of control.

Leon had admired Darcy since he first came to know the young lawyer at the legal gang's Friday lunches in Chinatown. Then circumstances would bring them together again, Leon as one of three Commissioners unravelling the largest fraud in Manitoba's history accomplished by an Austrian entrepreneur, Alexander Kasser, who had conned the prior government into giving him forest rights over much of northern Manitoba, and over 200 million dollars of government financing to build a pulp and paper plant in The Pas. Darcy became its counsel, and together they would expose a labyrinth of over two hundred dummy corporations around the world through which the money had moved and Kasser safely ensconced back in Austria out of reach with no extradition powers in place, and the monies in his hands.

Darcy's uncanny sense of the art of the possible took us to the doorstep of Leon Mitchell when searching for a mediator. He was the perfect choice. How could any of the parties refuse him? Who else could have ever fit the bill so perfectly in those circumstances at that time? In the initial meeting with all the parties crowded around a boardroom in some humble offices in the old Exchange area of Winnipeg, Stuart Martin offered what I can only presume he thought were comforting words to the Cree. He pronounced that that they should only expect the loss "of a few moose and fish," the clear underbelly of the point being "What's the big deal?" Buried inside Leon's bushy eyebrows was a glare in a flash as he sensed the hostile response that this would bring. Almost immediately, he adjourned the meeting on the basis that he considered it would be "helpful" for him to have more one-on-one conversations with each of the parties so he could be more helpful to them. Soon he was clanking around on his crutches bound to each arm in the communities across the North, under the Golden Boy in Winnipeg, and the Clock Tower in Ottawa. He journeyed from one group, piecing together some patchwork quilt of ideas, approaches, thoughts out loud, artfully vague and elastic to provide a platform to start growing a mutual conversation that everyone could own. Often I was with him, watching and learning.

Under Leon's skillful leadership through intensive negotiations over a four-year period, an agreement in principle was signed on July 31, 1977 following many days of round-the-clock negotiating sessions. As the possibility of an agreement loomed ever larger, we continued to fly in from the North additional leaders from the Cree communities to augment the negotiating team. Beside us was an unlikely colleague, an Australian, a brilliant physicist, then completing a post doc at the Atomic Energy Commission of Canada research station at Pinawa, Manitoba. Faced with a mountain load of studies and data, Darcy and I needed serious help. Serendipity answered the call in the form of Colin Gillespie, and his colleague Manfred Roehbock. With rigor and tenacity they passionately tackled the mountain of information and took on an army of engineers and experts. They were no less relentless with the other side than they were with the NFC team in advancing their rigorous view as to how the future should be shaped with a tsunami of logic and tenacity. There were days of exasperation as Darcy and I, often with Leon drawn into the room, pushed back with the pragmatics of what was doable. More than once I can recall protesting : "this team of logic horses will take us over a cliff and we aren't going over it." Fierce discussions aside, we each made the other better. The experience would also prove to be a conversion for Colin who would complete a law degree and become our partner at the firm.

Our final deliberations stretched deep into the night. "It takes courage to say yes. It is easy to say no," Darcy explained, and together we worked through the tangle of considerations the leaders needed to consider. Finally, at 4:00 a.m., after a lengthy final discussion in Cree, Chief Walter Monias of Cross Lake and Chair of the NFC turned to us and said, "There is no other alternative but to sign. But you and Glenn need to sign first." As disquieting as that might have been to some lawyers, Darcy and I picked up the pen and signed, first he, then me, then Walter and each member of the team.

The next day we were on a plane to the North. In packed halls in each community, we explained the agreement to community members and weathered the inescapable second-guessing and 20/20 hindsight to follow. Darcy captured the essence: "I know that we have a guitar that is playing music now, but if someone thinks it could play better music by tightening the strings further, let them do so. But the danger that also brings is that the strings might break and then it will play no music at all." I can still hear Chief Walter Monias booming out on more than one occasion, "I need no notes, because I speak the truth." Many others who had played critical roles in reaching the agreement attended to support the decision.

Chief Henry Spence and his councillors set the pattern in explaining to their community of Nelson House the events that led to the agreement and the steps needed to finalize it. Alongside Chief Spence were Chief Walter Monias, Chief Ken Albert from Norway House, Chief John Wavey of Split Lake, Ken Young, a young Cree lawyer from The Pas, and adviser to the NFC, Joe Keeper from Norway House, executive director of the NFC, and Allan Ross. We came back from the North it was with a strong endorsement of the decision to sign.

Leon combined tenacity with patience, creativity and sagacity: there was no such thing as not finding a way around a problem. One of the most intractable challenges was Premier Schreyer's insistence that the proactive policies for northern Manitoba his government had ushered in be acknowledged in any agreement reached with the Cree. Policy and agreements are not happy bedfellows, for policies can be changed by subsequent governments, and without certainty, the Cree people could have no confidence that what they were promised would be delivered. Ingeniously, Leon proposed a bridging device that would bring back to life as a building block of the agreement the earlier arbitration instrument, the strategy would give the arbitrator the power to convert into damages the loss of any benefits occasioned by a subsequent change in policy.

Shreyer accepted Leon's proposal, and authorized Len Bateman, the chair of Manitoba Hydro, to sign the agreement–in–principle at 4 am July 31, 1977. Within minutes we were over in Darcy's basement palace and the scotch bottles came out for a toast, or a few, and Leon clanked in, with Len Batemen happily alongside to join in the celebration. The next day Schreyer took the agreement to his cabinet colleagues. There, unbeknownst to us, he was meeting an im-moveable force in the person of Sid Green, the minister of natural resources. Green argued that the bridging provision constituted a fundamental encroach-ment on the exclusive mandate of government to govern and to formulate and change policy as it saw fit. Schreyer ultimately couldn't carry his cabinet in the face of this strident and determined opposition.

On August 25, 1977, he called a press conference to announce that he had not been able to carry his government and was reneging on his commit-ment to the agreement. There had been no forewarning, other than a call to the office moments before the press conference when word leaked that the premier was making a major announcement that would affect the agreement. Darcy rushed over; I was out of town. Schreyer explained. Darcy boomed: "You are a man who cannot be trusted to keep his promises." Darcy took no pleasure in that; but he had little choice. He knew this to be a cruel irony. The North had been a major focus for Ed Shreyer, whatever one's politics both personally and through his government's policies. An election was already planned, with the campaign slogan "Leadership You Can Trust" implanted firmly in the literature.

In the first two weeks of the campaign, Schreyer's inability to carry his government, and the deal he reneged on with the Cree, became a central issue in the election, fodder for the hotline radio host Peter Warren, and a flurry of cartoons in the *Winnipeg Free Press*. Almost immediately, we met with Sterling Lyon to secure the Progressive Conservative party leader's commitment to sign the document if elected. The backroom dealings were intense, with Ottawa pull-ing out all stops behind the scenes to pressure the communities to back down and sign the deal without the controversial bridging provision. They stayed clear of Darcy and I. The efforts were of no avail; no one backed down one inch. Schreyer lost the election.

In early December, we received a call from Lyon's legal adviser, who advised that some additional words in the clause would be a helpful step in reinstating the agreement in principle. Could we meet? After careful deliberation , we developed an approach that would accommodate the request without having any negative legal implications for our client. In early December, I returned home from an afternoon meeting in the attorney general's office to advise Darcy and Colin and the clients that the agreement in principle was reinstated with the addition of ten face-saving words. Premier Lyon signed.

Now came three months of heavy slogging, as we sought to have the agreement ratified through a vote in each of the communities. Over 50 Cree people, broadly representative of the communities, were brought into Winnipeg with a television crew hired to tape questions and answers about the agreement to be wrapped together as a video and shown in the halls and schools of the North, combined with endless meetings with fishers and trappers, elders, and youth, and open line radio shows on the community radios in many of the communities. There was then a final session where representatives of the parties sat and listened to community questions and the answers given to verify the accuracy of the information. On March 17, 1978, with a very solid majority in every community, the Northern Flood Agreement (NFA) was ratified by the Cree communities, and as promised the Lyon Government, Manitoba Hydro, and Canada, signed the agreement.

Above my desk hangs a framed collage of the people and places of those times. Included in the middle letter from federal Minister Hugh Faulkner, dated May 1, 1978, who wrote to Leon concluding his words of thanks and tribute:

> Not only did your contribution serve to overcome the initially wide differences dividing the four parties to the negotiations, but it also exemplified the highest order of dedication to the public service. Much of the credit for resolving this difficult claim belongs to you. I believe that time will show the Manitoba Northern Flood Agreement to be a fair and just settlement for all parties.

Reaching agreement on the words of the document had been tough, but giving effect to them would be much more difficult. The challenges of implementing the agreement proved enormous. In the heady final hours of the negotiation, to provide assurance there would be implementation teeth behind the words, in effect a "policing mechanism," Leon reintroduced the arbitration instrument in a much expanded form into the agreement. I never expected that it would need to be employed, as I had naively assumed that all the parties would do what they had committed to do. I would come to understand my naivety about the complexity of organizational structures, especially the institutions of government and publicly-owned utilities, over the years that followed.

It took four years for an arbitrator to be agreed upon and appointed. The legal capacity to give effect to the agreement was not achieved until 1984, during the last cabinet meeting presided over by Pierre Trudeau. Manitoba Hydro resisted at every turn. Facing limitation dates if we failed to raise claims, the entire agreement was ultimately reframed as a series of arbitration cases, which became the context for implementation. This is a much more complex story than can be told here, but the critical point it highlighted was the importance of ensuring that those who will be charged with giving effect to an agreement are also part of the negotiations to achieve it. It was a lesson I have carried with me since.

There were many other powerful lessons I took forward from those years, lessons that drew their power from remarkable people, but none more than from Sandy Beardy. He was a trapper who had spent his life canoeing the waters and traversing the ice around Cross Lake. He travelled hundreds of miles every winter in the lands north of the community to work his trap line. Cross Lake was downstream from the main Manitoba Hydro control structure that regulated Lake Winnipeg and turned it into a storage basin. When the demand for power was at its greatest in the winter (and potential price as well), the waters held behind the dam in summer were released. When the waters should have been high, they were low, and vice versa. Nature's normal cycle was reversed. In the winter, the churning of the water chewed the ice cover up like a ripsaw, and those who traveled by Ski-Doo faced the terrifying prospect of unexpected cracks and slush conditions, deadly perils when a man's feet became soggy with 20 miles to travel in 50 below weather.

Sandy had a warm and engaging way about him. He brought a thoughtful and dignified presence into every room. As a respected elder in the community and a very experienced trapper, Sandy and I spent countless hours together in meetings with the Trappers Association and the community. He was the perfect witness to put on the stand. He endured several hours of repetitive and often fruitless questions. Sandy answered and answered, but suddenly his demeanour changed. He stood up, and with a flash in his eyes and an unusual intensity, he spoke forcefully in English, much to the surprise of those from outside the community. Sandy typically spoke Cree on the witness stand, because he felt more comfortable in that language, especially with the incredible translation of Allan Ross at work. "Look here," he said, or words to like effect. "I've been in this bush all my life except for the four years I spent in the Canadian Army in uniform on the front lines in the Second World War. I know the outside world." Now he had their attention. "I have been across Europe, stood in its capitals, and walked those streets. When the war was over I came back here because this is where I chose to be. This was where I wanted to be. I could have chosen to do many other things and gone many other places. But I chose here, and now you are interfering in the life I chose to lead." That was that. The cross-examination ended quickly. The lawyer had no more questions. I don't think I knew that Sandy was a veteran, but in that moment I saw the power of moral authority spoken from the heart. It could have been my dad talking about fishing on Lake Winnipeg and his life choice.

"What will it take to postpone the hearing for a sufficient period to allow the completion of environmental studies?" I was asked as we were putting the papers back in our briefcases after the case had been recessed for the day.

"Let me speak with my clients," I responded. I had an idea. After a short meeting, I was instructed to provide the following response: "An arena."

"What kind of arena?"

"Just like the ones in Winnipeg, with bleachers and artificial ice. And we'll need funds to support its ongoing maintenance and operation." Soon a group from Cross Lake was touring Winnipeg arenas, and two years later a magnificent indoor rink opened. Darcy was there that cold December night, and with playful assurance he presented to the community a huge sailfish from one of his trips to Mexico punctuating the evening with "This was one of the mighty fish in Cross lake before Hydro arrived" as the kids swarming the ice laughed and elders manning the canteens chuckled along with them.

CHAPTER SIXTEEN
"Fish Eat That Stuff in Thermometers?!!"

The Winnipeg River system, which included the English and Wabigoon River tributaries, has been long famous for wilderness canoeing and world-class sport fishing. Since Dad's ominous phone call that fishing had been closed on Lake Winnipeg days after I started law school, these great natural jewels in the center of the continent would become famous for something very different.

In 1969, a young graduate student doing research on the river discovered unacceptably high concentrations of mercury in the fish stocks immediately below the pulp and paper mill in Dryden. Mercury was used in the processing operations. A crescendo of concern arose about the possibility that mercury contamination had affected not only the fish but the health of the people. Both their physical and economic health was at stake, because they depended on fish for food, paid guiding and other types of employment. Subsequent investigations only intensified the concerns. Almost immediately after the discovery of mercury in the water in 1969, the governments of Canada, Ontario and Manitoba moved to shut down recreational and commercial fishing operations throughout the Winnipeg River system and as far afield as Lake Winnipeg. While fishing resumed on Lake Winnipeg within two years, even today recreational fishing is allowed only on a restricted basis in the Winnipeg River system.

The greatest alarm was caused by the potential impact of low-grade chronic mercury ingestion through the consumption of the pickerel that thrive in the cold, clear waters of the Winnipeg River system. The Indian people of the region were at particular risk, because pickerel was a prime source of food for them. Medical investigations began immediately and included visits to Japan by the Indian people to learn firsthand of the effects of mercury contamination that had occurred in the fishing village of Minamata when a large portion of the population ingested high concentrations of mercury. In the English Wabigoon system, by contrast, the toxicity exposure was low-grade and chronic. The principal medical effects of mercury contamination are neurological with symptoms such as blurred vision, tremors, slurred speech, memory loss, dizziness and numbness. They also faced muscle weakness and loosening teeth. Extensive medical testing was soon underway.

Reed Inc.,the owner of the mill, stopped utilizing mercury in their processes upon the disclosure in 1969. The mill stumbled forward, but couldn't be operated efficiently without a massive reinvestment that Reed was reluctant to make. This became a particularly troublesome issue for the government of Ontario, anxious to see the community of Dryden, where the mill was located, emerge as the cornerstone of a revitalized economy in northwestern Ontario. When Great Lakes Forest Products Ltd. showed an interest in acquiring the mill, with assurances of millions in federal financing to assist in the modernization program, Ontario agreed to assist in one of the most difficult issues of the negotiations, relating to the threat of legal action. Ontario agreed to indemnify the companies who, in turn, co-shared liability up to 15 million dollars for any ultimate exposure over 15 million dollars.

In 1977, not long after I left law school, a writ had been filed in the Supreme Court of Ontario on behalf of the Ojibway communities of Grassy Narrows and Islington, commonly known as Whitedog, in seeking recovery of damages from Reed Inc., the owners of the mill at Dryden. Attempts to mediate a settlement were unsuccessful in the late 1970s. The environmental consciousness awakened by Rachel Carson's *Silent Spring* in the '60s was gurgling up in different ways and places across the continent. Close to home, the combination of the Cree of James Bay and Quebec, South Indian Lake, and mercury in the Winnipeg River system were creating a perfect storm of environmental angst sweeping through the media. Grassy Narrows and Whitedog were growing as powerful symbols of environmental degradation, energized by a broad base of external advocates, from church folks to an emerging community of environmental activists. In 1985 alone, 17 years after the mercury disclosures were first made, the topic was covered in three lead editorials in the *Globe and Mail*.

In the spring of 1982 two men walked into my office together. Roy McDonald, the Chief of the Whitedog community and Barney Lamm, owner of the famous Ball Lake Lodge a favourite recreational fishing destination for movie stars and celebrities. Ball Lake was just down river from Grassy Narrows, with many community members working in the lodge and as guides on the rivers. It was much more than a lodge; it was a community with multiple buildings, even a church, and a fleet of aircraft out of Kenora that serviced it daily. The lodge was often featured in the most famous of the outdoors magazines, *Field and Stream,* most likely because the likes of John Wayne and Frank Sinatra were frequent visitors. Roy and Barney had joined forces, and were here to ask our firm to represent them.

In the weeks following, we considered the case carefully. Coincidentally, I had first considered these issues in law school. A young professor, Barry Stuart, was pioneering the first course to be given in environmental law in Canada. Mercury was very much on my mind, and I enrolled in the course. The major paper I wrote for the course was on the legal implications of mercury contamination on the English Wabigoon rivers and the economy and wellbeing of the people of the region.

Much had been written on this topic over the intervening years. Our further research persuaded me beyond doubt that extraordinarily difficult questions of liability and damages were involved. Practical difficulties were everywhere. For one thing, proving damages would involve examining the individual avocations and lifestyles of the people affected. Whatever the outcome at trial, there would almost inevitably be appeals, likely to the Supreme Court of Canada. It would take years.

A negotiated outcome was the only possible path through this jungle of factual and legal difficulties, to say nothing of the enormous costs that would be associated with legal proceedings. And we were not the least confident that Ottawa would support the litigation to the conclusion. We concluded that if we couldn't bring about negotiations, there was no realistic likelihood of a resolution. I met with Roy and Barney, explained our conclusions, committed that I would do everything possible to initiate negotiations, but rejected litigation as a viable alternative. I explained that if the negotiations did go forward, I would represent Whitedog, and Barney would need to seek his own legal advice. They told me to go to work.

I made my first visit to Whitedog in the summer of 1982. Roy was showing me his community and sharing its history, and his own. He explained matter-of-factly that one day as a boy of twelve he saw some strangers on the shore peering through contraptions perched on three poles. He had no idea who they were or what they were doing. Later, he came to know them as surveyors who were working their way down the river configuring a huge hydro project. The men walked amidst the collection of small shacks on the side of the river, the small settlement where Roy was born and lived, and told the people they were going to be flooded and should "get the hell out of there." Then the men left. They were back within a couple of weeks. This time they told the people to get the hell out of there as they were going to burn their shacks down. It wasn't safe to stay, because the area would soon be under water. The residents departed fearfully, carrying what few possessions they could in their arms. Turning to gaze again at their homes, they could see the smoke rising as each hut was set on fire. It was 1955. Ontario Hydro had arrived, and the construction of the power stations along the Winnipeg River was underway. Roy's world had just been turned upside down.

When Roy and I first met, I noticed he walked with an unusual gait. Some months later, he shared more of his life story in a conversation in his office. As a young man, he had become a terrible alcoholic. One night while dead drunk, he passed out along the train tracks in Kenora. A train severed both legs below the knee. That night was his last drink. He went on to become a deeply spiritual man and a community leader. Now he was facing a challenge even more insidious and mysterious than anything he had faced before.

Roy related his initial reaction to mercury: "Who would ever believe that fish would want to eat that stuff in thermometers?" Not many people could have related to Roy's anguish over the mercury situation the way I did, for Dad had responded in almost the same way, except he had added that the damn scientists in Ottawa must have gone crazy, and in fact he may have been close to the truth, as years later I met one such scientist who shared with me the panic with which this revelation was greeted internally at the time.

My first step to jump start negotiations had been to fly to Toronto to meet with Reno Stradiotta, a senior partner at Borden Elliot, and counsel for Great Lakes Paper. Halfway through lunch, I had already concluded that Reno was a hell of a lawyer, and a guy with whom I could do business. We agreed that this case needed to be settled, but that would not be possible without Ottawa, and then Ontario, at the table. We went to Ottawa together, met with the Minister, and asked for the appointment of a federal negotiator. Months had passed since our meetings; we continued to press the matter. One day we received a surprising call: the Honourable David Crombie had asked former Supreme Court of Canada justice Emmett Hall to take on the role of counsel to the federal government in this very difficult situation. We were delighted with this news, but at the same time we wondered whether he would be up to this task at his age. Minutes after learning of his appointment, I called Justice Hall at his home in Saskatchewan. He answered within two rings. (I soon learned that was always the case when I called Emmett; if it rang a few more times I would become concerned.) I introduced myself. He said he would be in Winnipeg the day after next if I could meet with him. I knew that instant he was up for the task. I called Stradiotta and told him to expect us soon in Toronto.

The concept of a fund to which individual victims would have recourse seemed to be a possible pathway to start unlocking this legal puzzle. I knew we were aligned in our thinking when Emmett responded, "We should take a look at the fund that was created to compensate the victims of the Halifax explosion in 1917." It was a reference to the collision in the Halifax harbour of two ships loaded with munitions that blew apart the city. He urged me to look for guidance to the ongoing payments that had been the basis for a legislated settlement. From that day forward, Emmett and I worked seamlessly together to bring about such a result.

To be with Emmett was like being on a guided tour across decades of the people and events that had shaped Canadian history. His contribution to that history may have been a short one but for a blessing he was given at birth. During a long day of negotiations in a crowded boardroom, Emmett suddenly became disorientated; I was soon to discover that he had been born with only one functioning eye, and that the contact lens which covered his entire eyeball (and replaced every two weeks by an optometrist) had fallen off. That night as I expressed amazement at how he had functioned all those years reading and writing volumes he shared: "That one eye saved me. I wouldn't be alive had I not been born that way. Every young man I knew who went into service in World War One from Saskatchewan never came home. I was not eligible for military service."

Emmet's family had moved from Quebec to Saskatchewan when he was young boy. After an early career as a teacher, he went to law school. In the 1930s, he was appointed to prosecute the Ku Klux Klan which was trying to rear its head on the prairies. His life as a public personae at age 60 began partying on the train with John Diefenbaker as they returned to Saskatoon from Prince Albert after the election that made "Dief the Chief" prime minister of Canada. Emmett and Diefenbaker were law school classmates. Diefenbaker, the lone ranger criminal lawyer, had always maintained a relationship with Emmett, the establishment big firm lawyer, and turned to him for help when the occasion arose. That night Dief told him big things lay ahead. Soon Emmett was a judge, then on to the Court of Appeal of Saskatchewan, and within a year he sat on the Supreme Court of Canada.

The Hall-Dennis Report on educational reform in Ontario followed. Then Emmett completed the crown jewel of accomplishments, the Royal Commission that ushered in Canadian Medicare. On the Supreme Court, his was the decisive voice that gave legal credence to the concept of Aboriginal rights and title, he returned from Ottawa to Saskatoon in 1975 after retiring from the court, to the penthouse suite he bought in the Sheraton Hotel, still awaiting the next call for another assignment. And it came, a request to resolve the historical Crow's Nest Pass issues involving preferential railway tariffs on grain transport. Next, he took the call from Minister of Health Monique Begin to intercede in the so called "extra-billing" crises threatening to paralyze health care services in Ontario and spread across the country.

When Emmett received the call from the David Crombie, former mayor of Toronto, and now the Minister of Indian Affairs, to lend stature and leadership to the negotiations and serve as counsel to the federal government in the complex situation arising from mercury contamination in northwestern Ontario, the issue took on an international profile. As ever, Emmett answered the call to duty, but on a condition. He was 82. He was too old to waste time on governmental rigmarole, and: "I will keep you informed and tell you when I have written the cheque," or at least that is the way he reported the exchange to me, and from what I came to know I suspect it was just that! Crombie told him to get to work. We went to work together and kept working for four years until the job was done.

Emmett had access. There was no one who didn't return his calls. When he needed to speak to David Peterson, premier of Ontario, he picked up the phone. When there was an issue looming in the Senate over an Inuit senator's concern that the Inuit were not receiving the same attention, Emmett was on the phone to Allan McEachern and Duff Roblin, political legends and respective Senate leaders for the Liberals and Tories. He called me next, and without saying hello barked, "There's some problem raised in the Senate about your people getting preferential treatment over some Inuit group. Get a hold of your guys and tell them to talk to him. If he turns this into an issue it could stall the completion of this settlement."

Emmett got things done. Everything, small or big, was big until the deal was done, and nothing was too small for him to bird dog down. He knew the people that could make things happen, and even if he didn't, they knew him. He had moral authority, and when the situation required it to be used he knew how to do so. Never was there one hint of arrogance in these connections. They were earned over a lifetime.

Emmett was real, basic, not fancy. We made our first trip to Whitedog in a 1950s Otter seaplane. We left from a floatplane base in Selkirk. I had called Roy to ask where we should land on the river to access the settlement. He said, "By the big rock."

"Roy, isn't there a dock? The old man is with me."

"No dock, but there's a good path up the bank."

I was uneasy. So, too, was the pilot when he saw this very senior but clearly vigorous old man arrive. "Sir," he said, "the bank of the river there is pretty steep."

Emmett brushed that aside, mumbling something to the effect that he was not too old to get up a damn river bank. The pilot went on: "Do you guys have any lunch with you?"

"No, should we? There must be a café there for some lunch?"

"There's no restaurant. You better go into town and get some sandwiches before we leave."

Soon Emmett and I returned with two clubhouses wrapped in canvas, and off we went. The seats of the Otter were not pleasant, essentially canvas hammocks between two poles. But the forty-minute flight was uneventful. It was a clear, sunny day, and we glided smoothly in to the big rock, the pilot obviously not new to this junket. The pilot looked at the steep bank, then at Emmett, and said: "Sir, you better have your sandwich before you make that climb." He promptly pulled a seat out of the plane, positioned it on the granite under the wing out of the intense sunlight, and directed Emmett to his throne. My great regret is that I did not have a camera with me to take a picture of Emmett, and I unwrapping the tin foil and eating our lunch together on the Big Rock, then scrambling up the steep and irregular path up the bank. Emmett was not even breathing hard when we got to the top.

It was Friday, the day social assistance cheques were distributed, and there was action everywhere. The situation in Whitedog was tough. The community had taken serious blows from relocation, Hydro developments, and now mercury.

Roy greeted us enthusiastically. He was a gentle man, short, with a round face made even warmer by his infectious smile and quick wit. One of the band members approached him as we were leaving the band office, and after a short conversation the man walked off, obviously unhappy. Roy turned to me with a twinkle in his eye. "Glenn," he said, "you know the secret about being a good chief, don't you?" I knew enough not to answer, and Roy continued. "You only need to know one thing. You should always carry two wallets, one with money, and the other empty. Which one you pull out of your pocket depends on who you're talking to."

Emmett, like Darcy, walked with kings and paupers. He was comfortable with ordinary and powerful people alike. He saw people as people. I'm confident that without Emmett the institutional resilience and rigidity of the governments would have never been moved to resolution. Multiple examples to support that view could be extracted from those of us who worked with him. The clearest example of this came after the court approval in the settlement. As we walked down the Osgoode Hall corridor, a *Globe and Mail* reporter approached him and asked something like, "Sir that is quite an affidavit you signed today in support of this settlement. Do you believe everything you say in it?"

Emmett focused on him intensely and replied simply but with an edge, "This is the best possible conclusion in all of the circumstances. I am completely comfortable with what I said in my affidavit, and with what was concluded here today."

Emmett turned to me as we walked out. "What the hell is wrong with these guys?" he asked incredulously. Do they think I don't know what I'm signing or something? Does he think I would sign something that I did not believe?"

Clearly, Emmett believed the reporter thought an old guy like him didn't fully understand what he was signing. It irked him. Outside on the lawn, he turned to me and with the flash of a smile said, "Anyway, it will be long gone by the time anyone can catch up to me on what we did here today."

We went to a celebratory lunch where several of the lawyers joined us. We'd crossed two of three hurdles: federal legislation and court approval. Only one big piece of the puzzle remained, which was passing the agreed-upon legislation in the Ontario provincial legislature. Emmett opened up during lunch, directing his comments to Peter Jacobsen, lawyer for the province. "Peter, what the hell is taking so long over there in the legislature? I've got this done in Ottawa, and Ian (Ian Scott, Ontario's attorney general) and the Premier can't seem to get this through Queen's Park."

Peter tried to answer, but Emmett was onto an idea. "Get a hold of Ian," he urged, "and tell him that Glenn and I are coming down to the House this afternoon to see what's taking so long."

I sensed we were about to go on a very big roll. Within the hour, we were ushered into the front row of the Gallery. Emmett inadvertently waltzed right onto the floor of the Chamber as we turned the corner, and was intercepted by some guards who directed us to seats. The House was in turmoil because of a fuss that had erupted over one of the cabinet ministers. Television cameras were everywhere, and question period was raucous. Suddenly, at three sharp, the storm ended. When things settled down, half of the seats in the House were empty, as the legislators started their July weekend a few hours early. Ian rose in the afternoon session, having seen the two of us in the front row. He introduced Emmett to the members (with passing reference to my existence) and explained that two of the pieces of legislation on the order paper of the House were the contentious bill dealing with "extra billing by doctors" and the "English Wabigoon settlement." Both had Emmett's fingerprints all over them, he explained. There was a prolonged standing ovation.

Emmett and I sat centre stage in the Gallery as the work of the House began. The debate droned on over some amendments to the Municipal Act. Emmett was becoming agitated. "What the hell is going on here?" he mumbled. "Don't they know we need to get this done now?"

I have no doubt that Ian Scott could feel the intensity of Emmett's glare across the floor. Around four o'clock he walked across to the NDP House leader. I overheard him say, "While the old man is in the House we must get this English Wabigoon bill passed."

Soon the Conservative House leader came over to us, and said, "We're going to move the bill off the order table into the House now. If there are issues it will have to go into committee. We'd like to give it three readings today, but we have one issue that one of our members is concerned about, and he wants to speak with you. Can you speak to him?"

This time, I answered: "Yes, get him over here."

Emmett grumbled, "What the hell has this guy got to talk about? This has been in the courts, the federal House, every damn place."

"Emmett," I urged. "Let's just listen to him and get this sorted out."

The honourable member came over. He was concerned that the Ombudsman of Ontario had not been given the jurisdiction to receive and review complaints from anyone concerned about compensation they might be awarded by the Mercury Disability Fund. Emmett's mind was clearly elsewhere, sensing trouble and thinking of ways to avert it quickly with a phone call somewhere higher up. My mind was in overdrive. The answer came to me in a flash.

"Look, I hear you. I think the legislation has been drafted in a way that very effectively addresses your concern. Nowhere is the jurisdiction of the Ombudsman excluded in the bill. The Ombudsman's mandate is untouched, so whatever mandate the office has will apply with respect to this piece of legislation and anything created pursuant to it."

The legislator looked perplexed by my answer, but stymied as to any retort, he left, clearly puzzled as to what to do next. His powerful point had clearly been put into wobble mode.

Minutes later, Ian Scott rose in the House to introduce the bill for passage. He confessed to a "curious conflict of interest," indicating that he had been the lawyer who initially filed the writ on behalf of the claimants in Whitedog and Grassy Narrow. He went on to embrace the bill, describing the careful negotiation surrounding its development under the watchful and experienced eye of Emmett Hall. He asked that three readings be given today in the House. The NDP House leader spoke to the bill, and went on at length praising the work of Stephen Lewis in bringing it to where it was today. Stephen was the former NDP leader but hadn't been in the legislature for ten years. Emmett whispered to me, truly baffled at this prolonged recitation about the role of Stephen Lewis. "What is this man talking about?"

And then the Conservative House leader rose to speak. It was about 5:00 p.m. My apprehension rose as soon as he opened his mouth. He spoke of many things, but all I heard was the sound of a bell tolling with every mention of the word "ombudsman." For the next forty-five minutes, the pendulum swung between support and concern. Emmett was highly agitated, and kept mumbling something along the lines of, "What the hell is this guy talking about?"

There was no easy answer to Emmett's question, until the moment of truth: "But I have decided not to oppose the bill." Bang, bang, bang, one, two and three readings, the bill passed into law, and the House adjourned.

Emmett and I walked from the Gallery. We met Ian as he came off the floor of the Chamber. "Ian, thank you," Emmett exclaimed. "I never like to leave a job undone. I was beginning to wonder whether I was going to go before this was finished." He added, "This is the third anniversary since the death of my wife. It's an important day for me. Thank you for what you have done today." The always gracious Ian Scott, one of the great trial lawyers of Ontario, and a leading public figure, was clearly touched. He thanked Emmett for his enormous contribution to Canadian life and his work on this very difficult file.

The mercury pollution settlement agreement was approved in the Supreme Court of Ontario by Mr. Justice David Griffiths in June 1986, and took concurrent legislative effect in both the Legislature of Ontario and the Parliament of Canada. The preface said this:

> The complexities, uncertainties, and inevitable costs of litigation as a means to resolve the issues, and concern that the existing legal framework could not as comprehensively and satisfactorily resolve the issues in a manner consistent with the public interest and the interests of the parties has caused the parties to conclude that the issues must be resolved by agreement between them.

Each word was packed with meaning. The Honourable Emmett Hall; Robert Blair, now Justice Blair; his then associate John Olthius; and Reno Stradiotta, QC; all shared in its authorship. In subsequent years I came to realise that this one paragraph crystallized much of my growing disenchantment that the law, and its frameworks, was not structured in ways that could provide enduring solutions to the most difficult problems. No doubt, to have a serious conversation, you need to be taken seriously. And the power that punches out of rights established in a courtroom gets you into the negotiating room. But this power is not sufficient to get anything done once inside, and in fact liberating the participants from the fight became one of the fundamental challenges in making progress. Courts are in the rights and power business.

People fight for rights, to advance and protect them, and to defend themselves in the face of accusations that they have abridged someone else's. You need talk to achieve results. Moving from fighting to talking is the essence of the space where I work. Turning rights into results is the real challenge if you want to be part of making a real difference for real people in real places. What I was coming to understand is that the conventional wisdom with which I was working was trying to force problems into processes, rather than building processes to suit the problems. My professional lens shifted to "building processes for problems, not forcing problems into processes." Moving through that archway has taken me to many different people and places in my continuing swim against the current.

Over the years I have drawn many lessons from the mercury case. Perhaps the most critical is that the greatest challenge in solving big problems is big organizations, whether companies or governments, communities or civil society, First Nations or labour unions. Most large organizations do not think "transactionally." They think in lines and work in boxes called departments and ministries, with policies and programs. Others who interact with them soon adopt the same image. Working with these complex structural components and the dynamics that come with them is the most difficult of challenges. The extraordinary significance of Emmet Hall's engagement in this case was his ability to override much of this challenge using the incredible access that he deployed as an ambassador for the cause, once he was persuaded of the integrity and wisdom of the settlement taking shape. He became its champion, and our champion got us through doors that otherwise would have taken much longer to open.

I would start combining lessons from Leon Mitchell with my own evolving experience. Leon understood that there are reasons behind everyone's hopes and worries. Through understanding these reasons, he sought ways to build bridges. "People act in accordance with how they perceive their self-interest," he said, and how we see our interests evolves. It is in the course of this evolution that reconciliation amongst competing views can be built. Leon's quest was to create the space for conversations allowing people to explore their interests with others whose world impacted their own but who saw the world differently. Searching for ways to live together in spite of differences was the business of building relationships. Respect, relationships and reconciliation were the building blocks of the Leon Mitchell magic. By the time Leon died, he had opened many doors for me.

His work on the Northern Flood Agreement and the Public Service Staff Relations Board was gaining attention in the world of what was becoming known as "alternative dispute resolution." The acronym "ADR" was soon to be welded into popular use with growing frustration at the inability of courts to deliver timely, accessible and effective resolution of issues. The Society of Dispute Resolution Professionals was born in 1973, and while the majority of its founders and members were Americans, several became Leon's colleagues on the Public Service Staff Relations Board. The Harvard Negotiation Project had been initiated soon after United States Chief Justice Warren Burger in a major lecture exclaimed, "There must be a better way!" He bemoaned the rising tide and backlog of litigation overwhelming the courts. Harvard professor Frank Sanders had around the same time penned an article envisioning a "multi-door courthouse" in which cases would be streamed into alternative processes depending on the nature of each situation.

My work with the Northern Flood Committee had had an unexpected consequence. Shortly after the agreement's signing, there was a cloudburst of opposition in Thompson, Manitoba. This was the town that nickel built, which had grown from an Inco company town to Manitoba's northern capital, a city of around 15000. Someone had pressed an alarm bell that had everyone convinced that access to hunting and fishing as a resource and recreation was to be denied to all but the Cree under the agreement. Ken McMaster was not the only minister in the Lyon government who had signed the agreement, but his constituency was Thompson, and many of the fiercest protagonists emerging were among his strongest supporters. A meeting was called in January 1978 in the Steelworkers Hall. Ken called and told me, "It's not in the interest of your clients to have this thing go out of control anymore than it is for me. I want you to consider coming up to this meeting with your clients to help me explain what the agreement says, and what it does not say. If this doesn't get settled down with clear information quickly, it won't be in anyone's interest." I understood, and I agreed.

For five hours that night I stood with several of the Northern Flood Committee leaders before a crowd of about 600, explaining and answering question upon question, until there were no more. The government jet had us back in Winnipeg by 12:30. That was the last I heard of the issue.

About a year later I received a call from Ken advising me he wanted to appont me as Vice Chair of the Manitoba Labour Board. This was one of the directions we wanted to take the firm; I already had considerable labour relations experience, and it was agree that I should take what was a part-time appointment. Soon, I was among three icons, two of whom had been board members since its creation in the 40s— for labour, Jimmy James, short, rotund, sporting a red T-shirt, and for management, George Keats, sports coat, trim, and fresh after the quarter mile swim he did daily. The Chair was Obie Baizley, formerly a chiropractor, then politician and a highly respected Minister of Labour in the Roblin government of the 1960s, penguin-like in his dapper three piece suit with a dangling watch. The old boys, well beyond the immediate hurly burly of today's issues, almost always reached unanimous decisions.

Day One, Jimmy and George gave me marching orders in the only Board Office so tiny Obie had to leave for me to sit with them "only if we have not agreed, do we want to hear from you" and go on from that day to serve on the Board for nine special years. I would stay nine years. His term in Ottawa concluded, Leon re-entered my life as counsel to the firm, and was soon appointed as vice-chair of the Labour Board as well. We worked and wrote together. We went to the annual Society of Professionals in Dispute Resolution conferences. I slowly evolved a practice as a labour arbitrator and mediator, including for Inco and the United Steelworkers. Often when I boarded or returned on the flight from Thompson I would know every second or third person on the aircraft.

Dr. Gerald Cormick, a Canadian from Vancouver whose family roots were on the wheat fields of Saskatchewan, learned of Leon's work. Jerry was professor in the Schools of Business and Public Policy at the University of Washington in Seattle, pioneering a field he had described as "environmental mediation," and training and mentoring a cadre of young professionals to intervene in complex multi-party environmental, land use and resource disputes. Jerry had formed the Mediation Institute in 1976, with significant Ford Funding and soon a blue ribbon board including Bill Ruckelhaus, the attorney general fired by President Nixon for refusing to fire the Special Prosecutor. I took Leon's place on the board of the Mediation Institute when Leon died in 1984. Jerry Cormick invited me to join him in delivering courses at the Banff Centre, where he had been appointed director of the newly formed Environmental Dispute Resolution Program, and mentored by Jerry, a new layer of my life opened.

CHAPTER SEVENTEEN
"Let Me Buy You a Beer"

"Glenn, let me buy you a beer. Meet me at the Pembina Hotel at eight." I'm not sure I even had a chance to answer. There he was, in what I soon realized was probably his regular table. A hand reached out before I had a chance to even see that impish grin spread across his warm full face. The beer was already on the table and Maurice Eyolfson was ready to roll.

"Do you know what those guys are saying about Riverton?" he asked.

"No, Maurice, I have no idea. I could guess, but I think maybe you prefer to tell me." I didn't even bother to ask what "guys" he was referring to.

"They're planning to put a fence around the village and a sign, 'Gimli Zoo,' on the highway. Are you going to let that happen without a peep?"

"Well, Maurice, maybe you probably have some ideas for me." I knew some set-up was on its way.

"You have to join the Festival committee. Islendingadaggurin needs you. We can't allow these Gimli guys to run the whole show."

"Well, Maurice, you seem to be in pretty tight," I replied. "From what I saw last weekend at that annual meeting you had me come to at the Wildwood Club, those Gimli guys and the Loni Beach gang were buzzing around you as if you were the Queen bee."

"They let me onto the committee without really appreciating that I was from Riverton. I'd been around Winnipeg so long they thought I was harmless. But now they know that I'm a Rivertonian at heart," he continued.

"You're doing a hell of a job, Maurice. Far be it from me to take any of the Riverton glory away from you. Two guys from Riverton would be a crowd with that group."

"They may get a little nervous, but you're pretty diplomatic. I'm worried about the future. When I'm gone from the President's chair, where will Riverton be? Out of it, maybe for decades again. Your Dad is from Riverton, your Mom from Hecla. What would your Afi SV say?" Maurice was on a roll. Soon he'd have the ghost of his own Afi, Gutti, hounding me.

I knew there was no deterring him. "Okay, Maurice. I'm in. But I need a job to do so I'm not lost in the woodwork." I had in mind an imposing title like "Director General, Government and Legal Affairs."

"We need someone to take over the flea market, and take it to another level. That will be a good place to get you started. It needs to be better organized with tighter controls over who gets in and what gets sold." Remarkably, he didn't even crack a smile when he laid that one on me. Nor did I.

So it came to pass that I was anointed King of the Fleas by our esteemed President, Maurice Eyolfson doing business his inimical way with a smile, a laugh, and a beer. He was Gutti's grandson, and heir to the same wicked sense of humour that had served his Afi so well. Maurice was now also a master negotiator who worked his magic as Manitoba's deputy minister of labour. He donned his Shriner's tasselled red hat each year to take center stage as the ringmaster for the annual Shrine Circus. Taking down this lawyer was mere child's play. Maurice became the festival's president in 1981 and 1982. I followed in his footsteps as president in 1985 and 1986. But throughout, whenever asked where he was from, with his heart on his sleeve and a boom in his voice: Riverton, *Canada!*

My years in the festival connected me to the culture of Icelanders in North America and in Iceland in important new ways. It gave me an even closer relationship with Gimli, which has always been like a second home. The family had deep connections there, but I established my own roots. When I joined Richardson and Company one of the expectations had been that I would take over the fledgling office that had been started by the firm some years before. While I never lived in the community, I commuted regularly from Winnipeg, and over those years built deep personal relationships that have remained a cornerstone of my life, as well as a solid law practice which is still flourishing today.

Often I would walk about town, usually starting at the harbour which I knew so well from the many times I had been there with Dad on his gossip stops on the way home from Winnipeg, or to meet the *Spear* because the weather had been to treacherous to land at Hnausa. Before the dock, I would stop at the fountain constructed by the Rotary Club, one of the initiatives of the Gimli Harbour Park Development Corporation I helped to found and lead. The *Goldfield* had been tied to the dock at the front of the harbour, waiting patiently every year for the ice to let her free, with the classic barn-red icehouses and packing sheds owned by BC Packers immediately behind. Now, they'd been transformed into a museum. And since Sig Fish had acquired her in 1969 the Hnausa harbour had become the *Goldfield's* lonely home

I often thought back to 1975, the centennial anniversary of the Icelandic immigration to Canada. The *Goldfield* led a massive flotilla that assembled at Hnausa to make the two-hour trip down the lake to Gimli to commemorate the travels of the early settlers. The *Goldfield* pulled into her old berth and Sig Fish opened the boat and a makeshift bar at the bow became popular with the last stragglers leaving late into the evening. Onboard were several of my close friends and classmates from Osgoode Law School who had come to spend the weekend. The naval battalion coming down the lake, and the party for a town that followed are part of the folklore of our friendship, endlessly retold as part of the glue that binds us. RJ Grey, Associate Dean, an institution at Osgoode as the "students' dean" forgets nothing ever, and, while he was not part of the great voyage, reinforces these memories every reunion by greeting me with "Goldeye!"

When I walked down the Gimli dock during my years with the festival it was always to the *Blackhawk*. The *Blackhawk* is the Lake Winnipeg equivalent of a luxury liner. Its main deck is paneled in oak throughout, with a sitting area in the stern with a panoramic view out onto the water, and an open fireplace in the central area alongside a galley doing double duty as a bar tucked around one corner. The panelled wheelhouse blends seamlessly into the main deck. There are staterooms below, and a large open deck above for a quiet summer visit, a lounging in the afternoons and energetic parties at night complete the picture.

Irvin and Lois Olafson—my Dad's youngest sister and her husband—and their entire family opened the *Blackhawk* graciously to family, friends and community for many years, and never more openly than the weekend of the Icelandic Festival. They made my years as festival president particularly special by hosting many events for me on the boat, including the annual president's receptions after the traditional program, and special cruises for the Fjallkona. For many years, and often most especially for our distinguished visitors from Iceland, the *Blackhawk* was synonymous with the festival, and unforgettable hospitality.

This now glamorous lady hid a secret within her finery. She had started her life as a fish freighter, just like the rest of those workhorses of Lake Winnipeg. Northern Lake Fisheries brought the hull in from the great Lakes by rail and outfitted her as a Lake Winnipeg freighter in the '30s, whose waters she plied for decades, with her name changed from the *Alert* to the *Douglas M*. She met an undignified, but not fatal, end, beached on the shore at Hnausa, held upright by wooden crutches quietly rusting beside a lonely harbour for years. When Ray Senft—a contractor by occupation but a sailor at heart—stumbled across her, her fortunes began to change. His love affair with her was like Rex

Harrison's Henry Higgins working to refine Eliza Doolittle in *My Fair Lady*, Ray envisioned her in a different way in a new place. It was an effort of love to transform her. This would be his Queen on the lake. Most who boarded the *Blackhawk* did not know the history that made her what she was, much less the hours and money it took to remake her, but on the grand celebration to honour her hundredth anniversary Irvin made sure Ray was there in full glory ready to be proclaimed as her modern day saviour.

Ray almost beached his "Eliza" in a storm on one of his first voyages. He quickly realised that he was more a builder than an able seaman. He set in search of someone who could handle a vessel of this size. Irvin was one of a very few with the money to buy and the wherewithal to run her. An engineer, then a dentist, but a fishermen first, Irvin grew up in a troubled family; his boyhood was not easy. He was rowing out to his nets each day in the fall from the Black Bear station when he was sixteen, missing the first few weeks of high school. He and my Aunt Lois were little more than kids when they married, and Irvin became another son to Afi SV and Amma Kristrun. Irvin's relationship with Afi was profound, and not much Afi ever told this self-made man ever left his mind. One of many exchanges he shared with me, which tells much of my Afi SV was this: "Never make a deal where the other guy does not make money," to which a surprised young man asked "Why?" Afi answered "it will make you money."

The maritime museum was always another stop. The centrepiece was Afi Malli Brynjolfson's last boat, the *Baby Spear*, donated by my mother's family when he died. My eyes always shot immediately to the pump. A magnet for a kid, I'd grab hold of the curved metal handle, about the length of a hatchet, and start pulling it up and down, straining my neck around the corner of the cabin to see if any water had started to come. Usually the plunger caught hold of the water below in some mysterious way and pulled it up, but sometimes the pump just made a gurgling noise and nothing came. Then Afi would come over, and with a small can of water he pulled from the lake with a string, he would pour water into the pump to prime it. Soon I would hear the water splashing out from the spout. Sometimes it would take fifteen minutes of steady pumping until the last bit of water was sucked from the bottom of the hold of those leaky old wooden boats.

These were the whitefish boats, often referred to as "Gasboats", a curious name, but easily explained by the gas engine pulled out of old cars that was the centerpiece of the old wooden boats. The clutch and the brake were worked by long handles protruding from the gearing system at the back of the motor, like a floor shift on an old car from the '30s. You couldn't really call the three-sided structure a "cabin." Closed to the wind on the front and the two sides, it was open to the back of the boat. It was usually referred to as the "housing." On the front wall there was a door to the deck behind the bow on the right, and a window ahead of the steering wheel. The compass was on a small ledge between the wheel and the window. Whoever was steering the boat had just enough room on the narrow floorboards for a stool. If he went back another six inches, he'd fall into the motor.

There was no cover over the motor. Long experience had taught that the potential for gas fumes to build up under a cover could be fatal. Old Bill Hudson from Fisher River had been on a gas boat when a build-up of fumes had ignited, blasting him overboard and pulling apart the old wooden boat. Miraculously, he survived. The smell of gas never left you aboard, but when the boats were moving the steady winds worked better than any imaginable ventilation system. Otherwise, the men wouldn't have survived long, as they literally slept with the engine. There was a sloping gangplank that inclined to a back platform immediately behind the housing open to the stern. Across from the engine, on the other wall, were two bunks on hinges that dropped down to sleep on at night. A third bunk pulled down over the gangplank, the gas boat equivalent of the Murphy bed.

The only washing facility on the boat was a basin on a stand beside the pump, with a towel hanging from a nail and a bar of Sunlight soap on the two-by-four that held the side wall together. There was no toilet, but a dribble or a bum over the side worked fine. It wasn't a fancy place, but as a kid that thought never crossed my mind.

The harbour, the whitefish boats, the "white rock" where the original settlers were cast ashore —this is the soul of Gimli. In the winter, just to the south of the museum, all the whitefish boats used to sit quietly on the shore, held upright with crutches and waiting peacefully for the next season. Now they were all in the water, having just returned from the summer's fishing. Things have changed. Not as many boats ply these waters as the northern white fishery has declined, and they have been kicked out of their old winter nesting location to the dismay of many. As I wandered back down the dock my eyes were drawn to the huge anchors that had been placed out front of the museum, the original anchors of the Lady of the Lake.

In the spring of 1988, as recently retired president of the Icelandic Festival of Manitoba, I was chairing the Centenary Committee. Many significant projects were identified, including writing the history of the Icelandic Festival. I knew of, but had never seen, a copy of the constitution that had been developed by the colonists to regulate their affairs as a self-governing colony. We retained a young Icelandic scholar, Jonas Thor, then studying at the University of Manitoba. I asked Jonas if he could locate it, wondering out loud whether another project might be to have it displayed in some way as a historical site.

One afternoon he dropped by the office with "here is your constitution." We chatted as I thumbed through the document. My eyes riveted on the election of a conciliator, together with municipal councillors, in the first few paragraphs:

> The duty of Conciliators is to seek to compose differences in all private cases. The Conciliators shall summon before them, the parties to the dispute at some definite time and place, in accordance with the wish of either party to the case, and notification by letter shall be a sufficient notice of summons. If conciliation comes to naught the plaintiff shall pay each conciliator 1 (one) dollar for the attempt at a settlement, but if a settlement comes about, then both parties shall pay the same amount according to agreement. Payment is to be made when the attempt at conciliation is completed. Conciliators shall be obliged to record their settlements and their attempts at conciliation.

> If the attempt at conciliation does not succeed, or if either of the parties to the case does not attend after a legal notice of summons, then shall the parties, if either so demands, place the case before a board of arbitration of five impartial individuals which the parties to the case themselves select. Each party to the case shall nominate two, but the fifth member shall be the Governor or the Vice-Governor of the Regional Council if they cannot agree on the fifth one. The majority vote of the Committee of Arbitration decides the issues. Arbitrators are obliged to record their decisions.[60]

What would have inspired these Icelanders bordering on starvation, quarantined by smallpox, to devote their energies to creating this remarkable document?

It was a bizarre coincidence to come upon this within two hours of leaving for Toronto to a major conference, *Access to Civil Justice*, part of an initiative of the attorney general of the day, Ian Scott, to overhaul the civil justice system of Ontario. Our paths had crossed two years before during the mercury case. Ian was committed to streamlining a justice system beset by cumbersome procedures and overbearing costs to make it more accessible to the ordinary person through the development of creative new approaches to resolving disputes. He asked me to lead a discussion on the potential for mediation.

I pored over the document on the flight. I thought about the session I was to lead the next afternoon. These Icelanders had developed a unique system of civil justice elegantly integrated into a governance structure. The election of the conciliator would give the holder of the position moral authority and the office influence and stature within the community. Mandatory mediation prior to binding arbitration was always a concern, for mediation is traditionally voluntary, not based on compulsion like a court. It is the willingness of the parties to participate freely and to agree on a mediator of their choice, that empowers the process. But the election of a mediator was a compelling way of managing those concerns.

I put the Icelanders' clauses up on the screen and invited people to speculate on its origins. Not surprisingly, no one had the answer, and were even more dumbfounded to learn the time and the context.

Later I pursued the origins of this further. I could find no clear answers. There is a history of mediation within Scandinavian legal systems. I came across some suggestion that there was something akin to this in the land registry legislation of Ontario, of which some of the colonists may have been aware from their Kinmount experience. History aside, the important fact for me was that this practical arrangement had resonated for the New Icelanders who wanted a workable governance structure in their new home.

Since I had completed the mercury case, I felt an underlying tension growing inside me blossoming into an internal tug of war. I had deep loyalties to Manitoba—my family and my profound friends there, the communities, my clients, my colleagues and the firm. And yet, influences were at work telling me it was time to make a change. I started considering the possibility of moving to Vancouver, encouraged by my wife Maureen, who had spent much of her childhood visiting her grandmother a block away from English Bay every Christmas, Easter and summer, facilitated by her dad, a CN engineer who would put her aboard the train west. Since the day I met Leon I had been imperceptibly but surely moving to the field of what was then called "public dispute mediation." More career possibilities in that direction were starting to emerge over the horizon in British Columbia much more than Manitoba. I would be closer to Jerry Cormick. We were teaching together at the Banff Center. I knew the kind of pathbreaking work he was doing. I was on the board of directors of the Mediation Institute. The decision to move was not easy, and dragged on for three years.

Darcy helped me make that decision. He found a silver lining in a dark cloud. He told me that my career still had many directions to travel. He didn't want me to go, but go I must he said, so like the Icelanders I would go but stay. We would open an office of the firm in Vancouver.

So in 1989, Maureen and I, with our eleven-year-old son Paul and six-year-old daughter Sonja made the jump into a very uncertain future. Those first years rebuilding a career in a new place from a standing start with a young family, were not easy. Within a couple of years continuing the relationship with the firm in Winnipeg proved impracticable. Step by step, a new future opened, for the family and for my career.

Barry Stuart re-entered my life, big time. He had recently been appointed to the National Round Table on the Environment and the Economy as a member of the executive committee. Barry's long friend, David Johnston, then principal of McGill University, later to become governor general of Canada, was its first chair. Barry called and said he wanted to meet me for lunch at the Hotel Vancouver. Twenty years after our initial time together, he was once again working up the passions of his student. Barry had returned from Papua New Guinea, where he was a key architect in negotiating the constitution of a new republic after achieving independence from Australia (he would be awarded the Independence Medal at the United Nations 20 years later). He was now working as a judge in the Yukon Territory.

Barry always combined many careers into one, and his periods of intense activity on his circuit across the North afforded him the flexibility to integrate into his judicial duties his continuing commitment to the people, the land and the environment. For three years he had been on leave of absence, acting as chief negotiator and sealing a legacy as the leading figure in achieving the Yukon Land Claims Agreement.

Now, he had embraced with vigour the sustainable development charge of the World Commission on Environment and Development chaired by Gro Brundtland, the former prime minister of Norway. His experiences had persuaded him that the critical challenge was not to define and develop policy prescriptions for sustainability, but as a process of engaging diverse values and interests: reaching sustainable outcomes by building sustainable relationships.

Barry had a vision. He was not to be deterred. "It needs to be on one page," he said, "like a constitution on the wall, a set of user-friendly principles we can take into communities, businesses, environmental groups, First Nations and government departments, that will provide guidance on how to build processes to reach consensus on difficult decisions and resolve differences."

"Barry, that's a pipe dream," I replied, "and even if we could put something together, this sounds more like writing a text book than something we hang on the wall."

"We're not going to write it, we're going to negotiate it."

"Negotiate it! With who? Are you going goofy?" Barry and I often engage in frisky conversations.

"We'll negotiate it with all of the Round Tables of Canada. Every province and territory has established one modelled after the National Round Table, with broad ranges of stakeholders represented. The credibility of the principles will be based on their having been negotiated though a national process with every point of view represented."

"Who is going to do this?" If ever I defied the fundamentals of my legal training to not ask a question unless you knew the answer, that was it. Actually, the fact is that I knew the answer. I just wasn't sure I wanted to.

"We are. You, Jerry and me," he responded without even a glimmer of hesitation.

"Jerry? He's agreed to this boondoggle?"

"Not yet. That's your job to bring him aboard. This is what you guys are doing. He's the guy who invented this whole field, and even though he's living in Seattle, he's a Canadian, and you guys are teaching this stuff at Banff. And now you're doing it up here. Isn't he from an original settler's family from Saskatchewan?" It was clear that Barry, like Maurice, was about to turn my life, and Jerry's, in another direction. Soon he widened his net again and pulled others into his orbit, like my old Osgoode classmate Paul Emond.

Two-and-a-half years later, along with a task force of ten remarkable colleagues, with endless training sessions and countless discussion, from one end of the country to the other under Barry's tireless leadership, we finally all sat together in a restaurant in Montreal celebrating the successful negotiation of *Building Consensus for a Sustainable Future: Guiding Principles*. Every province and territory had signed on, including Quebec (one of the few documents it signed in the difficult years following the failure of the Meech Lake Constitutional Accord) and the Canadian Council of Ministers of the Environment. We didn't make it down to one page, but a highly user-friendly brochure was an incredible achievement. We sent 25,000 copies into publication and it was subsequently referenced in many international agreements.

Barry's mission was not complete. More breakfasts followed, and the next challenge was laid out as a "duty," not an odyssey. A practical handbook needed to be written to show how the principles could be put into action, based on the body of experience that we continued to accumulate. Jerry's track record was significant, and my own experience base was building. I always brought the enormous body of experience that came with me from Manitoba. I had also now provided leadership to a process resulting in an agreement amongst all the sectors of interest around the salmon fisheries on the Skeena River (First

Nations, recreational, commercial, the Department of Fisheries and Oceans). I had been asked to serve as chair, and for almost four years the unheard of was achieved, "every opening of the fishery was by agreement amongst all the sectors," in what had become a path-breaking process of integrated resource management. At the request of Bernie Wiens, chair of the Canadian Council of Ministers of the Environment, who I'd come to know through the Round Table work, I had led the development of a "wildlife diversification agreement" to more effectively exploit the wildlife resources on the land base given the dismal state of the agricultural economy. I had been involved in a situation on Haida Gwaii, in the Queen Charlotte Islands, in a complicated tangle involving the sitting of a marina promised in the South Morseby agreement to compensate the community of Sandspit as a result of the loss of logging.

Slowly, I realised that the tools I was using I had learned long ago, and I felt a deepening appreciation that wisdom in human affairs draws from a deep well. Looking backwards enables you to see forwards. My old history teacher's question again reared its head: "Is history bunk?" I could answer it now. The past is the future.

I came to see my forefathers, that ragtag group of Icelanders struggling to survive along the shores of Lake Winnipeg, as true pioneers of sustainable development. They understood in a visceral way that independence and interdependence can only survive together. Building an economy was essential, but not sufficient. Those poor people, struggling to live and make a living, and then build a life, knew that it would take more than food on the table and money in their pocket to realize their dream. As desperate as the times were, they were also going about the business of nation-building. They were developing their own institutions, obtaining a printing press and publishing a newspaper, creating a constitution, establishing local governments, building a school system, organizing churches, and dealing with fundamental faith-based differences. They understood the essential elements of building a sustainable future. Land and people, fish and water, culture, history and identity—this is clay with which a sustainable future must be moulded. Many forces are at work—power and values, rights and interests—and are energized by a constantly changing context.

To make a living and a life, they needed ways to make decisions and resolve differences. They needed to work with nature, and they required a governance structure to work with each other. The constitution they created to respond to these challenges was remarkable in its detail, with provisions for the establishment of four electoral districts with a governing council and executive committee with a duty to "stimulate civic consciousness, sociability, cooperation and ambition among their electorate," admistrators with extensive record keeping duties that were to be accessible to all; regulating elections, taxation and public works, promoting enterprise, and social assistance. Notably, the voice of the women had not yet made its presence felt at the ballot box, although one suspects the same could not be said at the breakfast table. What came into effect on January 14, 1878 was suitable for running a country.

What had these impoverished people brought from their history and homeland, now plunked down in this inhospitable place, to engage their hearts and minds so fervently in the enterprise of constitution-making? In the *Book of Settlements* which describes the original settlement of Iceland, the editors have this to say in the introduction:

> To begin with, there seems to have been a mere trickle of immigrants, but during the period c. 890-910 there was a steady stream, claiming possession of all the best farm lands. This "Age of Settlements" was over in 930 when the settlers and their sons adopted a common law for the entire country, instituted the legislative and judicial Althing, and organized their society on the new basis, by which political power was shared out between 39 chieftain-priests (godar) representing every part of the country. This was a peaceful farmers' union based on the equality of all free men. It had no monarch, no army, and no royal court. Above all, what gave it cohesion was the common law. The chieftains had judicial and legislative powers, and also priestly duties, but they depended on the support of other farmers. The highest official in the land, the Lawspeaker of the Althing, was elected by the chieftains, his period of office lasting three years, after which he could be re-elected for another term. The Althing met annually for a fortnight at Thingvellir to consider and change the laws and settle disputes. At the same time thirteen local assemblies were set up, one for every three chieftains. Soon after the middle of the tenth century, the country was divided into four Quarters—a decision reflected in the structure of the Book of Settlements—and each of these had a court dealing with legal disputes between litigants of different local assemblies within the same Quarter. This political organization lasted without major changes until Iceland came under Norwegian rule in 1262-4.

In his acclaimed book *Atlantic*, Simon Winchester adds this:

The first true parliament is reckoned by most to have assembled in Iceland—and somewhat symbolically, in the curiously fashioned valley in the west of the country known as Thingvellir where the world's

American and Eurasian plates are still tugging apart from one another and new ocean floor is being created.

There is a large basalt slab protruding upward from the western wall of the valley, and it was here beneath it that more than a thousand years ago farmers and peasants and priests and merchants passing through the valley would stop and camp and meet each year to hammer out in some fashion the manner in which each thought their island nation should be run. The assembly was called the Althing, and once it had a formal structure—the date generally agreed for this formation being 930A.D.—it became the sole body charged with fashioning Iceland's laws. The rock, from which the Icelandic flag flies still, day and night, is without doubt the most revered monument in the Atlantic north; the Rock of Laws, which set the pattern of governance of much of the rest of the world.[61]

The same values that inspired the creation of Iceland seem to have been at work in New Iceland. Even more remarkable is the fact that these values survived throughout centuries of a dark history of colonial domination.

The Althing Valley in Iceland is broad and magnificent. The serene vista reveals no clue of the world of fire and darkness far beneath the valley bottom, where the two continents collide, but the mysteries of this wondrous place are revealed in the walls around the valley; as the earth pulls the land down, the walls become taller, one millimetre a year.

I travelled to this valley once. It was a cloudy day in early spring. Gudmundur Magnusson, then the head of the University of Iceland School of Business and former president of the university, was my friend and guide whom I had come to know during my festival days when he was head of the Iceland/Canada liaison committee in North America.

As we drove along, I thought how hard it must have been for Sigurdur to leave this place of unique beauty. But those were different days, and this was a different part of Iceland than the northern region Sigurdur called home. We passed a luscious, fertile green mound, an oasis in the rocky terrain, where the thermal furnace deep below leaked its life-giving heat. Gudmundur explained how thermal engineers drilled deep into the earth to draw out the heated water and pipe it to Reykjavik, where it became thermal power to heat and light the houses, and showed me a large facility where this gift from god was unfolding.

Gudmundur pointed to a desolate farmhouse which he explained was the home of Halldór Laxness. This was definitely not America; there were no signs nor billboards. Here he brought to life Bjartur of Summerhouses who lived in his mind for days as he tracked a lost sheep over mountains and rivers in a compelling drama of resilience in his Nobel powerhouse, *Independent People*. I thought to myself: this man left his signature in the world with the power of his words and ideas, not his land and his house.

When we reached Thingvellir, Gudmundur led the way on foot along a gravel road, the valley walls rising alongside as we progressed down a gradual slope. Nature remained nearly untouched in this pristine place. The dark and moving contours of the hues of grey above, lying low over the valley, sharpened the lines of the rocky perimeter. Gazing out across the valley from a wooden platform, he explained that if we had walked there a thousand years ago, on this same road, we would have passed a collection of large tents and campsites, the camps of the great chieftains who travelled from across Iceland with their entourages to conduct the business of the nation. They traded and celebrated here, married and divorced. And they held trials and read the laws.

We were standing at the very place where the Lawman would read aloud one-third of the laws of the land each year. These words, memorized and passed down through successive Lawmen, were recorded in written form on vellum in the tenth century. This is *Jons Bok*. One of the Centenary events back home had been to bring an exhibition to the Winnipeg Art Gallery of the famous Icelandic manuscripts, one of which had been Jon's book. Mom and I helped the curator Jonas Kristiansjon unpack the exhibition, and when he saw *Jon's Bok*, he passed it to her. The script was tightly written. To my astonishment, she began to read from it aloud in impeccable Icelandic as Jonas listened in delight.

That the Vikings had stood as giants in the history of the rule of law, not of men, and had given their wisdom to the world with the institutional corner-stone of parliament, ran counter to their popularized image as savages cling-ing to the rigging of longboats destined for pillage on fearful shores. They had a drive within them to create something lasting and profound in a new place. Gudmundur and I were bound together by those Viking genes, standing here more than a millennium later. We could gaze outward from that place and share a common history of where we had come from, and who we were. My place in the world had become the middle of North America; Gudmundur's was still this bastion in the North Atlantic.

I return to the New Icelanders' collective act of constitution-making. How had they gone about it I asked? What I learned was this:

> With their newspaper established the colonists turned their minds to the *constitution* under which to operate their colony. Since they were in unorganized territory, and pretty much on their own, they felt that the

constitution needed to cover all phases of public administration. *To carry any authority it should have the sanction of all concerned.*

Two public meetings had been held early in the year (1877), one at Riverton, the other at Gimli. Each meeting chose a committee of five men to draw up a set of by-laws, the committees to act independently, and when both had their drafts ready, to meet together and consolidate these into one set of regulations to form a constitution. [emphasis added]

These folks understood in a powerful way the interface between "what" and "how"—and that what we measure first in human terms is not where we arrive, but the way in which we get there. A few simple words say a great deal: "to carry any authority it should have the sanction of all concerned." To ensure that was accomplished, they worked from the mandate that public meetings gave to independent work groups in the two key regions, who were in turn charged with integrating and reconciling the outcome of their efforts. The process was transparent, inclusive and reflective. My years within the indigenous communities taught me a basic truth—"A good way to a good place"—and in the business of constitution-making it is clear the Icelanders lived by the very same values and code of conduct.

A combination of assaults eventually traumatized the colony into submission, but, from near death, was able to rebuild on the back of growing economic self-sufficiency powered by fish, and together the colonists began to creatively answer the question of independence and interdependence in new ways reflecting new realities. Here they would build their new ways and new institutions, like Islendingadagurinn, the Icelandic Festival, an Althing of a different kind suited for a new land and a new beginning. They would provide a way and a reason to maintain connections among families, communities, and countries, a gathering where history is refreshed, and futures created. It has become part of Manitoba, and Canada, where anyone who identifies with this heritage can become Viking for a few days. For those few days each year "I" becomes "we," as we celebrate a sense of "us-ness" with anyone who wants to identify with this heritage.

When you add the Betel Homes, the Icelandic National League, the Icelandic Clubs in most major North American cities, *Logberg-Heimskringla,* as the inheritor of many newspapers, the *Icelandic Canadian* magazine, and a host of other groups and organizations, the visibility and knowledge of the Icelandic presence is remarkable. So is the pride that resides within the community. Within every community where there has been a significant Icelandic presence in North America, and most certainly in Manitoba, the descendants of the pioneers have written and published a book to remember and honour them.

Recent history has added a new perspective on events from the past. In 2008, Iceland, faced with the trauma of a complete national financial melt-down—which brought with it deep tensions internally and mockery from abroad—turned to the enterprise of constitution-making. They had long talked and bickered about replacing the Danish Constitution that had been in place when they seized independence in 1944. Now, they turned to the same wisdom as the New Icelanders, empowering a citizen's committee of ordinary people to lead the charge, now with three subcommittees and social media instead of a printing press. The committee invited every citizen to contribute ideas and hold discussions online through their own website and Facebook. Recommendations from this constitutional committee to the Althing, where final authority rested, helped build the foundations for the "constitutional remake." This caught the attention of the international press:

> Big in the news these last days is the high-tech revision of Iceland's constitution. The international media appear to be quite baffled about the fact that Iceland's constitutional committee—who are currently overhauling the country's constitution—has invited all citizens to participate in putting forward suggestions online.

In the course of developing the new constitution, one of the participants in the Constitutional Conference, Katrín Oddsdóttir, told CNN:

> [After the economic crisis], we were forced to do something about our democracy. The social contract is the basis of our society... Everything is open for discussion. What's happening is that we are creating owner-ship... Thousands of people are writing the constitution together, online.

Foreign Policy magazine could not resist these snide comments:

> This model may have worked in the Viking days—I'm guessing adminis-trative tasks were pretty minimal back then—but this new scheme seems to combine all the worst features of local government community forums and online comment boards. It will be interesting to see how much of the public input will actually be incorporated into the final draft.

What's to be snide about? The fact that citizens across this tiny nation nosed up to their laptops to voice their opinions can surely only be a good thing. And, unlike in many other nations, the fact that everything is open for all to see has all the smell of a powerful democracy. That smell has never reached many cor-ners of the globe, and if at all, a whiff at best.

Deeply held values about the power of inclusion and voice have once more risen to the surface at a time of great stress. Social dislocation and tension evoked the same response in modern times for the Icelanders as it did for the settlers in New Iceland, with echoes back to the distant time of the formation of the country a millennium earlier.

Responding to the challenges of building sustainable futures means finding ways to live together in spite of our differences. That is what governance is all about, whether within a partnership, a community or a country. Respect for each other's rights to be, to be different, and to differ, is the foundation. This value is given expression in different ways by different people in different places.

These are universal themes that resonate no less today than they have for centuries. Presently, I am leading the Responsible Minerals Sector Initiative (RMSI) bringing together companies, communities, and governments, in global dialogues around the question, "Mining. For what end? For whom?" The question inside the question is always "governance." And as you peel back its layers, it is inclusion and voice that is inevitably at the core.

CHAPTER EIGHTEEN

Leading without Owning

So "What do you do?" is always a perplexing question which leads me to the ledge of a lecture or a tangent. The simple fact is that the narrow community of professionals doing work of a similar nature to me are in search of a name, and have been for years. I worry that if I start to ramble on about fish and water, rendering plants and nuclear waste, municipal conflicts and treaty negotiations, hydro utilities and mining projects, sky trains and pipelines, and all the people and places I have worked, across Canada and many other places in the globe, the listener will almost certainly conclude I am some hopeless dilettante or aggrandizing fool or, if not, at least as someone spread too thinly to have worthwhile insight to contribute. In my case, if I were to add that I learned the essential tools of my trade as a boy in a fishing family on Lake Winnipeg, they would likely draw even more troubling conclusions.

If the word "dispute" arises, inevitably "so, I guess you're a lawyer?" is evoked. That gets me going in another direction. I have not made a dollar in more than 20 years from the practice of law. So a further rambling answer follows, with yes, but no. "I thought you had to be a lawyer to deal with disputes." Off we go again, and now I am dangerously close to slipping off into a lecture about how lawyers have corrupted the field by squeezing the problem and solution into a legal framework, as opposed to seeing the legal dimension as part of a wider problem. The Vikings understood the distinction centuries ago where it is said of the lawyer Njal, the central character in the great Icelandic *Njal's Saga*: "He was a wise and prescient man who remembered the past, and discerned the future, and solved the problem of any man who came to him for help." Where are the Vikings when you need them, I am inclined to ask?

"So if you don't have to be a lawyer, what are you? Can anyone get into this field? I have been thinking about making a change myself. This might be a good possibility for me." Everybody seems to be expert in what I do and presumes they can jump right in, so I feel another tangent coming on.

Why not just "a mediator?" you might wonder. The world I live in is most often in the middle of big fights around big projects and environmental and community concerns with different groups and organizations that, unlike the labour relations community, have no experience in working with each other. For them, mediator is synonymous with a labour relations mediator who they associate with high-handed tactics and "take it or shove it" recommendations to push folks into corners. As unfair as this may be to labour relations mediators, and I have often worked in that role, it is too often a perception that they draw from media reports. "Facilitator" seems to have become a more palatable term. The problem with that term is that it suggests someone on a fixed assignment to manage a meeting, while most of my assignments continue for months and years. A senior executive with whom I have often worked used to say to me, "When I'm introducing you to others, I never describe you as a facilitator, for what they take from that is something entirely different from what you do. What should I call you?"

Others like the term "Chair," and that may work in some contexts, but it creates an expectation that I am going to start ruling people out of order or telling them to shut up. No doubt I help manage interactions in a meeting to ensure a respectful environment, but you have to use more subtle strategies to achieve in conflicted rooms where people are struggling with whether they should even be in this room with "these people." "Process manager" is another term that has been hung on me, and my role does include management and administration of the process, particularly as it evolves into a continuing relationship with growing cohesion and purpose.

Tortured now by curiosity, and determined to leave no stone unturned, the last gasp of my new friend is often "so you must be kind of like a judge." I suppose it's not a surprising jump, especially if I've made some flippant remark about being a "recovered lawyer," for isn't that what judges are, former lawyers? On this one I have given some papers so I have a handy script.

Judges provide answers. I help others reach their own answers, which usually take the form of outcomes they can live with because they're better than other alternatives.

Judges are given questions. I help others agree on the questions that must be discussed to reach outcomes. Judges rule on relevant and appropriate issues and evidence. Relevance in my world starts with someone's need to talk about something, because that's important in how they see the problem, even though it may not be relevant to others. Judges work in their way to their solution with those "standing" before them. I help others agree on "our way" to "our solution." Who's in the room is whoever needs to be—typically, whoever can help or hurt or frustrate in giving effect to whatever outcome is sought.

In court, fewer parties and fewer issues are usually more conducive to orderly and efficient adjudication. In my world, more players and more issues is often better. In court, the rules of engagement are fixed. In my world, I work with parties to help them reach agreement on their own rules. Judges exercise the power residing within the institutions to which they are appointed, and do so graciously and predictably, while expecting, and if necessary compelling, those before them to do likewise. My power comes from each of the parties' right to fire me, "by whomever and however I am paid." I am there because the parties have asked me to be.

Power lurks everywhere in my world, and who exercises it and how and when are always uncertain and unpredictable. Unlike a judge, my only power is persuasion, not command or coercion. The values through which judges interpret their world are embedded deeply within institutions. In my world, diverse worldviews that must find an outcome enabling them to co-exist come from many places, often many lands. What is important to one is sometimes anathema to another.

The only time recognized in a courtroom is judicial time. In my world, the parties each bring their own clock, and synchronizing all clocks in the room is no easy task. Dealing with time is a central challenge that drills to the core of integrity of the process.

The mantra of the judge is "justice must be done and seen to be done." My mantra is "a good way to a good place."

As I put my earphones back on I have often reflected on how disquieting it seems to not be able to slot someone into a clear category with a label. The simple fact is that this work involves bits and pieces of all of these roles. But there is more to write, and more compelling questions to ask of myself. So what does all of this have to do with growing up in a fishing family on Lake Winnipeg? And being part of this unique slice of Canadian history?

I straddled both sides of the fish world growing up: the business of fishing and the fishing itself. The Sigurdsons were in the fish business—they started as fishermen, but then became company men, company men with a difference. They weren't ones for sitting in offices in Winnipeg selling fish in Chicago before it had even arrived on the dock in Selkirk. They spread out to stations around the lake and ran the operations where the fish came out of the water. They were doers. They built businesses. They operated boats. They constructed roads. They worked through problems. They made money; they lost money. They were bonded together as a family unit, always seeing their own personal interests inside the company which had an identity distinct from any of them.

Afi Malli, Mom's dad, on the other hand, stuck to fishing, the only business he knew or wanted to know. His fortunes rose and fell with the fish populations. Later in life, he told the *Winnipeg Tribune*, "... even if I could change, I probably wouldn't. We never made much more than a living ... but it was a good living." There had been good years, but in my time there were as many bad years as good, and even the good years were not "good." I think what Afi really meant was that he had a good life. Fishing was not a job. It was who he was.

The dynamic between the fishermen and the companies was often not easy. Within a company like Sig Fish, with its many tentacles of business activity, there were more ways to manage uncertainty. My friend Brian Oleson's dad, Kari, was a fisherman, and for his family getting everyone working together to supplement the family income was the only option. So Emily and her boys became wizards at seaming on nets, deftly manipulating a needle through each mesh to tie it to cord-like ropes, sidelines, to which corks and leads would later be attached to frame the net. Whatever one's circumstances, everybody lived and worked, and as kids, went to school, together. There were no suburbs to escape to. Settling accounts after a bad season with not a dollar left to take home was not easy for the fisherman, or for Dad.

The other side of this cycle was the inevitable scramble to get the whole operation mobile again the next year, with men arriving every day at the office from near and far to make their deals and seek an advance against the next season's catch with Steve agonizing over every dollar authorized by Dad, and leaving the Sig Fish account. As a boy I came to understand these tensions and feel their burden and pain, especially when too many beers brought anger to the surface.

There are also unique challenges in family businesses, where home comes to work and work comes home. The families and the business are interconnected; the families have to work together, just like the business partners. The family history was always alive in my world, as was the history of the Icelanders in Canada. While Stefan and Johannes went their separate ways, the following generations of Sigurdsons stuck together in the family business for nearly seven decades. These were all strong-willed and powerful individuals. But, paradoxically, each was at the same time the epitome of "the company man." They spoke always of Sig Fish as "the company." The company wasn't some thinly veiled disguise for their individual business enterprises. It was much more than a legal fiction; it was a fact of life, and it had a life above and beyond them. Each saw themselves as part of the company, and its history was their identity. They worried about it, they protected it. They managed it carefully, with great fiscal prudence. Owing money to the bank was not in their blood. They never raided the treasury in good days, nor went starving in bad days. That financial stability and independence helped them manage their relationships as partners and make it through any differences that surfaced. The company came first. They always had cash in the bank, and cut back their own incomes to ensure it was there. The company was always protected before the individuals, and that was a cornerstone of their success.

Yes, there were differences, strong words and strained relationships, although these were certainly the exception not the norm. But within the partnership, the integrity of the company was top priority; walking away was not an option. The talking continued for days or weeks or months until they were talked out. The fish always had the last word; they set the timeline. As the next season approached and the logistics of mobilization went into action, with everyone soon to be off to their stations, there was no more time for bullshit. There were jobs to get done, and done they would get! That was corporate governance Sig Fish style.

There were similarities in the tension between Afi SV and Steve, much like those between Stefan and Johannes a generation earlier. Afi SV always dreamed big and bigger. Steve wasn't into dreaming. Tellingly, Afi SV was invested in stocks; Steve in Canada Savings Bonds, and even those bewitched him after he realized that some long-maturing bonds he bought were subject to significant price fluctuations prior to maturity. SR, for his part, tended to follow his more forceful younger brother's judgments on business when push came to shove, but he didn't have Steve's zealous preoccupation with every dollar. Dad was probably in the middle of the gang, and I am not sure where Victor was in his investing style. In the mid-60s, with the continuing challenges in the fishery, Dad tried to build up the ancillary businesses, particularly the Shell dealership and the mink ranch. He spent some summers with Riverton as his headquarters, rather than up at Berens River. Steve believed in sticking to your knitting, doing what you know best and doing it to your best, and saw in this the rise of another SV. He urged Dad to return to the core business. That view soon prevailed, and Dad was back North.

Afi SV and Steve's differences worked for, not against them, in business, pulling them back from the excesses to which they were both prone. Afi SV's leadership expanded the networks and connections his dad had created, and dramatically expanded their business reach and stature. His energy was boundless, including rushing around Winnipeg in his massive buffalo coat appearing at the doorsteps of business associates or deputy ministers, most often to be met by their wives with whom he would engage in lively conversation as he dropped off a Christmas turkey. While Afi was thinking turkeys, Steve was thinking waybills. After the fall season, he would make his annual pre-Christmas examination into each and every invoice of fish shipments from the stations against Booth's purchase receipts in Winnipeg. Seldom did he fail to track down thousands of dollars. It was like an annual Christmas gift.

Notwithstanding the differences in personality, Steve and SR always supported Afi SV in his wide range of business pursuits, with their money beside his. Afi always pushed the boundaries, particularly with Monarch Construction in his last years, and Steve could never adjust to the potential agony of losing hard-earned cash. Occasionally, this underlying tension in perspective and personality came to the surface. Leaving $400,000 "on the table" on the last floodway contract was a particularly tough pill to swallow. Dad most often found himself drawn into the middle. He'd listen to each side's entreaties and do his best to interpret, and I guess "mediate" would be the best word. He was the glue, and became ever more so over the years.

My boyhood world was one where the realities of life both caressed you and slapped you. The young knew the old and the old the young. When someone died, whatever their age, it touched you, for you almost surely knew them. You remembered them, you missed them. Life was tough for people. For many, this was compounded by booze, too much too often, which could be either the cause or the symptom of their difficulties, Indians and Icelanders alike, including many near and dear to me. Even after a prolonged "bender" between seasons, on the lake everyone was soon sobered up, and you saw people for who they really were. Sometimes the sobering up took a few days. There were nights, only two to which I was exposed, when someone was struck with the DTs screaming about snakes around them and elephants on top of them—frightening stuff as a youngster. Mom and Dad helped me understand. Dad sat beside the man through his private horror. The madness would pass.

Dad died on May 30, 2012. Many who knew and respected him were in touch with me, and they offered some fascinating insights. Irvin Olafson, Dad's brother-in-law, sent this along shortly after his death:

> Stefan and our past neighbor Ted Kristjanson spoke at a meeting of the Manitoba Historical Society many years ago. Ted was anecdotal in a Mark Twain kind of way as he talked about fishing on Lake Winnipeg. Then your Dad came on, in his quiet inimitable way, and spoke seriously about the family's involvement on the lake. I sat back in the darkened room, as he illustrated his talk with slides, and came face to face with

the true character of this unique man. What impressed me the most was his descriptions of the activity of life on the lake. But then he defined the role of every individual pictured with a name and his importance to the job at hand. I learned a lot from and about your dad that day.

Dad looked through weaknesses to find strength. Everybody was important in their own way. Tom on the scales, Dollie at the stove, Jones at the wheel, Dori with a gasket, Roy with the keys, and Harrison, Jacob, Oli, Gestur, George and many others bringing in the fish. Dori was drunk on occasion out north, but in a couple of days he'd be sober. Sig Fish wasn't a factory where discipline slips were handed out or pay docked. Dori was a very important man, keeping fifty outboards running day in and day out, and generators and ice machines humming. If you found yourself with a dead motor in a big storm you'd want to know Dori was on his back in the engine room using every bit of ingenuity to get the pistons thumping again. Outboards, not booze, was where Dad focused, not in some conscious way; it was simply the way he was.

With a unique combination of gruffness and cajoling, and always another nickname, Steve had a different kind of charisma that bound him to the lake and the men and women with him. Often in the first week north, he'd shout at me "Goddamn Edgar Prince," as we steamed down the road with the fish heads off to a mink ranch. "He ate 19 eggs this morning. Can you believe it?" In moments like that my first lessons in economics came to mind, back when Steve spotted me heaving an empty Coke bottle into the river: "If you deal with every two cents that way you'll never have a pot to piss in." Against that backdrop, it was not a big jump to conclude that Steve was more worried about his kitchen costs than he was about Edgar's arteries. But every year, Edgar was back. He was a straight shooter, a man you could always count on, who people respected, and liked.

I did not know it then, but I do now. I was experiencing the wisdom of leadership, and seeing it in action by different personalities in different ways. They never pretended to be anything which they were not; they were authentic. I would come to understand and apply that in the work that lay ahead in my own way. I know that the wisdom of leadership is not deposited in a select few, but can be found everywhere, surfacing unexpectedly in different ways in different people. Some leaders are elected; many are appointed. Some rise through the ranks; some are brought in from outside. Some leaders lead one other; some lead millions. Some run governments; others lead companies. Some work on factory floors; others are on the open sea, or in shops, or are angels on the streets. Its mysteries are within the hearts and minds of ordinary people, very few of whom achieve greatness. Every day in every way, leaders are at work, and for all but the very few, the great work they do is unknown. Their leadership is no less because it is unknown. Leadership is far too important to leave to the famous.

Those are the kind of folks I often find in the rooms where I work. They are the people who care enough about an issue that they become involved. They enjoy the confidence of others. They worry about what others will think back home. Before they go to a meeting they take the pulse of others, and when they get home they keep them informed and onside. These folks are everywhere. It just takes the right issue or opportunity to bring them out of the shadows. That's when I bump into them.

Steve's oldest daughter Helen Kristjanson phoned me after Dad's death. We talked of many things, and then she added spontaneously, "I don't know why, but I often found myself questioning why I had just told your Dad something I intended to keep to myself. I don't know why that was."

I think I do. Dad was someone you could count on not to use something personal someone shared with him against them, or to hurt them.

Dad earned the trust of others, not in any conscious way; that was simply the way he was. I shared this exchange at Dad's memorial service the next day.

This exchange put a precise point on something that had a far deeper personal meaning for me. The core of my leadership challenge is to help others create the space where they can have the conversations it will take to reach outcomes that are and are seen to be theirs, not mine. Some may see this as philosophical meandering; I see it as profoundly pragmatic. Agreeing is one thing; getting done what is to be done is another. Deciding and delivering are always in a difficult relationship. What I do know is this. If you feel you are part of the agreement and the decision, you are much more likely to want to do it; if you are just told "do it," unless you are "in the army now," the more likely you will try to find ways to resist. I cannot be helpful to others if they do not have confidence in me. That is my most critical tool.

"Ownership" is much more than a legal or physical reality; it is an emotion. A fisherman has gear, nets and equipment and goes on the water to take his catch. He returns with his fish, sells them, and feeds his family. Ask him who he is and he will tell you, "I am a fisherman." He is not telling you about the boats and equipment he "owns," he is telling you who he is. Shakespeare made the point so elegantly, so simply: "an ill-favoured thing sir, but mine own."

The Sig Fish lessons have given me important tools in understanding dynmics within organizations, large or small, a company or a community. Ownership is like gravity. Leadership can give or take ownership. I understand that. In hockey, the lower your centre of gravity, the less likely you are to get knocked over. That's true for people and sports, and it's true for organizations doing business, whether public or private. Organizational structures are not built to migrate power downward, or across, so the force of gravity meets upward resistance, laterally reinforced. Ministries, departments and business units all like to work autonomously, defending their turf and their hierarchies. Universities have carved knowledge into silos called disciplines. It is becoming ever clearer, though, that alignment and integration are critical to organizational resilience. A critical measure of success will be how far the ownership bar is lowered within the organization and in its interactions with external parties who can help or hurt—the so-called "stakeholders." The lower the centre of gravity, the more resilient the organization or partnership among organizations will be. The royal jelly of great leadership is to understand that empowerment comes with empowering others, through persuasion, not compulsion. There is no greater leadership than that which enables others to reach that emotional place.

So what do you do? I hope others with whom I work see it in the same way as I do but they may use different words. What I think best characterizes what I and others like me do is to "lead without owning."

I learned from the people of the lake first, and then from many other places and people, that those who make their livelihoods from the water or the land understand the world viscerally. Watching, listening and remembering they see patterns and live with uncertainty. They observe how things and people work and feel when things are changing, while the experts with books and lab coats record, analyse and interpret. They derive their identity from their relationship with the world around them, while the experts build credentials with titles and papers. It is as if one is inside the apple looking out; the other is biting into it. The view from the inside is of the whole; the other sees chunks and slices. Knowledge does not begin or end with a credential, nor with experience and wisdom. We need them both; and they need each other to see how each needs the other. I have come to understand that when the voices that speak truth from the ground sit around the table with those who bring truth from a book they bring together a force of gravity that makes solutions to seemingly impossible challenges possible.

If the likes of Afi Malli had been brought around those tables many years ago, would Lake Winnipeg be in the trouble it is today? Let's not try to answer that question here, while acknowledging that the future he foresaw so clearly has arrived, sitting on top of the list of the world's most endangered lakes. There are many culprits. Fertilizers on farm fields have done double duty, growing crops on the land and algae in the lake. The golden wheat fields glisten while Lake Winnipeg exudes a murky green sheen visible from space. Phosphorus from far and wide and every direction has moved with ever greater speed into the lake through accelerated drainage programs and the transformation of the vital defences of wetlands and marshes into ditches and fields. No doubt if he were here Afi would be thundering that hog-tying the lake as a "storage tank" has lowered the flushing action and helped the algae grow, voraciously consuming the oxygen that keeps the waters alive.

Canadian Geographic reports in a recent article:

> For two decades, huge blue-green algal blooms have been plaguing Manitoba's Lake Winnipeg. Visible from space, the blooms signal an over-abundance of phosphorus and nitrogen running off a watershed that drains nearly a million square kilometers. The sources are obvious and are massive in scale: the rise of industrial farming and livestock production, a hydroelectric dam network on northern Manitoba's Nelson River that has limited natural nutrient outflow since the mid-1970s, widespread depletion of the watershed's marshlands, plus a deluge of sewage, fertilizers and detergents from growing cities.

Afi Malli was no less prescient in other ways. Nothing raised his ire more than this "goddamn government bullshit" that Indians couldn't go into the beer parlour. He ate, worked and slept with Indians all his life in camps and boats, but they couldn't go for a drink together—equals on the water, but not in the beer parlour. When Afi's fury was particularly aroused, he punctuated his forceful advocacy with a reddened face and bulging veins. Mom recalls the poignant moment when his long partner and close friend, Roy Murdock, an Indian, was about to join the gang "for a few." Afi was aching for a chance to put his rhetorical skills to work, making it clear that "he would take care of any trouble." Roy's wife was not as confident, and quietly urged, "Now, Roy, you know you're not allowed to go." Roy listened. Afi calmed down and backed off.

Men like Roy could go to war and fight for the country (not to mention drink while on leave during the war), but couldn't take a drink at a local Lake Winnipeg pub. Soon, at least, some Legions opened up for the veterans, and Roy could head in there to down a few. Wherever there was no Legion, though, it was some years until the Indian fishermen would enter a beer parlour without being in peril. The currents of social justice were starting to swirl in the country, and Afi's thunder was an early "wake up call." The marginalisation of the indigenous people throughout the hundred years since Confederation was emerging from the darkness, and I would feel throughout my life these currents that I first felt as a boy.

My deep connection to indigenous people since childhood has informed my work in many ways and many places, in difficult challenges across Canada and around the globe. Mother Earth is the indigenous soul, wherever on the globe you find yourself. There are few places in the world where resources are being hunted or exploited where there are no indigenous people whose lives and livelihoods are affected.

I came to know First Nations people as kids, just like me. I banged nails on the porch outside the cabin with Peter, and sat on the stool between the legs of his older brother Gestur who let me believe I was steering the "*Spear boat*" all by myself. I ate Dollie's bannock and chipped ice in the icehouse with Tom. I knew them as Indians, just like I was Icelandic. Often, as the men sat on the dock waiting for the wind to subside so they could get out to their nets, or dressed fish together in the shed, you would hear both Ojibway and Icelandic in the room. And then they switched seamlessly to English to talk together as Canadians. It was just life, no big deal. We were kids growing up together, and their elders were no less my elders than mine theirs. It all worked. It was no big deal.

Similarly, I came to know how their communities work. Family units, like in every society, were the fundamental building blocks around which the communities were organized. Grandmothers and grandfathers were often key figures in the lives of the young children, just like they were for me. Dollie always had a gang of her youngsters on the island and around the kitchen with her. I came to understand that "who's who in the zoo" was alive in their communities, just like every community I've ever known or studied. Like Riverton, some people had nicer houses than others, and better locations along the river, but the banners weren't rich neighbourhoods and big houses. The barometer, I have come to believe, was respect, built on the strength of the family's role and history in the community, and the inherited obligation of carrying it forward for the next generation. In my experience, this wasn't much different from most societies, although expressed in different ways through cultural traditions and practices. Chiefs, whether hereditary or elected, play a primary leadership role, just as the leaders do in any community with whatever name they might wear. Ancestors and elders are the cornerstones of social stability. When "push comes to shove" on internal community struggles, the counsel of the elders is sought.

Meetings are often structured in a circle, such a sensible way to make everyone feel that they are there on a level playing field. There are few meetings that I do not set the room up in that way, allowing everyone to see everyone else, communicating through their words and expressions, not hidden behind tables and stacks of papers. I couldn't count how many hotels across the country

I've irked by pulling their tidy rectangular furniture set-ups into crude circles or diamonds, almost coming to blows with one particularly intense woman welded to a sense of order in an Edmonton hotel. I now often just pull away the tables, leaving only empty chairs to greet the participants as they enter the room. Some look askance on seeing this configuration, some confused, some enthused, but whatever the response the message is that we are doing something different in the room. The typical opening prayer in the hundreds of First Nations meetings I have participated in recognizes the glory of the creator in the plants and animals around us, and calls upon the wisdom of the ancestors to guide us. It sets a mood, and creates a climate of respect. Reflect on how you would react to this setting as opposed to a courtroom with a judge on high or a row-by-row community hall with a chair at the front, and some form of "call to order." Ask yourself what effect this might have on how you saw others and interacted in the discussion. And how you would relate to the importance of the discussion.

Myths about Aboriginal people have littered Canada's history. People and institutions of all kinds and descriptions, including within the aboriginal community, vacillate between romanticizing the past or hell-bent on bulldozing it away. Some still see only "Indian fighters" or "Indian lovers," like in the cowboy movies we watched as Brother Cartier struggled with his old projector. They think it, but correctness precludes them from saying it. It's startling that the echoes of this detritus from history are alive today. There are many truths. We need to understand each other's truths.

There has been no greater truth more penetrating to understand and experience than the impact of residential schools on the aboriginal people of Canada, a truth from which there is no hiding, and for the many individuals affected, no escaping. In 1999, I was contacted by my friend, Phil Fontaine, who was then National Chief of the Assembly of First Nations, and George Thomson, the federal Deputy Minister of Justice. They asked me to develop, coordinate and lead across Canada what became known as the "Exploratory Dialogues" to bring together representatives of the survivor groups, the government and the churches to explore alternate approaches to resolving the growing avalanche of residential school claims in the courts. We traversed the country in a sequence of Dialogues comprising 50 to 70 people assembled in each centre for two long days.

I had many great partners in this exercise, including my friend Chief Mark Wedge from the Yukon, and, in the final dialogue, Barry Stuart, who had been a background counsellor throughout. A strong supporter was Robert Joseph, a distinguished hereditary chief with an honorary doctorate from the University of British Columbia, then the executive director of the BC Residential Schools Project chaired by Chief Steven Point, leader, lawyer and judge, who later became the lieutenant governor of British Columbia.

Often when Phil and I would connect we would wind the clock back to 1973 when Phil called his erstwhile lawyer. "I want to fire the teachers here at the Fort."

"Phil, small detail. You don't hire them."

"Yeah, I guess that's a point. What if I just issue an order that they cannot come on the reserve?"

"That should do it!"

Phil had no issue with the teachers. His goal was to give control of the school to the community, and away from Indian Affairs. Our reminiscences always reach a climax when we recall the three ever longer telegrams to the Head of the Public Service Commmission of Canada (he was unresponsive to letters and phone calls and there were no faxes or emails!) to negotiate the teachers out of the superannuation fund. We were ushered into a massive Ottawa boardroom. After an hour or so the man himself appeared. You could see bewilderment and bemusement all over his face at the spectacle of what he no doubt saw as two bushy haired kids that needed to be put in their place. Soon after, the Sakeeng Education Authority was borne, I believe the first of its kind in Canada, with Yngve Lithman as its first executive director. It has been a long road since those days.

I told Phil at the outset that without someone beside me who understood the residential school experience and its impact, and knew the survivors' groups, it would be impossible to manage the task reasonably and responsibly. He told me Maggie Hodgson was the person; she knew everyone and could accomplish anything. Of course, he was right. Maggie is smart, canny, wise and remarkably seems to know everyone in the Aboriginal world connected to residential schools, from one end of Canada to the other. Maggie stalked me around the mulberry bush, sizing me up in a Vancouver hotel for most of a day when we first met. I offered to drive her to another meeting at the end of the day, and as we chatted in the car before she got out, her last words were, "I can dance with you." My friend Maggie and I danced together just fine. She came with connections, sagacity, toughness and softness—quite the package. It's a combination many have recognized, and it earned her our nation's highest civilian honour, the Order of Canada.

What was shared in those meeting rooms was deeply troubling. It would shock most Canadians. I confess to often crying on the inside, and visibly on occasion. Kids, now sixty, pulled from their mothers' and fathers' arms under threat of imprisonment. Communities emptied emotionally with their children home only for annual visits. There were some positive stories recounted, for the experience was not universally bad. But there was no shortage of stories of abuse of every possible kind, including the widespread horror of sexual exploitation at the hands of pedophiles who migrated to those institutions like bees to honey. Students went on to become parents, without the experience of being parented themselves, triggering generational cycles of abuse.

The Dialogues were a breakthrough. A fundamental barrier was crossed. People had a voice, not just those who were students or families and communities who had felt the intergenerational consequences, but those within government and the churches who felt this pain no less deeply than I. They carried the burden of institutional responsibility and accountability for things of which they had had no personal knowledge, much less involvement. Conversations and understanding began, and networks were established.

We drew this body of work together in a final Dialogue that brought together representatives from each of the prior events to develop a concluding set of principles to inform how we might move forward together. Regrettably, the tangle of litigation that had already consumed these issues—between all the groups of actors, and at that point particularly between the government and the churches—sucked the momentum out of this remarkable achievement. Once more, the problem was forced into a process ill-designed to deal with it. A decade later a solution was reached. I leave to others to reflect at a later point with the full trajectory of history as to whether there were other and better ways this could have been handled.

If I have any underlying creed to the way I work and think, it is the belief that there is a common humanity that anchors us all, whoever we are or whatever our colour. It's on top of this foundation that I then layer on the differences that distinguish and define them. Hopes and fears, love and hate, jealousy and selflessness, suffering and healing, just like everywhere. Folks get along most of the time, but sometimes a fight breaks out, just like everywhere. Almost invariably, like Sigurdur, they dream that their children will have a better life than they did. That dream is still alive in much of the world, but for recent generations in the Western world the hope is increasingly that children will have as good a life as their parents, and that we're leaving the world sufficiently intact to make that possible.

Differences are at the heart of knowing who we are. Father Lou Menez gave me that lesson in 1971 as his guest in the mission home while I was working in Fort Resolution. Lou had found his way to Canada's North from France after spending the war years as a prisoner in a massive German armaments facility that he was astonished had not been blown to smithereens by Allied bombs. The priesthood followed, and then he became an Oblate Father. The Canadian North quickly became his home.

Every afternoon at five, I saw Lou pulling the cord on the bell at the front of the small church, and a few old ladies tottering in to join him in evening prayers. On Sunday afternoon the old ladies and some kids would pile into the back of his truck and he would ferry them into the bush for an afternoon of berry picking.

One night over rabbit stew and a beer, Lou was waxing eloquent about people, about his life, about the community. Suddenly, he fixed his gaze on me and said, "You know Glenn, without the French, the English would be nothing." I thought he might be opening a discussion about Quebec separatism and the dynamic leadership of René Lévesque.

"What do you mean?" I asked hesitantly.

"Without the French, the English would not know who they are." Lou had given me a penetrating insight, a seed that has continued to grow with experience. Becoming one while remaining different has the ring of paradox, but if that is so, then life is nothing but paradox. That night, Lou Menez taught me that difference is the essence of identity.

Toward the end of my stay Lou came into the house perplexed. An evangelical minister had arrived in the community about a year earlier to proselytise the Christian message with more determination and fervour than Lou's brand of faith prescribed. That day, he had decided to leave town, and his last act was to say goodbye to Lou and to give Lou his Bible. Lou was bewildered. The meaning came readily to me, but Lou struggled. Lou accepted people for who they were and how they lived within the community. The evangelist was trying to remake the community in his own image. The day he realized this, he had the courage to acknowledge that Lou possessed the wisdom he lacked. Lou was once more the sole cleric in town.

Lou's wisdom buried deep within me. He allowed himself to sink into a place and a people. Lou absorbed their truth. When others saw difference, he saw identity. He understood and accepted who and what they were, and respected them and their way of looking at the world. Making a difference is not about making differences go away, but dealing with differences. Differences are okay.

Seeing Canada through the lens of my Icelandic Canadian roots has enabled me to see Canada in my own way, and I think it is the way that most Canadians see it. That I bring my own point of different point of departure to my citizenship does not detract from Canada; it enhances it. Multiculturalism does no justice to the magic chemistry that is Canada, and becomes all too readily the playpen of politicians for or against it. Canada is the nesting ground of diversity—geographically, historically, ethnically, culturally, socially and politically—holding in its arms a prototype of global complexity. The elasticity of accommodation is what has held the country together. It is a country that does not work well when hard lines are drawn. The genius of Canada is strength through diversity, a point made eloquently by our current governor general, David Johnston, with almost 150 years of history in his wake:

> On whether there should be more uniformity among those taking the citizenship oath, or a greater expression of diversity: If I had to make a choice it would be the latter. I think it's quite appropriate in Canada that we can be hyphenated Canadians. If you ask me what kind of Canadian [I am], I'm Scottish-Canadian. I think it's attractive that we don't discourage but we encourage people to keep their language and their heritage, and to teach it to their children and their grandchildren. The great gift of this nation is that we respect diversity, and somehow we've been able to make a nation out of diversity and allow people their expression of their identity—as long as they don't hurt somebody else. That's John Stuart Mill, I'm on safe ground there.[62]

The saga of the Icelanders stands in testimony to the wisdom of the governor general. The Icelandic-Canadians became one with Canada, adding texture to what it means to be Canadian while preserving their sense of "us-ness." This duality provided a place from which to interpret the Canadian reality and to make a unique contribution to Canadian life. How could a people leave and become different, but somehow remain the same? Something was inside them, something invisible on the surface, something that came with them from Iceland that they continued to protect and nourish, as so many other Canadians from other backgrounds have done.

My cousin Heather Alda Ireland's wonderful vocal talents are often called into service in her consular duties as a senior member of the consular core in Vancouver. There is no greater expression of the mystery of the Icelandic-Canadians' duality than the passion and power with which she sings "O Canada" and "O Gud a Land" (Iceland's national anthem) one after the other. This same sense of duality is expressed by countless citizens in their own way, whether they roots are indigenous to these lands or connected to a land far away, all bonded together as "us" because they are all Canadians. A stronger and more resilient national DNA is evolving out of what might best be thought of as a fusion society.

CHAPTER NINETEEN
"Tomorrow Will Be a Good Day"

Every summer I return home to the cottage, and the Icelandic Festival. At sunset, I often take my camera to the shoreline. This the magic time when the picture of the same scene changes moment by moment as if a giant brush was quietly at work. As the sun drops behind the big, sloppy gobs of marshmallow clouds as they float down the channel at the whim of the wind, a reddish hue appears through their intricate folds. Boundaries sharpen; the mood shifts. Suddenly everything changes, as darkness descends and the full glory of the moon and the stars takes over. Life is not much different. Experience is like the changing light, and each experience brings with it changing perceptions. The way we understand the world and our place in it one day changes the next. Sometimes quickly and sometimes slowly, over time we look at the same scene and see something very different. What may have been in the background is now the most prominent, the once prominent fades away,

Inevitably, this is a time for reflection, and nostalgia, and the stories of the lake come to life again, which a multitude of friends who make the trip up past Riverton must endure yet again. Usually what is most prominent on their mind is the still unruly state of the gravel road. Usually that leads to stories of the building of the road, and the unsung heroes like Uncle Grimsi and Leslie Olafson who endured isolation and black flies for many months swinging their small buckets hour after hour day and night. When the Selkirks or Mowatts visit from Pine Dock or Matheson Island to spend an evening over a few beers and a barbeque, they add another layer of texture from more recent times.

Then there is the endless fodder of all the characters, and surprising endings, like Arni. Dad had quietly used his influence to have him admitted to the Betel Home in Selkirk. Here he pampered roses by day, and charmed his other beauties by night; unlike his shenanigans from the past, what happens in Betel stays in Betel. The thought of Arni inevitably triggers thoughts of Steve and SR. They were puttering together in the basement, when SR dropped dead in Steve's arms. I am confident that the fateful episode with Arni with Sister

Superior driving in the hypo needle had been locked that day into a sealed compartment of the mind and would not have featured in his last remembrances. And like them, Sig Fish is gone. The note Brian Oleson's brother Freddie, another of Riverton's PhD folksingers, wrote after Dad died comes to mind. "It was a well written farewell for your dad. I was thinking of what a role Sigfish played in Riverton and what an adventure it must have been working in the business during its developmental days. It played such a role in giving Riverton a strong heartbeat. Really an amazing group of guys."

Many stories of inspiration come to mind, but none more than Auntie Maggie, Afi Malli's older sister by a year, walking across the stage of the Winnipeg Concert hall in 1988 like the queen she was that day. With touching remarks Dr.Harry Duckworth, awarded her with a Bachelor of Arts degree, sharing that at age 87 she was the oldest graduate in the history of the University of Winnipeg, adding that as the dean of the Senior Students Association they had enjoyed many conversations president to president so to speak.Auntie's humble home always had a spare room for the family, and on many nights as a house guest, I would watch her labouring at her dining room table over an essay, the Hecla girl still young at heart studying night after night for over 20 years after her husband Ed's death determined to earn her degree before she left this earth.

Usually my brother Eric adds additional dimension with his mastery of accents and brings back to life the actual words and inflections of some of his favourite gang. One of his most memorable stories is of the fishing trip he and our neighbour Ingi Ingaldson (who like John and Jan Restall, friends from my days at Osgoode Hall, have been part of the Leaside family for 40 years and now institutions in their own right in those parts), took with Jack Clarkson. It begins with Bill Bennet, a long-time resident, then mayor of Matheson Island, pointing to Jack's plane coming in for a landing visibly tilted to one side. "You see that plane, Ingi, coming in with that big tilt? That's because the pontoon has a hole in it and is half filled with water." Moments later a young pilot jumps onto the pontoon, pump in hand. Bill, with his distinctive twang common to folks in the Narrows area, exclaims, "You see, I told you Ingi, that's why she was so lopsided coming in." As the last piece of equipment is strapped in and a canoe lashed between the pontoons, Ingi pulls himself aboard. First straight-faced, then with a bemused grin, Bill tells him, "Ingi, you've been a good friend all these years. It's been real nice knowing you, Ingi. Have a fine trip." Ingi, the account continues, had a ghost-like pallor wash across his face, but it was too late to turn back.

Often my dear friend Colin Gillespie is with us for a few days, and he punctuates the evening with his own brand of Australian insight. When we recall an evening's festivities the next morning over coffee, his perspective on the long and colourful chats is clear: "That was like breathing in living oral history!"

I think of my first visit to this place. It was 1962 when Mom, Dad, Elaine, Eric and I first came to this spot and looked out onto this vista. The spring thaw had begun, so there was water along the edges of the bay, but it was still mostly covered in snow and ice. The ground was heavy with snow, and it was a struggle to move around the property. When we got to the shore, we could see it was a magnificent beach, a panoramic shoreline, in a protected bay. The lot was in the middle of the bay, and the shore was high enough to give a panoramic view over to the Narrows. This location also worked for Dad as it integrated well with his life on the lake, especially as the business was increasingly drawn up and down the North road. The *Spear* was still making its way to Selkirk in those years, but when Dad came home, it was usually by car from here so he could do his business in the city and sneak a few hours at the cottage on the way back north. Soon the *Spear* would be using the End of the Road six miles north as its terminus and its load of fish from the north would go on truck trailers and into Winnipeg on wheels. That summer the cottage came down from Winnipeg, prefabricated and ready to go, and it was assembled over four weekends.

The lake is very different now. The big boats that I used to watch come and go in front of the cottage gradually disappeared, until there was only the *Goldfield*, now also retired and sitting lonely on the bank of the river in Riverton. Only the odd sailboat comes north, often heading up to find harbour at Black Bear. Of course, when the fishing is on in the summer and fall the skiffs are out, bobbing in the channel as the fishermen from Matheson Island and Pine Dock make their lifts. The last remnants of Hanny Hanneson's fish station have disappeared, except up the hill where you can see the remains of the timber foundation of the home where he and Bertha lived. Whenever a dragline has been in the area, we have re-dug the small harbour originally dug out behind the shale bar by Hanny intact, and installed docks for the pleasure boats darting around the bay with water skiers.

Black Bear has been returned to nature. Nothing but remnants of foundations is left of the five fish stations that once occupied almost every inch of land in the small harbour, with its narrow mouth opening to the south and the island behind as perfect shield from the norwesterlies. There are a couple of small camps used by fishermen during the season. The lighthouse at the tip of the island is gone, no longer bidding farewell as you leave the Channel and enter the 200 miles of water ahead. Its classic structure, so long the navigational lynchpin of the lake has been replaced by steel, and an electric beam driven by a faceless source has long replaced the lighthouse keeper.

Dad is gone now, but his presence is still very much alive. The day of his memorial service Eric and I tracked down Tom Bittern in Poplar River, his wife's home community north of Berens River. "Can I speak to Tom?" I asked when I called the fish station around nine that evening. "He's out on the gut boat." It was as if nothing had changed in 50 years. We spoke when he returned, told him of the news, and chatted for over an hour. We were all very excited to connect after all those years, and had many stories to share. He made a special point to say, "The old station, I took it down and rebuilt it a few years ago for the Band back on the island, in the same place where it had been and I ran the station for the first two years."

Dad always resisted the idea of putting the station on the mainland, believing that the island brought everyone closer to the fishing grounds, and the real icing on the cake was a minimum of flies. "Your Dad and Auntie Dollie, those two were great friends," Tom said. I told him that Bernard Selkirk had told me that George Kemp was Chief. I mentioned a picture I had long intended to send him of his dad and his mom, holding his baby brother Glenn in her arms, and his grandmother Ma in front of the Log Cabin Inn. He rattled off Ma's many grandkids raising their own families in Berens River. Ma is gone, but like so many other British names, hers will live forever in the First Nation world of Canada's North.

Sometimes, when the evenings are bright and the lake dead calm, the cottage gang goes out into the Channel to bid the day goodbye. The mystery of the lake lives on. On nights like these, it has a mystical inner peace. Every star shines brighter than you see it anywhere else. The Northern Lights dance with a dazzling fury, darting across the sky in curtains dripping with light and colour. The surface is alive with the glow of the moon. To the east are the granite rocks of the Canadian Shield; there it begins or ends, depending on where you stand.

Here, the lake holds the continent together. You can see East and West Dog Head clearly, the two points that define the closest reach across the lake. It was on East Dog Head that Stefan and Johannes established one of their first fishing stations, and when you walk those granite rocks you can find the remnants of the foundations that I presume underpinned the buildings they constructed more than a century ago. To the north lies a giant body of water, noble, but a speck of its former self. Catfish, Georges, Spiders are all up there. We can see them in our minds' eye as they once were. To the south is the Channel, then Humbug Bay, Hecla, Riverton, Hnausa, Gimli, the mouth of the Red River and Selkirk. Matheson Island and the End of the Road are just around the corner.

You can't see all this, but you can feel it. The next morning you may feel it in a very different way, for Lake Winnipeg is nothing if not moody, and her disposition can become quite different overnight.

When Dad was with us he would have the last word on that. If it had been a month later, he would have likely said that the wind is soon going to turn to the northwest—there is a big blow coming. But now, in the heart of the summer, he would say, "There's not a cloud in the sky. The barometer was steady all day, and the sun is red on the horizon. Tomorrow is going to be a good day."

ACKNOWLEDGMENTS

I have written more words than I can imagine over my career, but none have been more challenging to write, or more important to me, than those that you have just read.

What you have read might be thought of as a gathering of my friends from many worlds and places brought together at my invitation so that they can know each other in the same friendship with which I have known them. I thank them all for shaping my life, each in different and special ways, and for becoming part of this book.

I know my own family best, so that is what I am most able to write about. I hope this book honours my own remarkable extended family, as well as all other families who see some pieces of their own experience reflected in these pages.

My sincerest hope is that many within the Icelandic diaspora across North America and the First Nations people of the lake in the surrounding communities or wherever they now may be will see in this something of their own connections to Lake Winnipeg.

The Icelandic Festival of Manitoba, *Islendingadagurinn*, is at its heart a fellowship of all the people who identify through genetics or friendship with the Icelandic presence in North America. This event is akin to an annual reunion which I have never missed. It has been a key element in keeping my determination to complete this effort energized.

Some specific people have helped hold me up over what seemed like an endless road. Mitchell Gray has been throughout a sounding board, a guide with words, and an editing adviser. Scott McIntyre's friendship has been invaluable since seeing a much earlier version, and giving me confidence: "There is a book here. I know it. But there is much more to do." Many times Billy Valgardson came to my rescue as I tried to emerge from another period of drifting and wallowing. And in these last months, Chris Labonte has been my able friend and guide to get me and this over the finish line. Finally, I am grateful to Gregg Shilliday at Great Plains Publications for having the confidence in me and this book to bring it to life.

Labours of love are driven by passion and persistence. That was my burden but many others had no choice but to share by enduring me, endless conversations, most especially my wife Maureen who suffered my tedious compulsion over the years, and Paul and Sonja, my son and daughter, who have both at different times helped me with different aspects of this undertaking. Elaine and Eric, my sister and brother, lived through these experiences with me, and over the years through countless conversations have been key to keeping these memories alive. You can feel my brother's passion for the lake in his voice and words as he retells his vivid stories of the characters and events from his years on the lake. My Aunt Solveig Riddell has been a constant supporter throughout.

Many friends and family were drawn into my web. Some read parts of this book as it unfolded over the years, and their words sparked me on; others in informal conversations gave me important insights and gentle touches that they may see in the pages that follow. They know who they are, and they know how much I appreciate them.

Bringing back to life the many people on Lake Winnipeg has given me new energy and insights into my own life. They are the heartbeat of this book. And most of all, to my Mom and Dad, to whom I owe my own heartbeat and the soul that inspired this book.

ENDNOTES

1 *Manitoba History*, Number 42 (Autumn/Winter), 2001-2002.
2 C.B. Gill, *Lake Winnipeg: Route of the Adventurers*, page 27.
3 Margaret Wishnowski, *Train Stories from the Icelandic River.*
4 Helgi Skuli Kristjansson, professor of history, University of Iceland, personal communication.
5 Unit 4, "From Iceland to Hecla Island," *Hecla Island School Teacher's Guide*, page 44.
6 Beard 654.
7 Helgi Skuli Kristjansson, professor of history, University of Iceland, personal communication.
8 Jonas Thor, *Icelanders in North America: The first settlers*, 2002, University of Manitoba Press.
9 *York Boats of the Hudson's Bay Company: Canada's Inland Armada*, Dennis F. Johnson
10 Arngrimsson and Christie, page 89.
11 Arngrimsson and Christie, page 95.
12 Ingibjörg Sigurgeirsson McKillop, *Mikley—The Magnificent Island*, 1979, self-published. Christine Tómasson Jefferson recalls her grandfather (Helgi Tómasson of Reynistað, Sigurdur's long-time friend).
13 *Icelandic Canadian*, Summer 1975, pg. 41-50.
14 Ardis-Annual Report of the Lutheran-Women's League 1949 Vol. XVII, page 3.
15 Ethel Howard, ed., *Gimli Saga: The History of Gimli, Manitoba*, Gimli Women's Institute, 1975.
16 Steinn Thompson, *Riverton and the Icelandic Settlement*, 1976, Thordis Thompson, page 86.
17 "From the memories of Magnus Stefansson from Fjoll in Kelduhverfi."

18 Frederick Temple Black Dufferin and Ava, *Letters from High Latitudes*, page 24.
19 Dufferin, page 24.
20 Dufferin, page 44.
21 Dufferin, page 26.
22 *Framfari* compilation, November 17, 1877, Vol. 1 No. 3, page 26.
23 *Framfari* compilation, November 17, 1877, Vol. 1 No. 3, page 26.
24 Helgi Skuli Kristjansson
25 Helgi Skuli Kristjansson, professor of history, University of Iceland, personal communication.
26 *Framfari* compilation, November 17, 1877, Vol. 1 No. 3, page 29.
27 *Framfari* compilation, November 17, 1877, Vol. 1 No. 3, page 29.
28 *Framfari* compilation, November 17, 1877, Vol. 1 No. 3, page 26.
29 [details needed]
30 Bishop Tache, in a detailed report on the fisheries in 1872.
31 Barbour, 1955-56 season.
32 Tough 39, Spring/Summer 2000.
33 J. Straumfjord from Mikley The tenth issue of Framfari was released February 4, 1878.
34 *Framfari* compilation, March 6, 1878, Vol. 1 No. 4, page 134.
35 *Framfari* compilation, July 16, 1878, Vol. 1 No. 31, page 299.
36 Thor, pg. 161-162.
37 Some material in the preceding two paragraphs from the diary of Shafki Arnason.
38 Thor
39 Mikley Book, page 30.
40 "The Diary of Jon Jonsson," page 115.
41 Frank Tough, "The Establishment of a Commercial Fishing Industry and the Demise of the Native Fisheries in Northern Manitoba," *The Canadian Journal of Native Studies*, IV9 1984, pg. 303-319.
42 Thompson, pages 200-202.
43 Thompson, pages 205, 294.
44 Thompson, page 203.
45 Barbour, 1955-56 season.
46 Thompson, page 205.
47 Gimli Saga, page 711.
48 Captain Ed Nelson, "The Viking and the King of the Icelanders," *Winnipeg Free Press*, Saturday, June 23, 1962.

49   The legendary captain and ship builder Ed Nelson described Stefan in
     this way: "King of the Icelanders," he called himself. Standing well over
     six feet, with piercing blue eyes, ringlets of black hair hanging down
     to his powerful shoulders, and radiating health and heartiness, Steve
     Sigurdson was an outstanding figure in any company. He was a pop-
     ular monarch too. No man was better liked than Sigurdson, and no
     boat was more welcome than his Viking among the fishing settlements
     along the south end of Lake Winnipeg in the early years of this century."
     (*Winnipeg Free Press*, Saturday, June 23, 1962 "The Viking and the King
     of the Icelanders")
50   Howard, page 230.
51   Howard, page 233.
52   Thompson, page 209.
53   Howard, pages 65-66.
54   Howard, page 231.
55   Possibly the menu of the Charterhouse Restaurant?
56   Frances Russell, *Mistehay Sakahegan: The Great Lake*, Winnipeg:
     Heartland Publications, page 27.
57   Russell, page 27.
58   Clifford Stevens, "A Rugged East Shore," *Logberg*, May 2001.
     [i] Paul Deprez and Glenn Sigurdson, *The Economic Status of the
     Canadian Indian: A Re-examination.* 1969.
60   Agreements in Reference to a Temporary Constitution in New
     Iceland, Translated by Professor Skuli Johnson. Retrieved from:
     http://www.mhs.mb.ca/docs/transactions/3/icelandicsettlements.shtml#o6.
61   Simon Winchester, *Atlantic: Great Sea Battles, Heroic Discoveries,
     Titanic Storms, and a Vast Ocean of a Million Stories.* Harper, 2011.
     Page 274-275.
62   *Globe and Mail*, Saturday December 24, 2011 "David Johnston,
     unplugged."

INDEX